Are You Ready to Incorporate?

Saving Time & Money through Sound Business Tactics

By the Editors of Socrates

SOCRATES™
KNOW HOW TO DO MORE
AND SAVE

Socrates Media, LLC
227 West Monroe, Suite 500
Chicago, IL 60606
www.socrates.com

Special discounts on bulk quantities of Socrates books and products are available to corporations, professional associations and other organizations. For details, contact our Special Sales Department at 800.378.2659.

This publication is designed to provide accurate and authoritative information in regard to the subject matter covered. It is sold with the understanding that the publisher is not engaged in rendering legal, accounting or other professional service. If legal advice or other expert assistance is required, the services of a competent professional person should be sought.

From a Declaration of Principles Jointly Adopted by a Committee of the American Bar Association and a Committee of Publishers and Associations

ISBN: 1-59546-247-3

This product is not intended to provide legal or financial advice or substitute for the advice of an attorney or advisor.

Printing number 10 9 8 7 6 5 4 3 2 1

Are You Ready to Incorporate?

Saving Time & Money through Sound Business Tactics

Special acknowledgment to the following:

Lisa Holton, Managing Editor; Robert Barnett, JD, Associate Editor; Michele Freiler, Editor; Chip Butzko, Encouragement Press, Production; Jeannie Staats, Product Manager; Derek Vander Laan, Cover Art; Peri Hughes, Editor; Alison Somilleda, Copy Editor; Kristen Grant, Production Associate; Edgewater Editorial Services, Inc.

Get the most out of Are You Ready to Incorporate?

Saving Time & Money through Sound Business Tactics.

Get the most out of Are You Ready to Incorporate? Saving Time & Money through Sound Business Tactics. Take advantage of the enclosed CD and special access to Are You Ready to Incorporate? Saving Time & Money through Sound Business Tactics resource section of Socrates.com that are included with this purchase.

The CD and Are You Ready to Incorporate? resource section offer readers a unique opportunity both to build on the material contained in the book and to utilize tools such as forms, checklists, spreadsheets and appraisals that will save time and money. More than $100 worth of free forms and content are provided.

The CD bound into the back cover contains a read-only version of this book. Readers can access the dedicated Business Plan resource section by registering their purchase at Socrates.com. A special eight-digit Registration Code is provided on the CD. Once registered, a variety of free forms, checklists, appraisals, research articles, government forms and other useful tools are available at

www.socrates.com/books/ready-incorporate.aspx

From time to time, new material will be added and readers will be informed of changes in the law, as well as updates to the content of this book.

Finally, readers are offered discounts on selected Socrates products designed to help implement and manage their business and personal matters more efficiently.

Table of Contents

Section ■ One

What Is a Corporation Anyway?

1 Corporations & Other Types of Businesses

Which Legal Structure Should You Choose?

Forming a corporation today can be a straightforward process—file the appropriate paperwork and you are in business. Whether you should incorporate is an issue that requires more serious consideration.

When starting a business, you have four options from which to choose—a sole proprietorship, partnership, limited liability company (LLC) or corporation. From the relative simplicity of a sole proprietorship to the organizational complexities of a corporation, each business structure provides different financial benefits and corresponding tax and reporting obligations. To maximize your business profit and function, choose a structure that best suits your company's size, current financial needs and long-term plans for growth.

If you have already decided to incorporate, skip ahead to Chapter 2. If you are still unsure, take a few moments to read through this chapter and consider all your options carefully.

Sole Proprietorships

A sole proprietorship is the simplest business structure available and also the most common. It is a one-person business in which the owner is solely responsible for all aspects of the business. It is also the least costly way of starting a business. You can form a sole proprietorship by opening the door for business. There are the usual fees for registering your business name and for legal work in changing zoning restrictions and obtaining necessary licenses. Attorney's fees for starting your business will be less than other forms because less document preparation is required.

Most home-based businesses start out as sole proprietorships.

Advantages

- **The easiest corporation type to get started; hook up the computer and go:** Your municipality or state may require business name registration and impose tax or other registration rules, but most sole proprietorships simply apply for a DBA (doing business as) account at the bank and they are in business.

- **Simple tax treatment:** As a sole proprietor, all business profits and losses are reported on your personal income tax return each year. You are required to file Schedule C (Profit or Loss from Business form) with your 1040.

- **Easy transition:** Unlike a corporation, a partnership or an LLC, there are no administrative costs associated with sole proprietorships, other than those you may incur while setting up your business.

Disadvantages

- **All debts and legal liabilities are your own:** Unlike other business structures, which may protect owners against lawsuit damages and excessive business debts, sole proprietors bear exclusive financial responsibility for their business. Bottom line: Sole proprietors without business insurance can lose much more than their business when faced with financial problems.

- **Beware of huge success:** If your business starts to make significant money, your income will be taxed at your personal rate, which is typically higher than standard corporate rates. Many corporations with substantial earnings do income splitting, which allows them to keep some earnings in the business that are taxed at the lower rate.

Sole Proprietorship	
Ownership	Owned and operated by one person
Organizational paperwork	Give yourself a name, get a business license and start operating
Personal liability	Owners have unlimited liability—personal assets are at risk in event of failure or lawsuit
Tax forms (minimum)	Filed with personal income tax return—Form 1040, Schedule C, Schedule SE (Self-employment tax), Form 4562
Upside: You have sole responsibility for the business	
Downside: You have sole responsibility for the business	

Going Solo

Did you know that more than 70 percent of businesses in this country have no paid employees?

The U.S. Census Bureau reported in November 2004 that the number of businesses with one or more owners but no paid employees grew nationwide from 17 million in 2001 to more than 17.6 million in 2002, a growth rate of 3.9 percent.

The report showed that Nevada led the nation in small business growth with a 7.4 percent increase between 2001 and 2002. Georgia slipped from first place in 2001 to second place in 2002, with a 6.3 percent increase. Florida also experienced growth of 6.3 percent. Texas and Delaware, both with 5.2 percent increases, rounded out the top five states in nonemployer business growth.

These statistics reflect businesses that are run by one or more individuals. They range from home-based businesses to corner stores or construction contractors and are often part-time ventures with owners operating more than one business at a time.

Some examples of nonemployer businesses having significant growth between 2001 and 2002 are landscaping services (21.5 percent), janitorial services (20.4 percent), nail salons (8.7 percent), real estate agents (7.1 percent), child-care providers (5.9 percent) and beauty salons (5.6 percent).

Four economic sectors accounted for 60 percent of nonemployer receipts—real estate and rental and leasing ($161.8 billion or 21 percent); construction ($115.3 billion or 15 percent); professional, scientific and technical services ($96.4 billion or 12.5 percent); and retail trade ($77.9 billion or 10.1 percent).

Total nationwide revenue during this period was $770.0 billion.

Partnership

A partnership is a legal entity that is jointly owned by two or more individuals, corporations or other entities. Partners agree to be in business and to share the profits equally based on the kind of partnership they have structured. A partnership can be formed by simply making an oral agreement between two or more persons, but such informality is not recommended. Legal fees for drawing up a partnership agreement are higher than those for a sole proprietorship, but may be lower than incorporating. You would be wise, however, to consult an attorney to have a partnership agreement drawn up to help resolve future disputes.

Such partnerships include the following:

- **General partnership:** Two or more people in business together, sharing all profits, losses and liabilities equally (although a partnership agreement may allocate profits, losses and liabilities in whatever way the partners choose). Partners can contribute capital, services or both. The act or signature of any partner can bind the partnership, and partners file a U.S. Partnership Return of Income that shows how profits, losses and other tax issues are allocated. The partnership also issues individual Schedule K-1s to each partner at the end of the year that establishes their share of the above. These profits/losses are eventually reported on each partner's personal income taxes.

- **Limited partnership:** In a limited partnership, one or more general partners manage the business while limited partners contribute capital and share in the profits but take no part in running the business. General partners remain personally liable for partnership debts, whereas limited partners incur no liability with respect to partnership obligations beyond their capital contributions. This form of business encourages investors to invest without risking more than the capital they have contributed.

Advantages

- **Less costly to start than a corporation:** Partnerships tend to have less expensive filing fees than corporations.

- **Management flexibility:** Partnerships tend to have a broader management base than sole proprietorships and a more flexible management structure than a corporation.

- **Option to be taxed as a corporation:** Partnerships have the option of splitting earnings as a corporation so that part of those earnings can be taxed at a lower corporate rate. Check with a tax specialist to see if converting to corporate status makes financial sense for your business.

Disadvantages

- **Unlimited liability:** At least one partner, and possibly all partners, could lose everything in a business failure or lawsuit (except in limited partnership situations). Personal assets of the general partners are often used to satisfy partnership debts.

- **Politics:** The life of a partnership is unstable. A partner's death or departure can result in a funding crunch that could cause a partnership to terminate.

- **Raising capital:** Partnerships cannot raise funds through stock offerings or bonds as corporations do; to raise additional capital, they have to increase revenue or seek more funding from partners.

- **Unilateral decision-making:** The acts of just one partner, even unauthorized acts, bind all partners.

- **Difficult to sell:** An individual partnership interest cannot be sold or transferred easily.
- **Limitations on benefits:** Most tax-supported fringe benefits, such as pension and profit-sharing arrangements available to corporations, are unavailable to partnerships.

General Partnership	
Ownership	Owned and operated by two or more people
Your level of control	Evenly split among partners
Organizational paperwork	Easy to organize, but you need legal contracts drawn up for the partners
Personal liability	Owners have unlimited liability— personal assets are at risk in event of failure or lawsuit
Tax forms (minimum)	In addition to personal income tax forms (1040, Schedule SE, 4562) you must file a Form 1065 (Partnership Return of Income)
Upside: Both parties share in the investment and operation.	
Downside: Partners could end up disagreeing, creating legal problems.	

Limited Partnership	
Ownership	Owned and operated by two or more people
Your level of control	Amount of investment and responsibilities of the individual partners are determined by contractual delineation
Organizational paperwork	Give yourself a name, get a business license and start operating
Personal liability	Owners have unlimited liability unless stipulated by contracts between partners
Tax forms (minimum)	In addition to personal income tax forms (1040, Schedule SE, 4562) you must file a Form 1065 (Partnership Return of Income)
Upside: Other parties share in the investment and operation.	
Downside: Partners could end up disagreeing, creating legal problems.	

Partnerships May Take on Additional Forms

Secret Partnership—the partners are active in the ventures but are unknown to the public.

Silent Partners—Partners are usually inactive and have only a financial interest in the partnership.

Why You Need a Partnership Agreement

There are no laws requiring partnerships to establish a partnership agreement, but without one, state statutes determine many aspects of your ownership, decision-making, dissolution and winding-down rights. Consider the problems and disputes between partners that could potentially develop: a partner leaves, dies or becomes incapacitated; a partner takes a partnership opportunity for him or herself; or a partner causes harm to the partnership. For these reasons, it is always wise to create a document to outline each partner's obligations to the business. Drawing up a partnership agreement is very important when forming a partnership. Whether you are forming a partnership with family members, best friends, or business acquaintances, it is important to define the partnership on paper.

A legally binding partnership agreement should include the following:

- The legal name of the partnership.
- The nature of your business.
- The type of partnership—limited, general, secret, silent.
- How long the partnership is to last. As with most contracts, it needs a start and end date.
- What each of the partners will contribute to the partnership—capital, in-kind goods, services, etc. This is referred to as initial capitalization.
- Any sales, loans, or leases to the partnership should be listed in detail.
- The management structure of the partnership—who will be responsible for what areas or tasks.
- The sales of a partnership interest. A clause may be added that restricts a partner's right to sell his or her interest to third parties. It does, however, provide a method that allows the partner to divest his or her interest in the partnership without bringing in outsiders.
- A clause that will allow the partnership to be dissolved.
- A survival clause in the event one partner leaves or dies.
- Guidelines on how disputes will be resolved—either through mediation, legal, etc.
- Each partner's specific interest in the partnership.
- How profits and losses will be split.
- A plan to keep the partnership going in the event one partner leaves.

Hint

If a partnership agreement is not executed, then all partners are equal under the law.

An Example of a Limited Partnership Agreement

Limited Partnership Agreement

of

_____

_____

adopted _____

Limited Partnership Agreement

For _____

THIS LIMITED PARTNERSHIP AGREEMENT (the Agreement) is made and entered into as of the _____ day of _____, 20_____ by and among:_____, as the General Partner and _____, as the limited partners, and each individual or business entity as shall be subsequently admitted as a Partner. These individuals and/or business entities shall be known as and referred to as "Partners."

WHEREAS, the parties have formed a Limited Partnership named above through their initial registered agent _____ pursuant to the laws of the State of _____. NOW, in consideration of the conditions and mutual covenants contained herein, and for good and valuable consideration, the parties agree upon the following terms and conditions:

ARTICLE I: COMPANY FORMATION

1. The Partners hereby form and organize the company as a Limited Partnership subject to the provisions of the _____Limited Partnership Act in effect as of this date. A Certificate of Organization shall be filed forthwith with the _____ secretary of state.

2. The Partners agree to execute this Agreement and hereby acknowledge for good and valuable consideration receipt thereof. It is the intention of the Partners that this Partnership Agreement, or as may be amended, shall be the sole agreement of the parties. In the event any provision of this Limited Partnership Agreement is prohibited or rendered ineffective under the laws of _____, this Agreement shall be considered amended to conform to the _____ Act as set forth in the Code of _____. The invalidity of any provision of this Agreement shall not affect the subsequent validity of any other provisions of this Agreement.

3. NAME. The name of the Limited Partnership shall be _____. The business of the company shall be conducted under that name or such trade or fictitious names as the Partners may determine.

4. DATE OF FORMATION. This Agreement shall become effective upon its filing with and acceptance by the appropriate state agency.

5. REGISTERED AGENT AND OFFICE. The Limited Partnership's initial registered agent and registered office shall be _____.
The Partners may change the registered agent or registered office at any time, by filing the necessary documents with the appropriate state agency. Should the Partners fail to act in this regard, the General Partner files such notice of change in registered agent or registered office.

6. TERM. The limited Partner shall continue for a period of thirty (30) years from the date of formation unless:

a.) The term extended by amendment to the Agreement. Partners shall have the right to continue the business of the Partnership and may exercise that right by the unanimous vote of the remaining Partners within ninety (90) days after the occurrence of the event described below.

b.) The Partnership is dissolved by a majority vote of the Partners.

c.) The death, resignation, expulsion, retirement, bankruptcy, incapacity or any other event that terminates the continued Partnership of a Partner.

d.) Any event that makes it unlawful for the business of the Partnership to be carried on by the Partners.

e.) Any other event that causes the dissolution of a Limited Partnership under the laws of the State of _____.

ARTICLE II: BUSINESS PURPOSE

It is the purpose of the Limited Partnership to engage in _____.
The foregoing purposes and activities will be interpreted as examples only and not as limitations, and nothing therein shall be deemed as prohibiting the Partnership from extending its activities to any related or otherwise permissible lawful business purpose, which may become necessary, profitable or desirable for the furtherance of the Partnerships objectives expressed above.

ARTICLE III: CAPITAL CONTRIBUTIONS

1. INITIAL CONTRIBUTIONS. Each Partner shall contribute to the Partnership certain capital prior to or simultaneously with, the execution of this Agreement. Each Partner shall have made initial capital contributions in the following amounts:

Name of Partner	Value of Capital Contribution
_____	_____
_____	_____
_____	_____
_____	_____
_____	_____

No interest shall accrue on initial capital contributions.

2. ADDITIONAL CAPITAL CONTRIBUTIONS. If the General Partner decides that additional capital contributions are necessary for operating expenses or to meet other obligations, notice must be sent to each Partner setting forth each Partner's share of the total contribution. Such notice must be in writing and delivered to the Partner at least ten (10) business days prior to the date the contribution is due. Any such additional capital contribution is strictly voluntary and any such commitment is to be considered a loan of capital by the Partner to the Limited Partnership. Such additional capital contribution does not in any way increase the percentage of Partnership interest. This loan shall bear interest at _____ points above the current prime rate. Any loan under this subsection shall be paid in full before distributions are made under Article IV.

3. THIRD PARTY BENEFICIARIES. Nothing in the foregoing sections is intended to benefit any creditor or third party to whom obligations are owed without the expressed written consent of the Partnership or any of its Partners.

4. CAPITAL ACCOUNTS. A capital account shall be established by the Partnership for each Partner. The capital account shall consist of:

a.) The amount of the Partner's Capital Contributions to the Partnership, including the fair market value of any property so contributed to the Partnership or distributed by the Partnership to the Partner.

b.) Members share of net profits or net losses and of any separate allocations of income, gain (including unrealized gain), loss or deduction. The maintenance of capital accounts shall at all times be in accordance with the requirements of state law.

5. ADDITIONAL PROVISIONS:

a.) Capital accounts shall be non-interest bearing accounts.

b.) Until the dissolution of the Partnership, no Partner may receive Partnership property in return for Capital contributions.

c.) The liability of any Partner for the losses or obligations incurred by the Partnership shall be limited to: Payment of capital contributions when due, pro rata share of undistributed Partnership assets and only to the extent required by law, any previous distributions to that Partner from the Partnership.

ARTICLE IV: PROFITS, LOSSES, ALLOCATIONS AND DISTRIBUTIONS

1. ALLOCATIONS. Net profits, losses, gains, deductions and credits from operations and financing shall be distributed among the Partners in proportion to their respective interest and at such time as shall be determined by the Partners.

2. DISTRIBUTIONS. The General Partner may make distributions annually or more frequently if there is excess cash on hand after providing for appropriate expenses and liabilities. Such interim distributions are allocated to each Partner according to the percentage of Partnership interest.

ARTICLE V: Management

1. MANAGERS. The names and addresses of General Partners are:

_____

_____

_____

_____

The General Partners shall make decisions regarding the usual affairs of the Limited Partnership. A majority vote of the Partners shall name successors as the General Partners deem necessary and who is responsible for all management decisions and undertakings.

2. NUMBER OF GENERAL PARTNERS. The Partners may elect one, but not fewer than one, General Partner.

3. TERM OF OFFICE. The term of office is not contractual but continues until:

a.) A fixed term of office, as designated by the Partnership, expires.

b.) The General Partner is removed with or without cause, by a majority vote of the Partnership.

c.) The dissociation of such General Partner.

4. AUTHORITY OF GENERAL PARTNER. Only the General Partner and authorized agents shall have the power to bind the Partnership. Each General Partner is authorized on the Partnership's behalf to:

a.) Purchase, or otherwise acquire, sell, develop, pledge, convey, exchange, lease or otherwise dispose of Partnership assets wherever located.

b.) Initiate, prosecute and defend any proceeding on behalf of the Partnership.

c.) Incur and secure liabilities and obligations on behalf of the Partnership.

d.) Lend, invest or re-invest Partnership assets as security for repayment. Money may be lent to Partners, employees and agents of the Partnership.

e.) Appoint officers and agents and hire employees. It is also the province of the General Partner to define duties and establish levels of compensation. Management compensation will be determined by majority Partner vote.

f.) Execute and deliver all contracts, conveyances, assignments, leases, subleases, franchise and licensing agreements, promissory notes, loans, security agreements or any other kind relating to Partnership business.

g.) Establish pensions, trusts, life insurance, incentive plans or any variation thereof, for the benefit of any or all current or former employees, Partners and agents of the Partnership.

h.) Make charitable donations in the Partnership's name.

i.) Seek advice from limited Partners, although, such advice need not be heeded.

j.) Supply, upon the proper request of any Partner, information about the Partnership or any of its activities including but not limited to, access to Partnership records for the purpose of inspecting and copying Partnership books, records and materials in the possession of the General Partner. The Requesting Partner shall be responsible for any expenses incurred in the exercise of these rights set forth in this document.

5. STANDARD OF CARE AND EXCULPATION. Any General Partner must refrain from engaging in grossly negligent, reckless or intentional misconduct. Any act or omission of a General Partner that results in loss or damage to the Partnership, if done in good faith, shall not make the General Partner liable to the Partners.

6. INDEMNIFICATION. The Partnership shall indemnify its General Partner, employees and agents as follows:

a.) Every General Partner, agent, or employee of the Partnership shall be indemnified by the Partnership against all expenses and liabilities, including counsel fees reasonably incurred by him in connection with any proceeding to which he may become involved, by reason of his being or having been a General Partner of the Partnership, except in such cases wherein the General Partner, agent or employee is adjudged guilty of willful misfeasance or malfeasance in the performance of his duties; provided that in the event of a settlement the indemnification herein shall apply only when the General Partner approves such settlement and reimbursement as being in the best interests of the Partnership.

b.) The Partnership shall provide to any person who is or was a General Partner, employee, or agent of the Partnership or is or was serving at the request of the Partnership as General Partner, employee, or agent of the Partnership, the indemnity against expenses of suit, litigation or other proceedings, which is specifically permissible under applicable law.

ARTICLE VI: TAX AND ACCOUNTING MATTERS

1. BANK ACCOUNTS. General Partner shall establish bank accounts, deposit Partnership funds in those accounts and make disbursements from those accounts.

2. ACCOUNTING METHOD. The cash method of accounting shall be the accounting method used to keep records of receipts and disbursements.

3. YEARS. The fiscal and tax years of the Partnership shall be chosen by the General Partner.

4. ACCOUNTANT. An independent accountant shall be selected by the General Partner.

ARTICLE VII: PARTNER DISSOCIATION

1. Upon the first occurrence of any of the following events, a person shall cease to be a Partner of the Partnership:

   a.) Bankruptcy of the Partner.

   b.) Death or court-ordered adjudication of incapacity of the Partner.

   c.) Withdrawal of a Partner with the consent of a majority vote of the remaining Partnership.

   d.) Dissolution and winding up of any non-corporate Partner, including the termination of a trust.

   e.) Filing a Certificate of Dissolution by a corporate Partner.

   f.) Complete liquidation of an estate's interest in the partnership.

   g.) Expulsion of the Partner with the majority consent of the remaining Partnership.

   h.) Expiration of the term specified in Article I, Section 6.

2. OPTION TO PURCHASE INTEREST. In the event of dissociation of a Partner, the Partnership shall have the right to purchase the former Partner's interest at current fair market value.

ARTICLE VIII: DISPOSITION OF PARTNERSHIP INTERESTS

1. PROHIBITIONS.

   a.) No Partnership interest, be it a sale, assignment, exchange, transfer, mortgage, pledge or grant, shall be disposed of if the disposition would result in the dissolution of the Partnership without full compliance with all appropriate state and federal laws.

   b.) No Partner may in any way alienate all or part of his Partnership interest in the Partnership be it through assignment, conveyance, encumbrance or sale, without the prior written consent of the majority of the remaining Partners. Such consent may be given, withheld or delayed as the remaining Partners see fit.

2. PERMISSIONS. A Partner may assign his Partnership interest in the Partnership subject to the provisions in this article. The assignment of Partnership interest does not in itself entitle the assignee to participate in the management of the Partnership nor is the assignee entitled to become a Partner of the Partnership. The assignee is not a substitute Partner but only an assignee of Partnership interest and as such, is entitled to receive only the income and distributions the assigning Partner would have otherwise received.

3. SUBSTITUTE PARTNERSHIP. Only upon the unanimous consent of the remaining Partners may an assignee of a Partnership interest become a substitute Partner and be entitled to all rights associated with the assignor. Upon such admission, the substitute Partner is subject to all restrictions and liabilities of a Partner.

ARTICLE IX: MEETINGS

1. VOTING. All Partners shall have the right to vote on all of the following:

   a.) The dissolution of the Partnership.

   b.) The merger of the Partnership.

   c.) Any transaction involving any potential conflict of interest.

   d.) An amendment to the Articles of Organization or to the Limited Partnership Agreement.

   e.) The transfer or disposition of all Partnership assets outside the ordinary course of business.

2. REQUIRED VOTE. Unless a greater vote is required by statute or the Articles of Organization, an affirmative vote of the majority of the Partnership shall be required.

3. MEETINGS.

   a.) The General Partner(s) shall hold an annual meeting at a time and place of their choosing.

   b.) Special meetings of the Partnership may be called at any time by the General Partner(s) or by at least ten percent (10%) of the Partnership interest of all Partners. Written notice of such meeting must be provided at least sixty (60) business days prior and not later than ten (10) days before the date of the meeting. A Partner may elect to participate in any meeting via telephone.

4. CONSENT. In the absence of an annual or special meeting and in the absence of a vote, any action required to be taken may be permitted with the written consent of the Partners having not less than the minimum number of votes required to authorize such action at a meeting.

ARTICLE X: DISSOLUTION AND TERMINATION

In the event a dissolution event occurs the remaining Partnership shall have the option to elect to continue the Partnership as defined by Article I, Section 6.

1. MERGER. In the event the election to continue the Partnership following a dissolution event is not obtained, a majority vote of the remaining Partners may elect to reconstitute the Partnership through merger with and into another Limited Partnership pursuant to applicable state law.

2. WINDING UP. If the Partners do not elect to continue the Partnership or reconstitute it, the General Partner or other person selected by a majority vote of the Partnership shall wind up the Partnership.

3. FINAL DISTRIBUTIONS. After all Partnership assets have been liquidated and all Partnership debts have been paid, the proceeds of such liquidation shall be distributed to the Partners in accordance with their capital account balance. Liquidation proceeds shall be paid within ___ days of the end of the Partnership's taxable year or, if later, within ___ days after the date of liquidation.

4. DISSOLUTION. Upon completion of the winding up period, the General Partner or other person selected shall file with the secretary of state the Certificate of Dissolution or its equivalent and any other appropriate documents as required by law. IN WITNESS WHEREOF, the parties hereto make and execute this Agreement on the dates set below their names, to be effective on the date first written above.

Signed and Agreed this _____ day of _____, 20____.

By

General Partner:_____

Limited Partner: _____

Limited Partner: _____

Limited Partner: _____

The Limited Liability Company (LLC)

A limited liability company (LLC) is not a corporation but a separate business entity offering a combination of the benefits provided by sole proprietorships, partnerships and corporations. Because of this, it may be a better fit for some businesses than a corporation.

The LLC got its start in Europe and Latin America, and appeared for the first time in the United States in 1977 in Wyoming. It has since expanded to all 50 states and become popular with small business owners for its partnership-like pass-through taxation and liability protection similar to a corporation. The pass-through taxation feature was approved by the Internal Revenue Service (IRS) in 1988. A sole-owner LLC is treated like a sole proprietorship for tax purposes.

Different states have different rules regarding LLCs, so it is important to check with your secretary of state's office for state-specific provisions. Some states impose an annual fee or tax on LLCs, so make sure you check all costs.

To some business analysts, the LLC represents the best of both worlds. First, it offers the pass-through tax status of a partnership. Members are taxed on an individual basis. The company itself pays no taxes (unlike a corporation). Second, members also enjoy limited liability protection. Risk is limited to their business investment. Personal assets are not subject to seizure from the company's creditors. Both advantages come with relatively few structural and paperwork requirements.

An IRS ruling granted LLCs this special pass-through tax status. To qualify, organizations must exhibit no more than two of the following four corporate characteristics:

1. **Continuous life.** Prevent your LLC from existing as a separate entity in two simple steps. Specify a dissolution date, typically 30 years, in your Operating Agreement. Also, include a special directive written in the document that allows your company to continue to exist without amending the Operating Agreement following any member's death, resignation, expulsion, bankruptcy or retirement.

2. **Centralized management.** While corporations typically appoint a board of directors as management, an LLC must vest management power in its members to maintain pass-through status. Although one-member LLCs may have difficulty obtaining partnership tax status, husband and wife are recognized as separate members.

3. **Limited liability.** This one is pretty much a given, since it is a central reason for forming an LLC.

4. **Free transferability of interests.** Members may assign or transfer interests to a third party or creditor who is entitled to receive dividends but not allowed to vote without membership consent.

Advantages

- **Debt and liability protection:** Like a corporate structure, LLCs protect personal assets from business debt and other liabilities.

- **No double taxation:** Like a partnership, LLCs require owners to report business earnings and losses on their personal income tax returns. Owners do, however, have some choices regarding how they are taxed and can file accordingly.

- **Flexibility in management:** Though LLCs can certainly be managed by one owner, the law provides for member management—co-management by all owners of the company. Additionally, LLCs also allow for one or more specially appointed managers.

- **No foreign ownership restrictions:** S corporations often have foreign ownership restrictions; LLCs do not.

Disadvantages

The disadvantages of operating as an LLC include the lack of widespread familiarity and thus, acceptance of this type of organization. IRS rules governing insolvency may create problems for the owners of the LLC. LLCs do not enjoy the advantages of IRS ruling when there is a sale of worthless stock or stock is sold at a loss. The sale of 50 percent or more of the ownership of the LLC in any 12-month period ends any tax advantage the company may have had with the IRS. And, LLCs may not engage in tax-free reorganizations.

- **Limited life:** Most LLCs are ordered to terminate after 30 years. Corporations have no expiration requirements.

- **Raising capital:** Because LLCs cannot issue stocks or bonds, raising capital may be a problem.

- **Higher taxes:** Because LLCs are not corporations, they are taxed at a higher personal rate.

- **Higher fees:** Even without the help of a lawyer or an accountant, LLC fees average over $250.

Limited Liability Corporation	
Ownership	Owned and operated by members
Your level of control	Total
Organizational paperwork	For most states, you must file articles of corporation
Personal liability	Limited liability—owner's personal assets are not at risk
Tax forms (minimum)	Depending on the structure, taxed as a partnership or corporation
Upside: You have the control of a sole proprietorship with the protection of a corporation.	
Downside: You have to deal with the paperwork of a corporation.	

Like all the business structures described in this book, you can file for an LLC yourself. However, establishing an LLC can get complicated, so it is important to have an attorney or qualified tax accountant review your decision and look over your paperwork before you file.

The C Corporation

The most common form of corporation—known as a general corporation or C corporation—is a stand-alone legal entity owned by an unlimited number of stockholders who are protected from the creditors of the business.

C corporations are unique because they operate as legal and tax entities apart from any of the people who own, control, manage or otherwise operate the business. A stockholder's personal liability is usually limited to the amount of investment in the corporation and no more.

A corporation is formed and authorized by law to act as a single entity, although it may be owned by one or more persons. It is legally endowed with rights and responsibilities and has a life of its own independent of the owners and operators. It has been defined by the U.S. Supreme Court as "an artificial being, invisible and existing only in contemplation of the law." Think of it as a distinct and independent entity that exists separately from its owners.

Limited Liability

The owners are not personally liable for debts and obligations of the corporation. They can personally lose only to the extent of their investment in the corporation, with the exception that they may be personally liable for certain types of taxes, such as payroll taxes withheld from the employees' paychecks but not paid to the IRS and state tax authorities. If the business fails or loses a lawsuit, the general creditors cannot attach the owners' homes, cars and other personal property.

Transferable Interests

A corporation has the ability to raise capital by issuing shares of stock, whether public or private. Although the sale of public stock is highly regulated by both federal and state governments, ownership interest or shares of stock may be freely transferred to another party under the rules of the stockholder agreement. Once the interest is transferred, the new owner has all the rights and privileges associated with the former owner's interest. The Federal Trade Commission set strict rules for issuing and publicly trading shares.

Advantages

- **Liability protection:** Owners' personal assets are protected from business debt and liability.
- **Longevity:** Corporations have unlimited life extending beyond the illness or death of the founding owners.
- **Employee benefits:** Corporations can offer tax-free benefits such as insurance, travel and retirement plan deductions.
- **Capital availability:** Corporations can raise capital by issuing stocks and bonds.
- **Easy sale of assets:** Transfer of ownership may be done through the sale of all the stock in the corporation to a new owner.
- **Consistency of management structure:** A change in ownership does not require a change in management.

Disadvantages

- Corporations are more expensive to form than sole proprietorships or partnerships.
- Corporations are required to file a significant amount of tax and reporting paperwork annually.
- Corporations have more legal formalities.
- Corporations are subject to more state and federal rules and regulations.
- Double taxation requires the corporation and its owners to file tax returns.

Corporation	
Ownership	Owned by shareholders
Your level of control	Checked by your board of directors
Organizational paperwork	Must file articles of corporation and is continually monitored by local, state and federal agencies
Personal liability	Shareholders have limited liability of the corporation's debts
Tax forms (minimum)	Form 1120 Corporation Income Tax Return, Form 8109-B Deposit Coupon, Form 4265 Depreciation
Upside: You can raise money by issuing stock.	
Downside: Higher overall taxes because dividends to shareholders are not deductible from business income.	

The S Corporation

Once you have incorporated, you have the option of filing taxes under IRS Subchapter S. An S corporation, as it is called, has the corporate structure of a C or regular corporation but enjoys the same pass-through tax status as a partnership, sole proprietorship or LLC. This means the S corporation itself avoids double taxation, paying no federal taxes. There are a few things to remember. Your salary must be included on the payroll and is subject to employment taxes. Health benefits are not fully deductible as in a C corporation. However, an S corporation is allowed to carry back losses from prior years to offset current earnings.

	Control	Liability	Taxes	Administration
Sole Proprietorship	Total control of business operations and complete share of profits	All personal and business assets are at risk	All taxes reported on personal return	Local requirements may include registering a trade name and obtaining a business license
General Partnership	Management and profits are shared between partners under the partnership agreement	General partners are generally liable for obligations and tort damages incurred by other general partners	Each general partner is taxed directly on his or her share of the profits	No formal administrative requirements other than obtaining proper licenses and permits
Limited Partnership	General and limited partners share in the control and profits of the partnership according to the partnership agreement	Limited partners are not personally obligated for the liabilities of the partnership	Each partner is taxed directly on his or her share of the profits	Registration requirements are similar to corporations but no boardroom record-keeping or tax filing requirements
Limited Liability Company	Members share profits based on a written operating agreement	Generally, members risk only their investment in the LLC	Either partnership-style pass-through to personal returns or corporate income if elected	Similar to corporate requirements for formation and operation
Corporation	Shareholders hold ownership rights and elect directors; directors govern general affairs and appoint officers; officers manage operations	Officers, shareholders and directors are not liable for debts or judgments incurred by the firm	Double taxation unless it is an S corporation in which earnings are passed directly through	Formal incorporation process and annual registration with the secretary of state. Comprehensive record-keeping and tax filing requirements

Like the LLC, many entrepreneurs and small business owners prefer the S corporation because it combines the advantages of a sole proprietorship, partnership and the corporate forms of business structure. S corporations avoid this double taxation (once at the corporate level and again at the personal level) because all income or loss is reported only once on the personal tax returns of the shareholders. However, like standard corporations (and unlike some partnerships), the S corporation shareholders are exempt from personal liability for business debt.

Advantages

- **A single tax level:** The income generated by an S corporation is generally subject to just one level of tax. In other words, the income is taxed only to the corporation's shareholders. In contrast, a C corporation pays tax on its earnings, and its shareholders pay a second tax when corporate earnings are distributed to them in the form of dividends.

- **Availability of losses:** Shareholders of an S corporation generally may deduct their share of the corporation's net operating loss on their individual tax returns in the year the loss occurs. Losses of a C corporation, however, may offset only the corporation's earnings. This pass-through of an S corporation's losses to its shareholders makes this structure attractive to startup businesses expecting to generate losses during their initial stages.

- **Income splitting:** S corporations can serve as excellent vehicles for splitting income among family members through gifts or sales of stock.

Disadvantages

- **Tougher to sell or transfer stock:** The exclusion for up to 50 percent of the gain on the sale of qualified small business stock does not apply to the sale of stock in an S corporation. Stock in an S corporation can only be transferred to eligible shareholders (individuals, estates and certain trusts, certain pension plans and charitable organizations), and an S corporation cannot have more than 35 shareholders. These limitations restrict the sources and amount of equity capital.

- **Limitations on benefits:** Fewer tax-free benefits may be provided to shareholder-employees of S corporations than to shareholder-employees of C corporations.

- **Estate planning for shareholders:** This is generally more complicated when an S corporation is involved.

- **Tax rates applicable to many individuals:** Taxation rates are higher than the rates that would apply to a C corporation at the same income level.

- **Employee stock ownership plans:** Under S corporations these plans have fewer advantages than those under C corporations.

Keep in mind that this list does not affect every company considering S status. Choosing to file as an S corporation is a particularly good justification for bringing an attorney or tax accountant on board to help you consider your options.

S Corporation	
Ownership	Owned by shareholders
Your level of control	Checked by your board of directors
Organizational paperwork	Must file articles of corporation and is continually monitored by local, state and federal agencies
Personal liability	Shareholders have limited liability of the corporation's debts
Tax forms (minimum)	Form 1120 Corporation Income Tax Return, Form 8109-B Deposit Coupon, Form 4265 Depreciation
Upside: Raise money by issuing stock and treat earnings as distributions passing directly through to shareholders and their personal tax returns.	
Downside: Any shareholders working for the company must pay themselves wages, meeting the standards of reasonable compensation.	

Factors in the Decision to Incorporate

Legal liability: To what extent do you need to be insulated from legal liability? If you cannot personally afford the risk of a lawsuit, incorporation and the possibility of business liability coverage may be a consideration.

Tax implications: Based on your goals and those of the business, are there opportunities here to minimize taxation? Which type of corporate structure would best fit those goals?

The cost of incorporation: Starting and keeping a corporation going is expensive. It is important to total up all fees, not just filing fees. There may be fees to file with annual reports, and many states charge franchise taxes. Make sure that the benefits outweigh the time and costs associated with forming a corporation.

Estate flexibility issues: Do you know where you plan to be 5 years from now? It is important to consider the anticipated timeline of your business and your planned tenure because these factors may affect the type of business structure you choose.

Conclusion

The remainder of this book will take you through the basics of the incorporation process. When we say the basics, we do so with the knowledge that no two companies, and particularly no two owners, are alike. The best structural choice is the one that best fits you, your business and your long-term goals.

The Process of Incorporating

What It May Cost in Time & Money

Most businesses incorporate to obtain limited liability protection. With the protection of a corporate structure, all business risks belong solely to the corporation rather than management or shareholders. Shareholders—even a single shareholder of a solo operation—are typically not liable if creditors demand debts owed by the corporation.

As one small business owner put it, "I incorporated because I did not want to lose my house if I got sued." Though this belief in complete liability protection is generally true, the reality can be a bit more complicated. We address risk management issues later in the book.

Business owners also incorporate for other reasons, including the ability to set up certain retirement plans, such as 401(k)s, for themselves and their employees, the ability to sell the company more easily if they want to retire or start a new business and most important, easier access to capital for expansion.

These are all strong incentives to incorporate, but what costs are involved in setting it up? Though costs may vary, expect to pay anywhere from $200 to $1,000 in filing fees and related costs if you are working without the assistance of an attorney or accountant, and potentially thousands of dollars if you put the entire effort in the hands of experts. This does not include the additional time, tax and related expenses you will face after the corporation is established.

Incorporating on the Cheap

It is certainly possible to set up a legal and well-functioning corporation by yourself if are willing to invest the time and effort needed to accomplish the task. A legal or business background that provided exposure to how corporations are launched and operated is helpful but not necessary.

The Internet has made the process of incorporating a far simpler task. Today, all 50 states have Web sites (usually based within the secretary of state's office) that guide you through the incorporation process. Some Web offerings are better than others, but they all provide basic information on the various forms, filing requirements and costs you will face in the setup process as well as what you will need to do and pay as an ongoing corporate entity. (Refer to Appendix A for complete contact information and basic incorporation details on all 50 states.)

There are also a variety of Web-based businesses providing turnkey incorporation solutions for as little as a few hundred dollars. The best ones are generally reliable and may be a worthwhile investment if you are looking for a simplified corporate structure. A simple Internet search will reveal dozens of Web-based services that will help you incorporate for a flat fee, but check with your local Better Business Bureau (www.bbb.org) before paying any fees.

Seeking Professional Assistance

The purpose of this book is to provide you with the groundwork needed to incorporate. And though it is possible and cost-effective to handle most of the details yourself, we would not discourage anyone from seeking the advice of legal and tax professionals during this process.

All business owners have unique needs and concerns with regard to business operations and tax issues, many of which impact their personal financial situation. A corporation formed without proper due diligence in those areas may end up a costly and ineffective structure down the road.

Get Some Friendly, Free Advice First

When you are learning something new, it is not always necessary to have the answers immediately at your fingertips. Sometimes it is better to be armed with the right questions and know the right people to ask those questions. Check with friends and business associates about their experiences with incorporation. Ask them the following:

1. Why did you incorporate?
2. Do you feel you have benefited from incorporation from a business or tax standpoint? In what ways? Have there been pitfalls?
3. What is one thing you would not do if you were incorporating today?
4. Do you plan to remain incorporated or would you change your business structure for any reason? Why?
5. What did it cost you to incorporate? Knowing what you know now, how could you have saved money?
6. Is there anything in the filing process you would have done differently?
7. Do you also carry business liability insurance? Why or why not?
8. What surprises, if any, did you get after you incorporated?
9. Is it tough keeping up with filing and regulatory requirements?
10. Did you face any particular local licensing requirements for your business?
11. Describe the process of operating a corporation? Do you think it is worth the extra work?
12. Did you work with an attorney or an accountant who was helpful during the process? In what ways did the extra help prove beneficial?
13. Did you have any bad experiences during the process of incorporating?

14. How long did it take to become incorporated?

15. Are there attorneys, accountants or other professionals that you would recommend?

Incorporation should not be a rushed decision, so it pays to speak to people who have experience with the process. You need a sense of what it is like to operate as a corporation and how to make the best use of the business structure.

Remember, too, the importance of thanking your associates for their time and input with a handwritten thank you note or e-mail. It is an expected courtesy and a good business practice. You never know when and how your paths may cross again in the world of business.

Ways to Incorporate

Method	Time Frame
Research and file your own papers	Could be lengthy
Hire an attorney or accountant	Several weeks
Use an online service	Some promise 24-hour turnaround, but then it is up to the state to approve all forms

Your Next Stop—Your Secretary of State's Web Site

The Internet will save you time and simplify the incorporation process, regardless of whether you handle the task yourself or work with advisors. It is particularly helpful to understand the laws, procedures and fees required by your home state before you enlist the help of an attorney or a tax advisor, even if you decide not to incorporate in the state where you live.

In all 50 states, any business owner who wants to create a profit or nonprofit corporation, partnership or limited liability company must file documents with a state official, usually the secretary of state. A corporation filing process typically starts with the filing of the "Articles of Incorporation" or the "Certificate of Incorporation."

Fees

Fees can vary widely by state—some states charge as little as $50 to file the initial articles of incorporation; others charge upwards of $500. In early 2005, the state of Colorado was offering a $0.99 fee to file articles of incorporation if the entire

process was completed online. Though that is an extreme example, some states provide discounts to those filing by fax instead of mail, and others affix penalties if you handwrite your application instead of typing it.

Read all fee requirements carefully. If a lawyer is filing on your behalf, ask for an itemized statement of what fees are being paid to the state.

Online Incorporation Companies

To incorporate online, visit your state's secretary of state Web site to apply directly, hire an attorney or accountant to file the necessary papers or locate an online incorporation company to prepare and submit the necessary paperwork for you.

The number of online incorporation companies continues to grow. Compare services and prices before selecting a company. The types of services and support provided varies from company to company (as does their fees for their services).

Services typically provided by online incorporation providers may include:

Corporate Name Reservation

Many companies provide an initial name check for any of the 50 states to check on name availability.

Employer Identification Number (EIN)

Assistance in obtaining a taxpayer identification number (TIN or tax ID) also known as employer identification number (EIN). This number will be required if the company is going to open a bank account, withhold taxes for employees, hire employees, create a trust, purchase an operating business, change the company name or change the type of organization.

S Corporation Election

Companies electing to incorporate as a S corporation may have this form prepared for an additional charge.

Foreign Qualification

Corporations are primarily regulated on a state by state basis. As such there are three designations: domestic, foreign and alien. A domestic corporation is a corporation transacting business in the state of incorporation. If this corporation wants to maintain an office in another state it would first have to file with the state and would be considered a foreign corporation. A corporation organized in another country would be considered alien. Most online incorporation providers will assist in the preparation of the necessary documentation for you to qualify for foreign status so that your LLC or corporation may operate in another state.

Registered Agent Service

A registered agent is legally required by a corporation or limited liability company in nearly all jurisdictions. The registered agent accepts official documents and can help to insure that certain documents are filed in order to keep the company in good standing. As such, the registered agent should be available at the physical address listed in the public records from 9 a.m. to 5 p.m. weekdays. Most incorporation companies provide registered agent services in all fifty states and several overseas locations. Registered agents are legally required by most jurisdictions.

Corporate Kits

Upon completion of incorporation, the registering company will provide a corporate kit including an official hand-held corporate seal with your corporation's name (if registered as a C Corporation), state and date of incorporation, a corporate records book, an example set of bylaws, corporate minutes, a directors register and officers list, a shareholder's register, a securities register, shareholder agreements, corporate bylaws and several personalized stock certificates.

Corporate Seal/Embosser

Corporate seals are required by many states for certain transactions if the company is registered as a C Corporation. An online corporation company will provide a corporate seal/embosser with the completion of registration.

Stock Certificates

Personalized membership certificates are generally included in the kit.

Articles of Amendment

Most states require a certificate or articles of amendment if your corporation makes any changes to the articles of incorporation. Most online incorporation companies will assist you in the preparation and submission of articles of amendment in any of the 50 states.

Certificate of Good Standing

Certificates of authorization or certificates of good standing are official documents stating that the company is incorporated in a specific state, that it has paid all necessary filing and registration fees and that it is authorized to transact business within the state. An online corporation company will provide this certificate upon registration.

Articles of Dissolution

A corporation or LLC must file certificates/articles of dissolution with the state in order to terminate the existence of the company. An online corporation company can assist you in the filing of these papers in any of the 50 states and some foreign locations.

Vital Deadline Announcements

As deadlines occur, most online incorporation companies will send advance notice of upcoming deadlines as part of their overall service. Reminder notices may include quarterly tax due dates, annual report filing due dates and annual partnership tax due dates.

Remember to Register

In order to gain access to free forms, dictionaries, checklists and updates, readers must register their book purchase at Socrates.com. An eight-digit Registration Code is provided on the enclosed CD. See page iv for further details.

Bylaws

As part of the filing process, you will need to prepare a set of bylaws that describe how the corporation will run, including the responsibilities of the shareholders, directors and officers; when stockholder meetings will be held; and other details important to running the company. Once your bylaws are accepted, the secretary of state's office will send you a certificate of incorporation.

Example of Bylaws (A Delaware Corporation)

ARTICLE I
OFFICES

Section 1.01 **Offices**. The Corporation shall have its registered office in the State of Delaware, and may have such other offices and places of business within or without the State of Delaware as the Board of Directors may from time to time determine or the business of the Corporation may require.

ARTICLE II
STOCKHOLDERS

Section 2.01 **Place of Meetings.** Meetings of stockholders for any purpose may be held at such place or places, either within or without the State of Delaware, as shall be designated by the Board of Directors, or by the President with respect to meetings called by him.

Section 2.02 **Annual Meeting.** The annual meeting of stockholders shall be held on such date as may be determined by the Board of Directors. At such meeting, the stockholders shall elect a Board of Directors and transact such other business as may properly come before the meeting.

Section 2.03 **Special Meetings.** Special meetings of stockholders may be called at any time by the Board of Directors or by the President, and shall be called by the President or Secretary at the written request of stockholders owning a majority of the shares of the Corporation then outstanding and entitled to vote.

Section 2.04 **Notice of Meetings.** Written notice of the annual meeting or any special meeting of stock shall be given to each stockholder entitled to vote thereat, not less than 10 nor more than 60 days prior to the meeting, except as otherwise required by statute, and shall state the time and place and, in the case of a special meeting, the purpose or purposes of the meeting. Notice need not be given, however, to any stockholder who submits a signed waiver of notice, before or after the meeting, or who attends the meeting in person or by proxy without objecting to the transaction of business.

Section 2.05 **Quorum.** At all meetings of stockholders, the holders of a majority of the stock issued and outstanding and entitled to vote thereat, present in person or represented by proxy, shall constitute a quorum for the transaction of business, except as otherwise provided by statute, the Certificate of Incorporation or these By-Laws. When a quorum is once present to organize a meeting, it is not broken by the subsequent withdrawal of any stockholder.

Section 2.06 **Voting.** (a) At all meetings of stockholders, each stockholder having the right to vote thereat may vote in person or by proxy, and, unless otherwise provided in the certificate of incorporation or in any resolution providing for the issuance of any class or series of stock adopted by the Board of Directors pursuant to authority vested in the Board by the certificate of incorporation, shall have one vote for each share of stock registered in his name. Election of directors shall be by written ballot.

(b) When a quorum is once present at any meeting of stockholders, a majority of the votes cast, whether in person or represented by proxy, shall decide any question or proposed action brought before such meeting, except for the election of directors, who shall be elected by a plurality of the votes cast, or unless the question or action is one upon which a different vote is required by express provision of statute, the Certificate of Incorporation or these By-Laws or an agreement among stockholders, in which case such provision shall govern the vote on the decision of such question or action.

Section 2.07 **Adjourned Meetings.** Any meeting of stockholders may be adjourned to a designated time and place by a vote of a majority in interest of the stockholders present in person or by proxy and entitled to vote, even though less than a quorum is present, or by the President if a quorum of stockholders is not present. No notice of such adjourned meeting need be given, other than by announcement at the meeting at which adjournment is taken, and any business may be transacted at the adjourned meeting which might have been transacted at the meeting as originally called. However, if such adjournment is for more than 30 days, or if after such adjournment a new record date is fixed for the adjourned meeting, a notice of the adjourned meeting shall be given to each stockholder of record entitled to vote at such meeting.

Section 2.08 **Action by Written Consent of Stockholders.** Any action of the stockholders required or permitted to be taken at any regular or special meeting thereof may be taken without any such meeting, notice of meeting or vote if a consent in writing setting forth the action thereby taken is signed by the holders of outstanding stock having not less than the number of votes that would have been necessary to authorize such action at a meeting at which all shares entitled to vote were present and voted. Prompt notice of the taking of any such action shall be given to any stockholders entitled to vote who have not so consented in writing.

Section 2.09 **Stockholders of Record.** (a) The stockholders from time to time entitled to notice of or to vote at any meeting of stockholders or any adjournment thereof, or to express consent to any corporate action without a meeting, or entitled to receive payment of any dividend or other distribution or the allotment of any rights, or entitled to exercise any rights in respect of any change, conversion or exchange of stock or for the purpose of any other lawful action, shall be the stockholders of record as of the close of business on a date fixed by the Board of Directors as the record date for any such purpose. Such a record date shall not precede the date upon which the resolution fixing the record date is adopted by the Board of Directors, and shall not, with respect to stockholder meetings, be more than 60 days nor less than 10 days before the date of such meeting, or, with respect to stockholder consents, more than 10 days after the date upon which the resolution fixing the record date is adopted by the Board of Directors.

(b) If the Board of Directors does not fix a record date, (i) the record date for the determination of stockholders entitled to notice of or to vote at a meeting of stockholders shall be as of the close of business on the day next preceding the day on which notice of such meeting is given, or, if notice is waived as provided herein, on the day next preceding the day on which the meeting is held; (ii) the record date for determining stockholders entitled to express consent to corporate action in writing without a meeting, where no prior action by the Board of Directors is necessary, shall be the close of business on the day on which the first signed written consent setting forth the action taken or proposed to be taken is delivered to the Corporation; and (iii) the record date for determining stockholders for any other purpose shall be at the close of business on the day on which the resolution of the Board of Directors relating thereto is adopted.

ARTICLE III
DIRECTORS

Section 3.01 **Board of Directors.** The management of the affairs, property and business of the Corporation shall be vested in a Board of Directors, the members of which need not be stockholders. In addition to the power and authority expressly conferred upon it by these By-Laws and the certificate of incorporation, the Board of Directors may take any action and do all such lawful acts and things on behalf of the Corporation and as are not by statute or by the certificate of incorporation or these By-Laws required to be taken or done by the stockholders.

Section 3.02 **Number.** The number of directors shall be as fixed from time to time by the Board of Directors.

Section 3.03 **Election and Term of Directors.** At each annual meeting of the stockholders, the stockholders shall elect directors to hold office until the next annual meeting. Each director shall hold office until the expiration of such term and until his successor, if any, has been elected and qualified, or until his earlier resignation or removal.

Section 3.04 **Annual and Regular Meetings.** The annual meeting of the Board of Directors shall be held promptly after the annual meeting of stockholders, and regular meetings of the Board of Directors may be held at such times as the Board of Directors may from time to time determine. No notice shall be required for the annual or any regular meeting of the Board of Directors.

Section 3.05 **Special Meetings.** Special meetings of the Board of Directors may be called by the President, by an officer of the corporation who is also a director or by any two directors, upon one day's notice to each director either personally or by mail, telephone, telecopier or telegraph, and if by telephone, telecopier or telegraph confirmed in writing before or after the meeting, setting forth the time and place of such meeting. Notice of any special meeting need not be given, however, to any director who submits a signed waiver of notice, before or after the meeting, or who attends the meeting without objecting to the transaction of business.

Section 3.06 **Place of Meetings.** (a) The Board of Directors may hold its meetings, regular or special, at such places, either within or without the State of Delaware, as it may from time to time determine or as shall be set forth in any notice of such meeting.

(b) Any meeting of the Board of Directors may be held by means of conference telephone or similar communications equipment whereby all persons participating in the meeting can hear each other, and such participation shall constitute presence at the meeting.

Section 3.07 **Adjourned Meetings.** A majority of the directors present, whether or not a quorum, may adjourn any meeting of the Board of Directors to another time and place. Notice of such adjourned meeting need not be given if the time and place thereof are announced at the meeting at which the adjournment is taken.

Section 3.08 **Quorum of Directors.** A majority of the total number of directors shall constitute a quorum for the transaction of business. The total number of directors means the number of directors the Corporation would have if there were no vacancies.

Section 3.09 **Action of the Board of Directors.** The vote of a majority of the directors present at a meeting at which a quorum is present shall be the act of the Board of Directors, unless the question or action is one upon which a different vote is required by express provision of statute, the Certificate of Incorporation or these By-Laws, in which case such provision shall govern the vote on the decision of such question or action. Each director present shall have one vote.

Section 3.10 **Action by Written Consent of Directors.** Any action required or permitted to be taken at any meeting of the Board of Directors or of any committee thereof may be taken without a meeting, if a written consent thereto is signed by all members of the Board of Directors or of such committee, and such written consent is filed with the minutes of proceedings of the Board of Directors or committee.

Section 3.11 **Resignation.** A director may resign at any time by giving written notice to the Board of Directors, the President or the Secretary of the Corporation. Unless otherwise specified in the notice, the resignation shall take effect upon receipt by the Board of Directors or such officer and acceptance of the resignation shall not be necessary.

Section 3.12 **Removal of Directors.** Any or all of the directors may be removed with or without cause by the stockholders.

Section 3.13 **Newly Created Directorships and Vacancies.** Newly created directorships resulting from an increase in the number of directors or vacancies occurring in the Board of Directors for any reason except the removal of directors without cause may be filled by a vote of the majority of the directors then in office, although less than a quorum. Vacancies occurring by reason of the removal of directors without cause shall be filled by a vote of the stockholders. A director elected to fill a newly created directorship or to fill any vacancy shall hold office until the next annual meeting of stockholders, and until his successor, if any, has been elected and qualified.

Section 3.14 **Chairman.** At all meetings of the Board of Directors the Chairman of the Board or, if one has not been elected or appointed or in his absence, a chairman chosen by the directors present at such meeting, shall preside.

Section 3.15 **Committees Appointed by the Board of Directors.** The Board of Directors may, by resolution passed by a majority of the entire Board of Directors or by written consent of all of the directors, designate one or more committees, each committee to consist of one or more of the directors. The Board may also designate one or more directors as alternate members of any committee who may replace any absent or disqualified committee member at any committee meeting. Any such committee, to the extent provided in the resolution, except as restricted by law, shall have and may exercise the powers of the Board of Directors in the management of the affairs, business and property of the Corporation, and may authorize the seal of the Corporation to be affixed to all papers, which may require it.

Section 3.16 **Compensation.** No compensation shall be paid to directors, as such, for their services, but the Board of Directors may authorize payment of an annual retainer and/or fixed sum and expenses for attendance at each annual, regular or special meeting of the Board of Directors. Nothing herein contained shall be construed to preclude any director from serving the corporation in any other capacity and receiving compensation therefore.

ARTICLE IV
OFFICERS

Section 4.01 **Offices, Election and Term.** (a) At its annual meeting the Board of Directors shall elect or appoint a President and a Secretary and may, in addition, elect or appoint at any time such other officers as it may determine. Any number of offices may be held by the same person.

(b) Unless otherwise specified by the Board of Directors, each officer shall be elected or appointed to hold office until the annual meeting of the Board of Directors next following his election or appointment and until his successor, if any, has been elected or appointed and qualified, or until his earlier resignation or removal.

(c) Any officer may resign at any time by giving written notice to the Board of Directors, the President or the Secretary of the Corporation. Unless otherwise specified in the notice, the resignation shall take effect upon receipt thereof, and the acceptance of the resignation shall not be necessary to make it effective.

(d) Any officer elected or appointed by the Board of Directors may be removed by the Board of Directors with or without cause. Any vacancy occurring in any office by reason of death, resignation, removal or otherwise may be filled by the Board of Directors.

Section 4.02 **Powers and Duties.** The officers, agents and employees of the corporation shall each have such powers and perform such duties in the management of the affairs, property and business of the Corporation, subject to the control of and limitation by the Board of Directors, as generally pertain to their respective offices, as well as such powers and duties as may be authorized from time to time by the Board of Directors.

Section 4.03 **Sureties and Bonds.** If the Board of Directors shall so require, any officer, agent or employee of the Corporation shall furnish to the Corporation a bond in such sum and with such surety or sureties as the Board of Directors may direct, conditioned upon the faithful performance of his duties to the Corporation and including responsibility for negligence and for the accounting for all property, funds or securities of the corporation, which may come into his hands.

ARTICLE V
CERTIFICATES AND TRANSFER OF SHARES

Section 5.01 **Certificates.** Unless otherwise provided pursuant to the General Corporation Law of the State of Delaware, the shares of stock of the Corporation shall be represented by certificates, as provided by the General Corporation Law of the State of Delaware. They shall be numbered and entered in the books of the Corporation as they are issued.

Section 5.02 **Lost or Destroyed Certificates.** The Board of Directors may in its discretion authorize the issuance of a new certificate or certificates in place of any certificate or certificates theretofore issued by the Corporation, alleged to have been lost, stolen or destroyed. As a condition of such issuance, the Board of Directors may require, either generally or in each case, the record holder of such certificates, or his legal representative, to furnish an affidavit setting forth the facts of such alleged loss, theft or destruction, together with proof of advertisement of the alleged loss, theft or destruction, and a bond with such surety and in such form and amount as the Board may specify indemnifying the Corporation, any transfer agent and registrar against any claim against any of them relating to such lost, stolen or destroyed certificates.

Section 5.03 **Transfer of Shares.** (a) Upon surrender to the Corporation or the transfer agent of the Corporation of a certificate for shares or other securities of the Corporation duly endorsed or accompanied by proper evidence of succession, assignment or authority to transfer, the corporation shall issue a new certificate to the person entitled thereto, and cancel the old certificate, except to the extent the Corporation or such transfer agent may be prevented from so doing by law, by the order or process of any court of competent jurisdiction, or under any valid restriction on transfer imposed by the certificate of incorporation, these By-Laws, or agreement of security holders. Every such transfer shall be entered on the transfer books of the Corporation.

(b) The Corporation shall be entitled to treat the holder of record of any share or other security of the Corporation as the holder in fact thereof and shall not be bound to recognize any equitable or other claim to or interest in such share or security on the part of any other person whether or not it shall have express or other notice thereof, except as expressly provided by law.

ARTICLE VI
INDEMNIFICATION

Section 6.01 **Indemnification.** The Corporation shall indemnify the directors, officers, agents and employees of the Corporation in the manner and to the full extent provided in the General Corporation Law of the State of Delaware. Such indemnification may be in addition to any other rights to which any person seeking indemnification may be entitled under any agreement, vote of stockholders or directors, any provision of these By-Laws or otherwise. The directors, officers, employees and agents of the Corporation shall be fully protected individually in making or refusing to make any payment or in taking or refusing to take any other action under this Article VI in reliance upon the advice of counsel.

ARTICLE VII
MISCELLANEOUS

Section 7.01 Corporate Seal. The seal of the Corporation shall be circular in form and bear the name of the Corporation, the year of its organization and the words, "Corporate Seal, Delaware." The seal of the certificates for shares or any corporate obligation for the payment of money, or on any other instrument, may be a facsimile, engraved, printed or otherwise reproduced.

Section 7.02 Execution of Instruments. All corporate instruments and documents shall be signed or countersigned, executed, and, if desired, verified or acknowledged by a proper officer or officers or such other person or persons as the Board of Directors may from time to time designate.

Section 7.03 Fiscal Year. The fiscal year of the Corporation shall be as determined by the Board of Directors.

ARTICLE VIII
AMENDMENTS

Section 8.01 Amendments. These By-Laws may be altered, amended or repealed from time to time by the stockholders or by the Board of Directors without the assent or vote of the stockholders.

ARTICLE IX
STOCKHOLDERS AGREEMENT

Section 9.01 **Stockholders Agreement.** Should the Corporation at any time, or from time to time, be party to a stockholders agreement (a "Stockholders Agreement"), then notwithstanding anything to the contrary contained in these By-Laws, in the event of any conflict between any provision of such Stockholders Agreement and any provision of these By-Laws, such conflicting provision of the Stockholders Agreement shall be incorporated herein as a By-Law and shall control.

Reporting

Corporations, even those run by soloists with no employees, need to issue stock, file annual reports and hold yearly meetings to elect officers and directors, even if they are both shareholder and owner. Meeting minutes need to be kept, and some states require witnesses.

Why all the fuss for a corporation running out of your attic? Consider if you get sued or if for any reason state or federal authorities—like the IRS—need to investigate your business. Any failure to keep and file appropriate corporate records correctly and on time could lead to a piercing of the corporate veil, which means that the corporate structure that protects your home and assets may not be effective. You could lose everything.

Your state may also require that all stationery, including letterhead, business cards, and product packaging, reflect your newly incorporated status by adding Inc. or LLC after your company name. The additional cost is a worthwhile investment. Many businesses prefer to work with incorporated companies because they have additional liability protection and additional confidence in the structure of your business could lead to more business.

Summary

The most important factor in creating a successful corporation is a solid understanding of the process and ongoing operational requirements. Talk to colleagues familiar with incorporating and take advantage of the information available on your home state's Web site.

Free Forms and Checklists

Registered readers can visit www.socrates.com/books/ready-incorporate.aspx for free forms, letters and checklists. To register, see page iv for details. Among the many items available are:

Commercial Lease • Estimated Startup Capital Worksheet • General Partnership Agreement • Minutes: First Meeting of Shareholders • Stock Ledger and Transfer Ledger • Corporate Resolutions • Personal Net Worth Worksheet • Profitability Worksheet Analysis • And more!

A Closer Look at Types of Corporations

Which Inc. Is Right for You?

Launching a business is a tremendous amount of work, and the corporate structure you choose impacts many of your business operations, including reporting procedures, stock ownership and federal and state tax requirements.

Incorporation can take weeks or months, depending on how much of the preparation you plan to do yourself. It is also the most expensive category of business formation, at founding and on an ongoing basis. For these reasons, it is critical to select the type of corporation that best fits your business model, growth expectations and personal tax issues.

Later in this chapter, we take a more detailed look at the three corporate structures as well as one noncorporate structure—the LLC. But first, lets look at the nuts and bolts of the incorporation process.

Establishing a Corporation

We will assume that you have an established business that you are thinking of incorporating. If you are still at the business formation stage, turn to Chapter 4 for a discussion of the importance of a business plan and other key steps in starting a business.

One disclaimer before we begin: This book is not a substitute for professional legal, financial or tax assistance in the establishment of a corporation. It serves as a tool to guide you through the process yourself or with the help of experts.

For those of you incorporating in Canada, much of the information provided here is applicable. However, Chapter 11 offers more specific information on incorporating in Canada.

The following are key steps in the incorporation process:

1. Decide whether to incorporate.
2. Decide where to incorporate.
3. Decide the type of corporation appropriate to your business (C corporation, S corporation or close corporation).
4. Select a corporate name.
5. Select a registered agent, if necessary.
6. Draft a certificate or articles of incorporation.
7. Sign the certificate of incorporation and file with your secretary of state with the appropriate filing fees.
8. Hold the incorporator's initial meeting to elect directors and transact first business.
9. Hold the first organizational meeting of the initial board of directors.
10. Select a corporate seal and stock certificate, issue shares, elect officers and open corporate bank accounts.
11. Apply for an EIN.
12. Choose a fiscal year.
13. File a Doing Business As (DBA) certificate, if necessary.
14. Apply for foreign incorporation in other states if you are planning to do business in states beyond where you plan your initial incorporation (subject to those states' requirements).
15. Obtain necessary state and local licenses and/or permits.
16. Hold the first regular, official meeting of directors and stockholders.
17. Document actions and maintain accurate corporate records.

Note

If the foregoing tasks sound complicated, we strongly urge you to consider hiring legal and tax assistance in setting up a corporation. Professional guidance can be invaluable, and a single meeting may be all you need to secure the advice and information necessary to proceed. Legal and tax professionals can offer more detailed information about the process, fees and ongoing tasks of incorporation required for your state than can be provided here.

After completing these steps, you are free to transfer reasonable assets and liabilities of the business to the new corporation for a set value, for which you receive shares of stock in exchange. This signifies your ownership in the corporation. You will also need to notify all customers and creditors of your change to a corporate status as appropriate. In some states, all that is required is a personal letter to each customer or creditor; in other states, you may need to place a legal ad in the classified section of your local paper. Again, check the rules of your state.

Why Selecting a Name Is Important

Once you have chosen a name for your company, make sure it complies with the naming rules of the state in which you operate; otherwise, you will be required to change it. In general, the following words cannot be used: acceptance, endowment, national, architect, engineering, pharmacy, bank, federal, savings, banking, guaranty, state, police, board of trade, indemnity, thrift, certified, accountant, insurance, trust, chamber of commerce, lawyer, underwriter, cooperative, loan, United States, credit union, urban development, mortgage, urban and relocation. These words can be used in the names of organizations or corporations, but only in fields in which special licensing or regulation is required.

The state-by-state incorporation rules (Appendix A) gives a brief description of each state's naming conventions, but the information may be only a fraction of the state's full rules. Consult the Web sites listed for each state for complete information.

Size Matters

When it comes to issuing stock, a corporation with $60,000 in annual revenues faces different obstacles than one with $60 million in revenues. Regulators generally do not get involved when stock is issued to one or two employees of a business. However, when stock is sold to 25 or more people (inside and outside the business), it is generally considered a public offering and subject to securities regulations on the state and federal level.

Because stock ownership is a key component of any corporation, it is vital to understand the purpose and ownership of stock, how it will be used in the business going forward and most important, how regulators view that offering. Failing to issue stock properly can lead to larger problems later.

Where to Go for Reliable, Free Advice

The Small Business Administration (SBA) of the federal government was established by Congress to provide prospective, new and established small businesses financial and management training and counseling. Check your local Yellow Pages for the nearest office or visit www.sba.gov.

The SBA offers free counseling through the Service Corps of Retired Executives (SCORE). SCORE is extremely helpful and may offer free on-site counseling services, workshops and seminars. Many local trade associations and chambers of commerce also provide assistance.

A Closer Look at Corporate Structures

Before choosing a corporate structure for your business, it is important to understand the various types available. Your decision should factor in your ownership provisions, your current company size and your long-term plans for growth.

DBA (Doing Business As)

A fictitious business name, assumed name, or DBA allows you to legally do business as a particular name at minimal cost, and without having to create an entirely new business entity. You can accept payments, advertise and otherwise present yourself under that name. In fact, if you present your business under a name other than your proper legal name without proper notification, it may be considered fraud. Fortunately, filing for an assumed name is so easy and inexpensive, there is really not much excuse for not filing one.

Filing an assumed name allows you as a sole proprietor to use a business name rather than your personal name. In most states, you cannot open a business bank account or accept payments without a registered DBA.

The exact rules vary from country to country and from state to state within the U.S., so check with your local business regulatory authority regarding your area. If there is any implication that there are more people involved (e.g., Sanford & Sons, The Mehle Group, etc.), or if you just use the first name (e.g., Sam's Hardware Store, Fred's Boathouse, etc.), you have to file an assumed name. It also lets you use a typical business name without creating a formal legal entity (i.e., corporation, partnership, LLC, etc.). You can even open a business checking account and get a business phone listing for the name. For sole proprietors, this is the least expensive way to legally do business under a business name.

A DBA also allows a single legal entity (corporation, LLC, etc.) to operate multiple businesses without creating a new legal entity for each business. For example, if you are planning to operate a series of Web sites, or a chain of stores, you might set up a corporation with a generic name, such as ABC Web Enterprises, Inc., or The Retailer, LLC, and then file an assumed name for each Web site or store. Since there is significant expense in filing and maintaining a corporation, this helps control costs while still allowing you to expand your business.

Applying for an Assumed Name

In some U.S. states you register your assumed name with an individual state's secretary of state or other state agency, but in most states, registration is handled at the county -level, and each county may have different forms and fees for registering a name. The process is simple: you perform a search through the state or county database to make sure the name is not already in use, then submit a simple form, along with the correct filing fee (anywhere from $10 to $50). Some states also require that you publish a notice in your local newspaper and submit an affidavit to show that you have fulfilled the publication requirement. Call your county clerk's office to find out the local fees and procedures in your area.

General Corporations or C Corporations

General, or C, corporations are the most common legal structure for larger corporations and ideal for companies that plan to go public in the stock market someday. A C corporation is a legal entity that is owned by an unlimited number of stockholders who are personally shielded from debts or obligations related to the business. C corporations are generally subject to dual taxation. This means that the profits of a corporation are taxed first as income to the corporation and then as income to the shareholders when profits are distributed as dividends. C corporations are also subject to higher regulatory scrutiny and other restrictions that may make this category of filing less desirable for smaller companies seeking the same liability protections.

Close Corporations

Though guidelines vary from state to state, close corporations are generally owned and operated by a few individuals—often members of the same family rather than public shareholders. Close corporations may have simplified tax provisions, and state laws permit close corporations to function more informally than general corporations. For example, shareholders can make decisions without holding meetings of the board of directors, and can fill vacancies on the board without a vote. These corporations often have less than two dozen shareholders and no ready market for the corporation's stock. Most company shareholders actively participate in the management of the corporation, which makes this corporate structure an attractive option for family owned and managed companies.

S Corporations

In previous incarnations, S corporations were known as subchapter S corporations or small business corporations. This type of corporation provides the limited liability benefits of incorporation but eliminates dual taxation. Essentially, it allows income, deductions, credits and losses to be passed through to shareholders, who are liable for taxes due.

Because an S corporation is limited to 75 shareholders, consider converting to a C corporation when:

- Your business becomes profitable and you want to expand your earnings by issuing stock to a greater number of shareholders. A C corporation allows unlimited shareholders.

- You have owned a profitable service business for several years and now want to diversify, reinvesting your earnings in the corporation. The lower corporate tax rates offered through a C corporation will leave you more cash for reinvestment. It may also be possible to pull sufficient income out of the corporation as salary to avoid double taxation.

- You formed your S corporation several years ago as a tax shelter. Earnings have grown and your company is now highly profitable, resulting in substantial taxes due on your personal income tax return. Converting to C status allows the profits to be taxed at corporate rates.

- You have encountered considerable passive losses through tax credits, depreciation or real estate investments. Though the losses result from accounting strategies, these items should be placed under ownership of a C corporation or held personally.

S Corporation Warning Signs

S corporations are subject to numerous regulations. You may risk losing your S corporation status if any of the following events occur:

- One of your stockholders transfers shares to a trust, partnership or corporation.
- Any new stockholder files a formal refusal to consent to the S corporation election.
- Stock is accidentally sold to more stockholders than permitted by law.
- In any one year, your corporation receives less than 80 percent of its gross revenue from inside the U.S.

Limited Liability Company (LLC)

An LLC is not a corporation but a corporate alternative. It is a business entity similar to an S corporation, partnership or sole proprietorship in terms of simplified taxation.

Most small business owners choose between an S corporation and an LLC. Review the following information to compare the two business structures and decide which one best suits your needs:

- Both LLCs and S corporations allow pass-through taxation.
- S corporations allow for up to 75 owners; LLCs allow an unlimited number of members, considered the same as owners.
- LLCs can have non-U.S. citizens as members.
- S corporations cannot be owned by C corporations; LLCs can.
- LLCs can be more flexible in distributing profits. LLC income is not directly tied to ownership stake, though a percentage needs to be set in the LLCs operating agreement.
- In most states, S corporations may be formed by a single individual, whereas LLCs may require more than one person.
- S corporations do not have to end with the death or departure of one or more owners. LLCs have strict dissolution dates and conditions—some states mandate that LLCs dissolve within 30 or 40 years.

Setting Your Fiscal Year

IRS Form SS-4, "Application for Employer Identification Number (EIN)," requires you to state your fiscal year, the 12 months of your financial activity upon which the IRS bases its tax calculations. In some states, you are also required to state your fiscal year on your certificate of incorporation.

The calendar year is often considered the most convenient fiscal year because fewer tax forms are required. However, there are several tax advantages to choosing a fiscal year that is not the calendar year. Consult with a tax advisor before making this decision.

When corresponding with the IRS, be sure to include your EIN. The EIN identifies your business to the IRS.

Summary

Incorporating a business yourself can be a daunting task. The various corporate structures available—including the non-corporate limited liability company—all offer specific benefits and drawbacks, each of which requires serious analysis. The business structure you choose should reflect your current tax situation, the type of business you own and your long-term plans for your company.

Section ■ Two

Getting a Corporation off the Ground

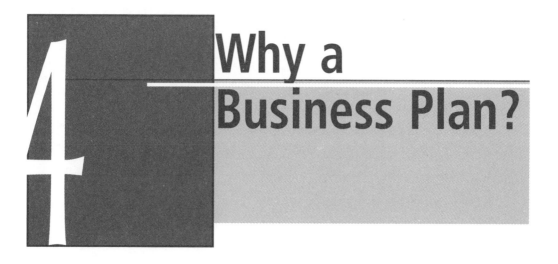

Why a Business Plan?

How Making One Can Help You Focus on the Goals of Your Corporation before You File

It is important to have a business plan in place before you decide to incorporate your business. Though this may seem an obvious task, many business owners jump into management without carefully considering the specifics of day-to-day operations or planning their short- and long-term business goals.

Creating a written business plan helps you focus your business objectives while mapping out strategies to meet those objectives. It forces you to articulate what it is you want to do and how you want to do it.

A business plan is also vital to securing financial support for your business. Your growth expectations will impact your need for capital, and most lenders are unwilling to provide funding until they see a workable business plan. A well-written business plan may also attract investors to the business.

Business plans have other benefits besides influencing lenders and investors. They are also useful tools for recruiting talent to your business. By outlining your company history, management, operations and goals in your business plan, you provide prospective employees a ready overview of your business and insight into the management philosophy and organization of the company.

If you made a business plan years ago when you launched your business and are now ready to incorporate, it may be time to rewrite it. Revising your business plan is a great way to update your view of the business and re-evaluate the benefits and drawbacks of incorporation for your company.

Benefits of Writing a Business Plan

• Support a loan application

• Raise equity funding

• Define objectives and describe programs to achieve those objectives

• Create a regular business review and course correction process

• Define a new business

• Define agreements between partners

• Set a value on a business for sale or legal purposes

• Evaluate a new product line, promotion or expansion

Creating a Business Plan

Writing a business plan is a difficult process for many people, one that requires you to evaluate why you are in business and what you hope to get out of it. And perhaps more difficult yet, developing a strategy to meet your goals. Resolving these issues on paper forces you to strip away any illusions you may have about the relative simplicity of starting and running a business.

A business plan should cover the following:

- **Executive Summary:** An executive summary is a one-page description of your franchise, products, services, risks, opportunities, target market, marketing strategies, competition, finances and above all, projected return on investment. Though perhaps the most essential part of your business plan, the executive summary may be best written after you have had the chance to work through the rest of the items.

- **Mission Statement:** A mission statement is a one- or two-sentence statement that describes the culture of your business and its goals. Some states require you to write a statement of corporate purpose as part of your application for your certificate of incorporation. You should think in those terms while writing the business plan.

- **Business Concept:** The business concept is an explanation of your company's function and the technology, concept or strategy on which it is based.

- **The Team:** A list of all key management members by name, experience and past successes.

- **Industry Analysis:** The industry analysis reviews changes in market share, leadership, players, market shifts, costs, pricing or competition that provide the opportunity for a company's success. It is important to update this section every few years.

- **Competition:** This section should describe the competitive challenges that exist in your industry and how you plan to overcome them.

- **Goals and Objectives:** This is your 5-year plan. State measurable objectives for market share, revenues and profitability. It may be helpful to seek the advice of an accountant.

- **Description of Day-to-Day Operations:** Describe staffing options and training. Also discuss resource needs, such as supplies, advertising and marketing.

- **Financing:** Outline your funding source(s) for the business, including short- and long-term capital needs. Explain clearly your plans to repay this debt efficiently.

- **Appendix:** Include in this section tax returns, articles related to the franchiser and any other third party information that may help further explain the business.

Projecting Income and Cash Flow

Creating financial projections is a key element of any business plan, and a task that you may need to enlist the help of an attorney or accountant to complete accurately. It is worthwhile to create a 5-year projection, totaling all projected expenses to determine your need for short-term capital. It is far safer to underproject your income than your expenses. If your business income outpaces your costs, you can always repay your creditors early.

Cash Flow and Income Projections

Cash flow projections are the most important projection because they detail the anticipated cash inflow and outflow. How much capital will you need to finance your startup? This can be difficult to judge, especially before you have a few months' figures to rely on. To ensure you always have enough cash on hand, your projections need to be as accurate as possible.

For projected expenses, begin with fixed costs, including rent, utilities, insurance, equipment and salary. Add variable costs, such as inventory, supplies, production costs and delivery. For projected income, use industry standards and demographic analysis to project how many customers you will draw. Estimate the average price customers will spend on your goods. Take into account the impact of major competitors, the scope of your promotional efforts and the attractiveness of your location. Subtract a quarter of your modest income estimate, as it inevitably takes time to develop customer awareness and loyalty. If expenses outweigh income, you need to rework your plan order to cut expenses, obtain a loan, or conduct a sales promotion to increase income. The categories to be shown in your cash flow statements include monthly, quarterly and annual.

Develop a Cash Flow Forecast

Once you have determined how much money you will need to open your doors, plan out how much cash flow you estimate you will take in each month to determine how quickly your business will start showing a monthly profit.

Calculating a cash flow forecast will help you determine how much investment is required to start your business and it will also highlight potential problem months. Complete the cash flow worksheet to forecast the first 2 years of your business.

Cash Flow Worksheet	
Beginning Cash Balance	$_____
Cash receipts:	
Collection of receivables	$_____
Interest income	$_____
Other income	$_____
Total	$_____
Cash disbursements:	
Accounts payable	$_____
Direct materials	$_____
Direct labor	$_____
Equipment	$_____
Salaries	$_____
Rent	$_____
Insurance	$_____
Leases	$_____
Advertising	$_____
Taxes	$_____
Other expenses	$_____
Income tax payments	$_____
Total	$_____
Net cash from operations	$_____
Sale of stock	$_____
Decrease (or increase) in funds invested (interest)	$_____
Short-term borrowings (repayments)	$_____
Ending Cash Balance	$_____

Note: If any of your figures are losses, place brackets around them or change the type color to red. This will effectively show where trouble spots may be occurring. Once you have your cash flow forecast complete, compare it each month with your actual cash flow to see how accurately you forecasted and to pinpoint months that may need additional promotion to increase sales. Complete the Cash Flow Forecast worksheet.

Cash Flow Forecast

Month	1	2	3	4	5	6	7	8	9	10	11	12	Year Total
Profit/Loss													
Less: Credit sales													
Plus: Collections of credit sales													
Plus: Credit purchases													
Less: Payments for credit purchases													
Plus: Withholding ____ % of total wages													
Less: Quarterly withholding payments													
Plus: Depreciation													
Less: Principal payments													
Less: Extra purchases													
Other cash items in/out													
Monthly net cash													
Cumulative net cash													

A major factor in your financing is liquidity, or the ability to pay your bills. Liquid assets include cash and possessions that can readily be turned into cash, such as checks, credit receivables and inventory—some more easily than others. Will you have enough liquid assets to cover all impending bills? To be solvent, you must be able to pay your bills as they fall due. Your assets must exceed your liabilities. The ratio should be at least 2-to-1; 3- or 4-to-1 is safer. A sound practice in initial stages of starting your company is to add cash and other assets while cutting expenses such as your personal salary.

Experience will tell you to add 30 percent to the most generous expense estimate. Then add another 15 percent to the adjusted total for emergencies and other unexpected expenses.

Cash to Be Paid Out Worksheet

Projecting the amount of cash to be paid out is as important as knowing where the cash will come from. The following is an example to help you calculate your cash expenditures.

Cash to be Paid Out		
Business name:	Period covering: Jan. 1 to Dec. 31	
1. Startup costs		$2,600
Business license	$100	
Corporation filing	$1,000	
Legal fees	$1,000	
Other startup costs:	$500	
A.	$0	
B.	$0	
C.	$0	
D.	$0	
2. Inventory purchases		
Cash out for goods intended for resale		$40,000
3. Variable expenses (selling)		
Advertising/Marketing/PR	$10,000	
Freight	$2,500	
Fulfillment of orders	$1,000	
Packaging costs	$500	
Sales salaries/Commissions	$20,000	
Travel	$2,500	
Miscellaneous	$500	
Total selling expenses		$37,000

4. Fixed expenses (administration)		
Financial administration	$2,000	
Insurance	$1,500	
Licenses and permits	$200	
Office salaries	$15,000	
Rent expense	$10,000	
Utilities	$3,000	
Leasing contracts	$1,000	
Miscellaneous	$500	
Total administrative expense		$33,200
5. Assets (long-term purchases)		
Cash to be paid out in current period		$10,000
6. Liabilities		
Cash outlay for retiring debts, loans and/or accounts payable		$10,000
7. Owner equity		
Cash to be withdrawn by owner/ partners		$25,000
Total cash to be paid out		$157,800

Source of Cash Statement

Provide a source of cash statement to any lending institution to show your company's cash potential.

Source Of Cash Worksheet	
Business name:	Period covering: Jan. 1 to Dec. 31
1. Cash on hand	
2. Sales (revenues)	
Product income	
Services income	
Deposits on sales or services	
Collections on account receivables	
Retainers received on sales or services	
Total sales	$0
3. Miscellaneous income	
Interest income	
Payments to be received on loans	
Total miscellaneous income	$0
4. Sale of long-term assets	$0
5. Liabilities	
Loan from lending institutions, investors, SBA, angels, etc.	
Total liabilities	$0
6. Equity	
Owner investments (sole proprietors/partners)	
Contributed capital (corporation)	
Sale of stock (corporation)	
Venture capital	
Total equity	$0
A. Less product sales	$0
Total cash available	$0
B. With product sales	$0

Personal Financial Statements

Most lenders require you to project your salary as part of overall expenses. If you agree to a low salary, it proves your willingness to sacrifice immediate personal gain to ensure a profitable venture—especially if you sacrificed a lucrative career to do so. Include with your fiscal projections a record of your personal finances, and list each asset you will contribute along with the market value of each.

Can you afford to wait while the company struggles to show a profit? How much equity will you invest in the venture? Complete the following worksheet, which summarizes your Personal Financial Statement.

Personal Financial Statement

			Assets	
Cash and cash equivalents				
Checking and savings accounts—include money market accounts				
Institution name and location	Account type	Account no.	Current balance	
1.				
2.				
3.				
		Total checking and savings $_____		
Time deposit accounts—including CDs				
Institution name and location	Account type	Account no.	Current balance	Maturity date
1.				
2.				
3.				
		Total deposits $_____		
Miscellaneous cash on hand				
Institution name and location	Account type	Account no.	Current balance	
1.				
2.				
		Total deposits $_____		
Marketable securities				
Institution name and location	Account type	Account no.	Current balance	
1.				
2.				
		Total value $_____		

Cash value of life insurance			
Policy holder	Policy type	Policy no.	Cash value
1.			
2.			
		Total cash surrender value	$_____
Trusts, deeds and mortgages	Description		
1.			
2.			
		Total	$_____
Real estate			
1.			
2.			
		Total holdings	$_____
Other assets			
1.			
2.			
		Total assets	$_____

Profit & Loss Forecast

Complete monthly and yearly profit and loss statements by combining expense and income ledgers. Under income, leave out sales tax and nonbusiness income. Subtract net inventory used (amount you started with plus purchases made minus current stock) to determine your gross profit. Subtract all other operating expenses, except sales tax and any nondeductible expenses, and you discover your magic number—net profit. Refer to your accounting ledgers and profit and loss statements frequently to find trends, such as slow sales cycles, overspending and stock shrinkage that you need to account for to survive.

Profit & Loss Forecast

Month	1	2	3	4	5	6	7	8	9	10	11	12	Total
Sales revenue													
Cost of sales													
(Percent of sales)													
Gross profit*	$0	$0	$0	$0	$0	$0	$0	$0	$0	$0	$0	$0	$0
(Percent of sales)													
Fixed expenses:													
Wages/Salaries													
Payroll tax													
Rent/Lease													
Equipment leases													
Marketing/Advertising													
Insurance													
Accounting													
Interest expense													
Depreciation													
Utilities													
Telephone													
Supplies													
Bad debts													
Freight													
Miscellaneous													
Total fixed expenses	$0	$0	$0	$0	$0	$0	$0	$0	$0	$0	$0	$0	$0
Profit/Loss**	$0	$0	$0	$0	$0	$0	$0	$0	$0	$0	$0	$0	$0

*Gross profit is calculated by subtracting cost of sales from sales revenue
**Profit/Loss is calculated by subtracting total fixed expenses from gross profit

Balance Sheet Pro Forma

Balance sheets provide an accurate picture of your company's financial health at any one particular point in time. It shows what your company owns and owes and how much it is worth at a certain date. It lists the assets you need to support your company and the liabilities show how assets are financed. It is suggested as a new company that you create a balance sheet each month or at least quarterly.

The following information is the basic categories you should include in your balance sheet pro formas:

Balance Sheet	
Assets:	
Current Assets:	
Cash	$_____
Investments	$_____
Accounts receivable (minus bad debt accounts)	$_____
Notes receivable	$_____
Inventory	$_____
Prepaid expenses	$_____
Total current assets	$_____
Fixed Assets:	
Land	$_____
Buildings	$_____
Equipment	$_____
Total fixed assets	$_____
Other assets	$_____
Total assets	$_____
Liabilities and Stockholder's Equity:	
Current liabilities	$_____
Short-term debt	$_____
Accounts payable	$_____
Taxes payable	$_____
Income taxes payable	$_____
Accrued liabilities	$_____
Total current liabilities	$_____
Long-term debt	$_____
Stockholder's earnings (deficit)	$_____
Total	$_____
Total liabilities and stockholder's equity	$_____

Summary

Though a business plan is not needed to file for incorporation, it is a valuable way to determine the feasibility of a business idea. If you have a business plan from your early days of a sole proprietorship or partnership, now is the time to revisit and revise the document. Doing so will help you re-evaluate your business goals as you revise your business status.

Business Plan Example

Wheel Sports International

Plan Number:

Presented To:

Date:

This business plan has been prepared by the management team of Wheel Sports International and is being furnished to select individuals for the sole purpose of providing potential financing to the Company. This business plan is a confidential document that contains ideas, concepts, methods and other proprietary information. Readers are to treat the information contained herein as confidential and may not copy any of these materials without the written permission of the Company.

1. Executive Summary

1.0 Executive Summary

Wheel Sports International is the premier in-line skate accessory manufacturer for the in-line skate industry. Wheel Sports has developed three innovative and practical skate accessories. Wheel Sports is able to produce worthwhile products because the company is built on skaters designing and making products for skaters. Wheel Sports will quickly gain market penetration and establish themselves as an innovative in-line skating product company.

Wheel Sports is a limited partnership located in Seattle, WA. Seattle was strategically chosen to provide Wheel Sports with credible product feedback since Seattle is considered by many as the future skating capital of the world.

The Products

Wheel Sports currently has three unique products available or soon to be released. The first is SkateCover, a fabric wheel cover that allows skaters to enter retail establishments or travel anywhere with their skates on while protecting the skates and the surface that they tread on. Wheel Sports' second product is SkateSurf, an innovative product that has created a new niche sport that combines in-line skating and windsurfing. Not only has Wheel Sports released this innovative product, but they are supporting and growing the niche sport as a legitimate extension of in-line skating. Their last product is SkatePac.

The Market

Wheel Sports will supply the rapidly growing in-line skating market with useful accessories. The market has been established with over 41 million pairs of skates sold during a 15-year period. Of this number, 30 million have been sold to recreational and fitness skaters, the primary segment that Wheel Sports will target. Wheel Sports' market can be broken down into five segments: recreational, fitness, speed, hockey and extreme skaters.

Management Team

Key to Wheel Sports' success is the fact that the entire focus of the company is to provide the ultimate skating experience to skaters. Not only are the products for skaters but every employee of the company is an experienced in-line skater. Sam Taylor, CEO, has 30 years of skating experience. He is so dedicated to skating that he commutes to work by in-line skates. Sam has worked for three different companies in the design department and has also spent years in retail environments giving him first hand knowledge of skater's preferences.

Veronica Meyer is Wheel Sports' Vice President and is also a true enthusiast. Veronica has 10 years of product experience at Rollerblade®, the industry leader. Lastly, Elizabeth Cohen is the Administrator and Web Master. Elizabeth's Internet experience and her excellent computer skills will support Wheel Sports' ambitious Internet effort. Elizabeth has come from In-line Skaters News, the premier Internet-based industry newsletter.

Wheel Sports is an exciting business that leverages employee's passions for the greater good of the company as well as the sport of in-line skating. Wheel Sports will reach profitability quickly. Sales are forecasted to be $485,000 for year 1 and rise to $1.65 million by the end of year 3. Wheel Sports will generate net profits of $230,000 and $571,000 for year 1 and 3 respectively.

1.1 Objectives

- To fulfill the aftermarket skate accessory demand with top quality products.
- To develop and manufacture SkatePac by January 2007.
- To develop skate tours by spring 2007.
- To reach sales of $485,000 by the end of our first year in business and reach sales of $40,000 monthly.
- To break even by the end of the first year in business.
- To encourage our customers to live healthy lives by making skating more fun, convenient and safer for them.
- To offer skaters support through our Web page, such as interviews with medical experts who will answer skater-specific questions about foot and joint problems.
- To develop a solid e-commerce market and to maximize our profit margin. We make full retail profit through e-commerce.

1.2 Mission

Wheel Sports International is planning on fulfilling the need for after-market products, a market we have identified, based on the large volume of skates that have been sold in the past 5 years.

Wheel Sports International will establish a service network for in-line skaters by providing products that help people incorporate more skating into their daily lifestyles. Our goal is to:

- Expand skating as an alternative to driving to do local errands.
- Form a network of skating enthusiasts with an emphasis on health and fitness.
- To encourage skate surfing as a recognized international sport.
- To develop SkatePac and other new products now in the idea and production stage.
- Improve the safety features included on skates to make them safer for enthusiasts.

1.3 Keys to Success

1. Developing quality in-line skating accessories through feedback from skaters.

2. Develop a niche market for our unique skating accessories.

3. Maximizing profits by selling through the Internet at full retail price.

4. Maintaining low overhead costs by monitoring and scheduling production.

5. Developing a network with other businesses and experts, through interviews published on our Web site.

2. Company Summary

2.0 Company Summary

Wheel Sports International was formed by skaters who created practical ideas and designs for in-line skating accessories. Being avid health and fitness advocates, we promote in-line skating as a lifestyle.

Our products make the trip to the local store or coffee shop easier and an enjoyable way to get exercise. This will eliminate the stress of driving in traffic and having to search for parking.

The main problem skaters experience now with most skates is poor fit. Lateral ankle support is essential due to the narrow wheel footprint of in-line skates. Because of this, skate boots have to be worn tighter than shoes. Wheel Sports has invented a solution to this problem and we are excited about its application to other footwear as well. We have also identified a lack of inexpensive accessory products available and will address those needs. Other needs can be addressed with new products.

2.1 Company Ownership

Wheel Sports International is currently a Limited Partnership.

Presently, **Sam Taylor** is Chief Executive Officer and owns 80 percent (80%) of the company.

Presently, **Veronica Meyer** is Vice President and owns 20 percent (20%) of the company.

Upon incorporating, **Sam Taylor** and **Veronica Meyer** will change their partnership agreement so profits will be divided as follows: 45 percent (45%) to Veronica and 55 percent (55%) to Sam.

Ten percent (10%) of Internet sales will go to Elizabeth Cohen, Wheel Sports' Web Master and Office Administrator.

2.2 Startup Summary

Our startup cost has been $10,000. The money has primarily been for materials for prototypes, product development, trademark acquisition, rental equipment, operating and administrative costs and establishing a Web site.

Upon receiving our loan for the first month, we plan on heavy advertising through the Internet, skating publications, and on-site events such as skating races. The startup costs are shown in the following table.

Startup Requirements	
Startup Expenses	
Legal	$698
Office/Computer supply	$1,473
Advertising	$1,000
Consultants	$0
Insurance	$0
Rent	$2,500
Research and development	$1,800
Expensed equipment	$233
Other	$1,500
Total startup expenses	$9,204
Startup Assets Needed	
Cash balance on starting date	$9,996
Startup Inventory	$1,500
Other current assets	$0
Total current assets	$11,496
Long-term Assets	$0
Total assets	$11,296
Total requirements	$20,900
Funding/Investors	
Paul Latos	$3,000
Greg Nelson	$3,000
Terri Lani	$2,000
Elizabeth Cohen	$3,000
Larry Chase	$3,000
Jonathon Plees	$2,000
Total investment from investors	$16,000
Current Liabilities	
Accounts payable	$200
Current borrowing	$4,500
Other current liabilities	$0
Current liabilities	$4,700
Long-term liabilities	$0
Total liabilities	$4,700
Loss at startup	($9,204)
Total capital	$6,796
Total capital and liabilities	$11,496

2.3 Company Locations and Facilities

At present, we are located in Seattle, Washington. From our location, we will warehouse, package and ship our products. We will find a larger site, within the area, as the business expands.

Several manufacturing companies have expressed an interest to subcontract our large production jobs. We plan to produce products on a monthly basis (utilizing a Just-in-Time production schedule) to cut our need for large inventory space.

3. Products

3.0 Products

Wheel Sports International now offers several products:

- The first product we have developed is SkateCover, a cover for the wheels and frame of in-line skates, which allow skaters to enter places that normally would not allow them in. SkateCover comes with a small pouch and belt, which converts to a well-designed skate carrier.
- The second product we have invented is our SkateSurf. These wind sails are specifically designed for use while skating. Initial feedback we have received from skaters indicates this could become a very popular sport. The process to trademark this product has been initiated.
- The third product will be referred to as SkatePac and be in production by January.

Other ideas for products are under development, but we must hold back until we can protect ourselves through pending patent applications.

3.1 Product Description

We have two products now being marketed on our website www.wheel sportssportsint.com, with two more products to be introduced in the near future.

- SkateCover's are made from Cordura, a nylon composite cloth that is extremely durable. SkateCover enables the skater to enter places that normally do not allow skates. Our cost to manufacture is $10.00 per set, and retails for $24.95 per set. The packaging is simple, inexpensive, elegant, and done in-house. One size will fit all skates.
- SkateSurf is made of Lycra and Dacron. The window of the sail is made of carbon fiber-reinforced Mylar. This product is an original concept and design. The sails come with an Alpha design, known for being very stable and easy to use. We incorporated a swallow-tail design for better upwind performance, speed, and excellent maneuverability. Consumers will have a choice of three exciting colors. The manufacturing cost is $100 and retails for $350 to $500, depending on the sail size.
- We are developing SkatePac, a new product that we feel has a large potential in this market. The estimated cost to manufacture each unit is $10 and retail for $45. This product is in its advanced development stage so a pending patent and a trademark have been applied for.

> • Our fourth product is a service: Skate Tours. We are currently working out details with a popular local skate outlet shop on the pier, and a major skate manufacturer. This tour will take skaters out to sail with SkateSurf.

3.2 Competitive Comparison

Our products are unique in the existing skate accessory market. While there are other accessory companies, none produce products as versatile as ours. Our ideas come from listening to what other skaters have to say.

3.3 Sales Literature

For the upcoming year, we are developing a company brochure, which will include our products.

We are targeting our market by focusing on Internet sales. A large portion of our advertising budget will be used for Internet advertising such as banners and site-promoting services.

We also plan on a mass postcard mailing media blitz to skate shops and to advertise in most of the major in-line skate magazines by spring.

Sales literature will also be distributed at the annual in-line skaters convention. A massive public relations effort will be launched to generate media interest in our new products.

3.4 Sourcing

Our Seattle, Washington location is ideal, since Seattle is a health-conscience city with miles of bicycle lanes and trails already built into the areas infrastructure. Major local skate shops in the area are now carrying our products.

Our supplier for Cordura is the major distributor on the West Coast. We have a supplier of Lycra and Dacron (the sail cloth) and a source for aluminum.

All of our costs are at the manufacturer level and the prices should drop as our production increases.

3.5 Technology

Wheel Sports International is a progressive company that has been able to combine high-tech materials and innovative ideas to produce new products with little competition. We own a trademark on SkateCover and we are in the process of acquiring trademarks on our other products along with corresponding patents. Some of our high-tech implementation will be more noticeable when we introduce SkatePac. This product should make skating more comfortable due to the new chemical products. Our SkateSurf are made of aircraft-quality aluminum, the lightest and strongest of sail materials.

We have already designed the next two generations of sails, and this should keep us ahead of any spin-off products that will try to copy us.

3.6 Future Products

We constantly survey and talk with skaters in order to develop unique products. We feel our new products will be very useful, functional and practical. There are several more product concepts on the drawing board. SkatePac, the newest product, will be in production by January of 2000. This product is being developed with the aid of a licensed, medical foot doctor who is also an avid skater.

4. Market Analysis Summary

4.0 Market Analysis Summary

With 41 million skates sold and little or no support products available, we have an opportunity to reach a market of approximately 30 million recreational and fitness enthusiasts.

There is now a growing trend towards fitness skating. With this large potential market, our products will be there to address their needs.

4.1 Market Segmentation

With a world skating market of over 41 million and steadily growing (statistics released by the Sporting Goods Manufacturers Association), our niche has been created. Our aim is to expand this market by promoting skate surfing, a new sport which is popular along the western coastline.

The Sporting Goods Manufacturers Association survey indicates that in-line skating now has more participation than football, softball, skiing, and snowboarding combined. The breakdown of participation in in-line skating is as follows: one percent speed (growing), eight percent hockey (growing), seven percent extreme/aggressive (declining), 22 percent fitness (nearly 7 million–the fastest growing), and 61 percent recreational (first timers). Our products are targeting the fitness and recreational groups, as they are the fastest growing. These groups are gearing themselves towards health and fitness, and combined, they can easily grow to 85 percent (or 26 million) of the market in the next 5 years.

Market Analysis			
Potential Customers	Growth	2000	2001
Recreational	10%	23,890,876	24,129,785
Fitness	15%	9,820,000	10,311,000
Speed	10%	787,500	795,375
Hockey	8%	3,080,000	3,104,640
Extreme	-10%	2,570,000	2,313,000
Other	10%	1,732,500	1,749,825
Total	9.13%	41,880,876	33,635,000

2002	2003	2004	CAGR
24,371,083	24,614,793	24,860,941	10%
10,826,550	11,367,878	11,936,271	15%
803,329	811,362	819,476	10%
3,129,477	3,154,513	3,179,749	8%
2,081,700	1,873,530	1,686,177	-10%
1,767,323	1,784,996	1,802,846	10%
36,646,650	40,075,019	43,965,810	9.13%

4.2 Target Market Segment Strategy

Our target market is the recreational skater and the health and fitness enthusiast. This segment can be reached over the Internet and through skate magazine advertising.

We plan on developing the skate shop market through an inexpensive postcard method.

SkateCover and SkateSurf are now sold at the two major skate shops in Seattle and Tacoma, Washington. Surveys indicate that in the fitness and speed market, the average age is 34 years, breaking down to 48 percent women, 52 percent men, an average of 1.8 years of college education, an average household income of $52,600 and 71 percent skate on four-wheel in-line skates.

4.2.1 Market Needs

We recognize the need for accessories for the growing market of skaters.

- We promote skate surfing as a new sport by providing excursions to wide open areas. A major skate company is willing to lend us the new large-wheel skates for our skate surfing excursions. However, conventional in-line skates will work just as well.
- We will soon offer SkatePac. The sheer number of existing skates purchased has created a whole new market for products to help increase the life of skates.

We have learned what skaters need for accessories by interviewing experienced skaters.

A person does not have to make time to exercise if skating becomes a lifestyle and is worked into daily activities. Skating is fun and a great cardiovascular workout at the same time, and this is something everyone is looking for.

4.2.2 Market Trends

We will distinguish ourselves by marketing products not previously available to skaters. The emphasis in the past has been to sell skates and very few replacement parts.

There is a world market of skaters. We have products for virtually every group of skaters.

The fastest growing segment of this sport is the fitness skater. Therefore, our marketing is being directed to service this group. SkateCover will enable them to enter establishments without having to remove their skates. SkateCover will be aimed at the recreational skater, the largest segment; however SkatePac is great for everyone.

There is one more way the sport of skating will grow, and that is through skate surfing. This sport is primarily for the medium to advanced skater. The growth potential for this sport is tremendous. The sails we have manufactured to date have ended up in Europe. The same thing happened with windsurfing. It started out on the West Coast but did not take off until it had already grown big in Europe. More and more groups are getting together on skate excursions in cities all over the world. For example, San Francisco has night group skating that numbers in the hundreds of people. The market trends are showing continued growth in all directions of skating.

4.2.3 Market Growth

With the price of skates going down due to competition by so many skate companies, the market has had steady growth throughout the world, with 22.5 million in 1995 to over 41 million in 1999.

By January 2007 we will get the growth statistics for this year; it is estimated to be over 42 million. More and more people are discovering, and in many instances, rediscovering, the health benefits and fun of skating.

4.3 Industry Analysis

Skate sales have undergone tremendous growth and distribution throughout the country.

Presently we will concentrate on Internet marketing. This will maximize our profit.

The Internet is probably the best communication medium for skaters all over the world, and we believe this is the best way to retail our products. The sales on the Web are now over $28 billion, as quoted by Forester Research, on e-commerce (January 1999).

4.3.1 Industry Participants

The number of skate companies is very large, as many shoe companies have joined in; however, the biggest companies are Rollerblade®, Roces®, Solomon® and K2®.

Some companies make skate bags whose price is in the $20 range. None of them address the problem of entrance to areas that will not allow you to enter while wearing skates and those products are for the most part bulky and impractical to skate with.

4.3.2 Distribution Patterns

We plan on shipping our products using UPS™ and FedEx® as our main mode of distribution, because it is the least expensive method and provides a shipping receipt for easy tracking.

We are also negotiating with three foreign distribution companies that have contacted us and are interested in distributing our products overseas.

4.3.3 Competition and Buying Patterns

Each segment of skating has its own buying patterns, depending on its own needs. The table in 4.1, Market Segmentation, illustrates this.

Wheel Sports International is forming its own market. While there are a few companies that make sails and foils that few skaters are using, our sails and foils are the only ones that are truly designed for and by skaters. Our competitors' sails are not designed for skating, but for windsurfing or for skateboards. In the case of foils, storage and carrying are not practical.

We need the capital to protect our inventions through patent application and trademark registration. Our other products do not have competition at this time.

5. Strategy and Implementation Summary

5.0 Strategy and Implementation Summary

Our involvement in roller skating goes back 25+ years. We have the reputation and skill that has gained respect from some of the most skilled skaters. We remain close to the skating community through contact with the local skate shops and by giving lessons. Close contact with the public has put us in a unique position to be able to get feedback from skaters of all types on our products and ideas, designed for them.

5.1 Value Proposition

At Wheel Sports International our emphasis is on quality at a fair price. Our pricing is determined by the cost of production and customer demand, so we pace production by need.

Speed skating demographics, as shown in Sections 4.1 and 4.2, show affluent and prime candidates for our higher ticket items. We develop our products for all skaters, but some of our products are more segment-specific, such as our SkateSurf which are more for the experienced to expert skater. For example, the speed skating segment is only 1.5 percent of the entire market, but this is roughly 7 million skaters.

5.2 Competitive Edge

Our company's competitive edge exists because we are the only company addressing the needs that have resulted from the extensive sales of in-line skates. We wish to fill the need for items which could double the life of a pair of skates.

Accessories such as SkateCover encourage people and make it more convenient to include skating into their lifestyles.

5.3 Marketing Strategy

The key to our marketing strategy is focusing on the speed, health and fitness and recreational skaters. We can cover about 80 percent of the skating market since we produce products geared towards each segment.

The speed and fitness skaters are an average age of 34 years, with a salary of about $54,000/year and an average of 2 years of college. This is our SkateSurf market. We are in the process of designing more advanced safety equipment that is well-suited for skate sailing in the future.

Our SkateCover and SkatePac are items that can be useful to all segments of the market.

5.3.1 Positioning Statements

We design our products for the skaters who depend on their skating products to be well-designed and practical. We want to help lengthen and improve the life of our customers' investment—their skates.

The present skate companies concentrate on new skate sales with no support for products already sold and that is our strength.

5.3.2 Pricing Strategy

Wheel Sports products are priced to encourage the customer to impulse buy, experiment and repeat buy.

SkateSurf are priced from $350 to $500. Lower-priced items are SkateCover at $24.95 and SkatePac for $45.

5.3.3 Promotion Strategy

Our long-range goal is to gain enough visibility to expand the product line into peripheral industries and other regions and to generate inquiries from potential inventors. To do that we need $50,000 investment money or a line of credit.

We also plan on promoting our goods at various skating races held throughout the country.

5.3.4 Distribution Strategy

We plan to enter the now extensive specialty skate shop market with SkatePac. We feel this is the competitive edge skate shops need to compete with the large chain discount distributors. The additional products, such as SkateCover and SkateSurf, should also help stimulate skate shop sales.

5.4 Sales Strategy

For now, our products are sold through our Web site www.wheelsportssportsint.com. This earns us full retail price.

In 9 months, we will gear sales towards the skate shops with SkatePac. Through retail skate shops, we will increase our sales.

Visibility will be very important, and we will gain exposure at skate racing events. We will target our advertising through the major in-line skate magazines and on the Internet.

5.4.1 Sales Forecast

We feel that our sales forecasting is conservative. We will steadily increase sales as our advertising budget allows. Please refer to the Sales Forecast Chart on the following page.

Sales Forecast			
Unit Sales	FY 2000	FY 2001	FY 2002
SkateCover	1,140	2,200	3,400
SkateSurf	1,072	2,100	3,200
SkatePac	1,560	7,000	11,000
Total Unit Sales	3,772	11,300	17,600
Unit Prices	FY 2000	FY 2001	FY 2002
SkateCover	$24.95	$24.95	$24.95
SkateSurf	$350.00	$350.00	$350.00
SkatePac	$45.00	$45.00	$45.00
Sales	FY 2000	FY 2001	FY 2002
SkateCover	$28,443	$54,890	$84,830
SkateSurf	$375,200	$735,000	$1,120,000
SkatePac	$70,200	$315,000	$495,000
Total Sales	$473,843	$1,104,890	$1,699,830
Direct Unit Costs	FY 2000	FY 2001	FY 2002
SkateCover	$10.00	$10.00	$10.00
SkateSurf	$100.00	$100.00	$100.00
SkatePac	$7.00	$7.00	$7.00
Direct Cost of Sales	FY 2000	FY 2001	FY 2002
SkateCover	$11,400	$22,000	$34,000
SkateSurf	$107,200	$210,000	$320,000
SkatePac	$10,920	$49,000	$77,000
Subtotal Direct Cost of Sales	$129,520	$281,000	$431,000

5.4.2 Sales Programs

Our sales program consists of Internet advertising and skating magazine ads in order to target our market. On the Internet, banner advertising utilizing link exchange services and high search engine placement will be our primary method of selling.

We presently accept credit card orders through our Web site. We plan to capture the impulse buyer market, which makes up 80 percent of all Internet sales.

5.5 Strategic Alliances

Cooperation between Wheel Sports International and the local skate shops is very good. We hope that our growth will be mutual, since some of our products are designed for the skate shops.

Since the local coffeeshop is situated in a parking lot, where skate sailing can be taught and SkateSurf can be sold, this can be our home site where we also can arrange the skate sailing excursions.

5.6 Milestones

Sam Taylor will concentrate on sales and promotion, teaching skate sailing lessons in addition to overseeing product development.

Veronica Meyer will be in charge of production by making sure we have ordered the products needed to maintain a smooth production. Veronica will see to it that our orders will be filled and shipped to their destination.

Elizabeth Cohen will be in charge of the administrative functions. Her duties will be to run the office. Elizabeth is also our Web Master and will maintain and update our Web site.

We will work as a team and help each other with all the work required for a smooth running company. Together, we will do whatever it takes to succeed.

Milestones					
Milestone	Start Date	End Date	Budget	Manager	Department
Sam Taylor	10/10/1999	10/10/2000	$20,000	CEO	Sale-Research
Veronica Meyer	01/01/2000	12/01/2000	$15,600	Vice Pres.	Production
Elizabeth Cohen	12/01/2000	12/01/2000	$0	Admin.	Administrative
Totals			$35,600		

6. Management Summary

6.0 Management Summary

Our group has very diverse talents that seem to complement each other well. Our common bond is our love for skating and fitness. We will create small businesses by teaching independent producers how to make our products. We have developed partnerships so we can control production quality and maintain exclusivity of all products produced.

6.1 Organizational Structure

Wheel Sports International is organized in three main functional areas: production, sales and administrative. We all have our assigned jobs but can and will help each other in other areas whenever necessary.

Sam and Veronica will continue to cooperate on product development. Sam Taylor and Veronica Meyer, as owners, are willing to accept the wages of $20,000 for Sam and $15,000 for Veronica for the first year, in order to help Wheel Sports International grow past the break-even point, with the expectations of a steady growth in salary as Wheel Sports International becomes more successful.

6.2 Management Team

Sam Taylor, CEO, has over 30 years of skating experience and is the main force behind our company, having earned the respect and good standing in the skating community. He has not driven an automobile in 5 years, instead skating for all his transportation needs. Because of skating instead of driving, he has not only regained his health, but is now in the best health condition ever thanks to skating. He has worked as a designer of skate products in the past for companies such as ZFlex, Dog Town and Cheap Skates. This has given him some insight into product development. For the past 3 years, he worked selling skates at local skate shops and has developed a feel for skaters' needs and market trends. In college, he majored in chemistry and physics, which has helped tremendously in identifying and developing products that are applicable to our needs.

Veronica Meyer, Vice President, loves skating for fitness and speed, which is a real asset for the company. Her ability in the inventing process is invaluable. Veronica's ability to input ideas when developing products and production procedures makes her a perfect partner in our endeavors.

Elizabeth Cohen, our Administrator and Web Master, has been skating for many years. Elizabeth has been doing our administration work and has been helping to make Wheel Sports International a reality. Her computer and organizational skills are an imperative part of our development.

6.3 Management Team Gaps

To maintain a lower startup budget, Sam and Veronica will be the only salaried employees until at least 9 months into our operation. We wish to bring Elizabeth into a salaried position as soon as possible. Elizabeth will receive a 10 percent commission on Web site orders until the company can afford to hire her full-time. Elizabeth will receive 10 percent of Wheel Sports International ownership.

6.4 Personnel Plan

The personnel plan calls for increasing head count by one more employee by December 2000, since an increase in forecasted sales necessitates more administrative help.

Our aim is to increase salary and compensation in line with a projected increase in sales and profits. Our overall personnel costs will be $35,000 for the first 12 months, which includes principals only. The present personnel cost figure is subject to change as business demands it.

Personnel Plan			
	FY 2000	FY 2001	FY 2002
Sam	$20,000	$40,000	$50,000
Veronica	$15,000	$40,000	$50,000
Other	$0	$200,000	$300,000
Total People	2	10	15
Total Payroll	$35,000	$280,000	$400,000

7. Financial Plan

7.0 Financial Plan

Our goal is to borrow $50,000 for 10 years. Our present plan is to utilize the borrowed money for the first year's operating capital, with cash input on a monthly basis. Such cash input will aid our operating costs and salaries. We should reach our break-even point after our first year. Upon receiving our loan, we would like to incorporate, as this will protect our company, investors, lenders, products and stockholders. We expect sales to reach $473,843 after the first year, $1,104,890 after our second year and $1,699,830 after the third year.

If sales do not measure up to our expectations, this could add an additional 6 months and an influx of another $20,000, which could be carried by credit card, but we do not expect this to happen.

These are our strong points:

- We want to finance growth mainly through cash flow. We recognize that this means we will have to grow at a slower pace than we would like, but this will enable us to build sales through investing in more advertising.

- Our most important asset is inventory turnover. Our ability to schedule production from month to month will help to control inventory costs.

- Collection is not a problem, since we will be credited payment to our bank account in two days by American Merchant Center for all our credit card sales over the Internet.

7.1 Important Assumptions

The financial plan depends on important assumptions, most of which are shown in the General Assumptions table. The key underlying assumptions are:

- A slow-growth economy, without major recession.

- No unforeseen changes in technology to make our products immediately obsolete.

- Access to equity capital and financing sufficient to maintain our financial plan as presented in this table.

General Assumptions			
	FY 2000	FY 2001	FY 2002
Plan Month	1	2	3
Current Interest Rate	12.00%	12.00%	12.00%
Long-Term Interest Rate	10.50%	10.50%	10.50%
Tax Rate	25.42%	25.00%	25.42%
Sales on Credit (%)	0.00%	0.00%	0.00%
Other	0	0	0

7.2 Key Financial Indicators

The most important indicator is inventory turnover. We have to make sure that turnover stays above 10, or we are clogged with inventory.

- Collection is not a problem, since payment to our bank is 2 days after receiving our orders via credit card. However, by October 2000, we will initiate skate shop sales and experience an approximately 30-45 day average payment delay. This could cause a change in cash flow, but can be easily managed.

7.3 Break-Even Analysis

Aside from the standard financial break-even shown, the following is a simplified breakdown of our first year's overall numbers in broad terms:

First Year's Projected Sales:	$473,843
Less 25% Tax:	- $11,846
Subtotal:	$461,997
Less Production Costs:	-$129,520
Subtotal:	$332,477
Less Operating Costs:	- $71,450
Profit:	**$261,027**
Plus Loan:	$ 50,000
Cash at End of the First Year:	**$311,027**
Production Costs for Year 2001:	-$281,065
Projected Profit First Year:	**$29,962**

Break-Even Analysis:	
Monthly Units Break-Even	70
Monthly Revenue Break-Even	$8,756
Assumptions:	
Average Per-Unit Revenue	$125.62
Average Per-Unit Variable Cost	$34.34
Estimated Monthly Fixed Cost	$6,363

7.4 Projected Profit and Loss

Our goal is to borrow $50,000 for the total of 10 years. Our present plan is to utilize the borrowed money for the first year's operating expenses, with cash input on a monthly basis. Such cash input will aid in our advertising, operating costs and salaries. This loan should help us maintain production and operating costs while developing our customer base and sales. Should sales lag, we plan to maintain solvency with credit card financing. We should reach our break-even point after our first year. We expect sales to hit $473,843 the first year, $1,104,870 our second year, $1,699,830 the third year. Our sales projection is very conservative, considering the sales potential.

Pro Forma Profit and Loss			
	FY 2000	FY 2001	FY 2002
Sales	$473,843	$1,104,890	$1,699,830
Direct Costs of Goods	$129,520	$281,000	$431,000
Other Costs of Goods	$0	$0	$0
Cost of Goods Sold	$129,520	$281,000	$431,000
Gross Margin	$344,323	$823,890	$1,268,830
Gross Margin %	72.67%	74.57%	74.64%
Expenses			
Payroll	$35,000	$280,000	$400,000
Sales & Marketing/ Other Expenses	$18,650	$36,300	$49,500
Depreciation	$0	$0	$0
Leased Equipment	$1,800	$5,000	$10,000
Utilities	$600	$1,500	$2,000
Insurance	$6,000	$12,000	$12,000
Rent	$10,800	$12,000	$15,000
Payroll Taxes	$3,500	$28,000	$40,000
Other	$0	$0	$0
Total Operating Expenses	$76,350	$374,800	$528,500
Profit before Interest & Taxes	$267,973	$449,090	$740,330
Interest Expense	$80	$1,811	$5,434
Taxes Incurred	$66,760	$111,820	$186,786
Net Profit	$201,133	$335,459	$548,110
Net Profit/Sales	42.45%	30.36%	32.24%

7.5 Projected Cash Flow

- We want to finance our first year's growth through a loan.

- The most important indicator is inventory turnover. Our ability to schedule production from month to month will help control inventory costs.

- Collection is not a problem since we will be credited payment to our bank account in 2 days by American Merchants Center, our credit card company for Internet sales.

- Selling our products over the Internet will allow us full retail price and maximize our profit.

Pro Forma Cash Flow			
	FY 2000	FY 2001	FY 2002
Cash Received			
Cash from Operations:			
Cash Sales	$473,843	$1,104,890	$1,699,830
Cash from Receivables	$0	$0	$0
Subtotal Cash from Operations	$473,843	$1,104,890	$1,699,830
Additional Cash Received			
Sales Tax, VAT, HST/GST Received	$0	$0	$0
New Current Borrowing	$0	$0	$0
New Other Liabilities (Interest-Free)	$0	$0	$0
New Long-Term Liabilities	$0	$34,500	$34,500
Sales of Other Current Assets	$0	$0	$0
Sales of Long-Term Assets	$0	$0	$0
New Investment Received	$0	$0	$0
Subtotal Cash Received	$473,843	$1,139,390	$1,734,330
Expenditures			
Expenditures from Operations:			
Cash Spending	$26,087	$49,178	$73,871
Payment of Accounts Payable	$227,845	$712,164	$1,066,796
Subtotal Spent on Operations	$253,932	$761,342	$1,140,667
Additional Cash Spent			
Sales Tax, VAT, HST/GST Paid Out	$0	$0	$0
Principal Repayment of Current Borrowing	$4,500	$0	$0
Other Liabilities Principal Repayment	$0	$0	$0
Long-Term Liabilities Principal Repayment	$0	$0	$0
Purchase Other Current Assets	$2,000	$0	$0
Purchase Long-Term Assets	$0	$0	$0
Dividends	$0	$0	$0
Subtotal Cash Spent	$260,432	$761,342	$1,140,667
Net Cash Flow	$213,411	$378,048	$593,663
Cash Balance	$223,406	$601,455	$1,195,117

7.6 Projected Balance Sheet

As shown on the balance sheet in the following table, we expect a healthy growth in the net worth to more than $1,091,499 by the end of the third year.

Pro Forma Balance Sheet			
Assets			
Current Assets	FY 2000	FY 2001	FY 2002
Cash	$223,406	$601,455	$1,195,117
Accounts Receivable	$0	$0	$0
Inventory	$25,950	$56,300	$86,353
Other Current Assets	$2,000	$2,000	$2,000
Total Current Assets	$251,356	$659,754	$1,283,470
Long-Term Assets			
Long-Term Assets	$0	$0	$0
Accumulated			
Depreciation	$0	$0	$0
Total Long-Term Assets	$0	$0	$0
Total Assets	$251,356	$659,754	$1,283,470
Liabilities and Capital			
Current Liabilities			
Accounts Payable	$43,427	$81,866	$122,972
Current Borrowing	$0	$0	$0
Other Current Liabilities	$0	$0	$0
Subtotal Current Liabilities	$43,427	$81,866	$122,972
Long-Term Liabilities	$0	$34,500	$69,000
Total Liabilities	$43,427	$116,366	$191,972
Paid-in Capital	$16,000	$16,000	$16,000
Retained Earnings	($9,204)	$191,929	$527,388
Earnings	$201,133	$335,459	$548,110
Total Capital	$207,929	$543,388	$1,091,499
Total Liabilities/Capital	$251,356	$659,754	$1,283,470
Net Worth	$207,929	$543,388	$1,091,499

7.7 Business Ratios

Standard business ratios are included in the table, based on SIC code 3949. The ratio shows a plan for balanced and healthy growth.

Ratio Analysis				
	FY 2000	FY 2001	FY 2002	Industry Profile
Sales Growth	0.00%	133.18%	53.85%	-2.30%
% of Total Assets				
Accounts Receivable	0.00%	0.00%	0.00%	22.80%
Inventory	10.32%	8.53%	6.73%	26.00%
Other Current Assets	0.80%	0.30%	0.16%	26.30%
Total Current Assets	100.00%	100.00%	100.00%	75.10%
Long-Term Assets	0.00%	0.00%	0.00%	24.90%
Total Assets	100.00%	100.00%	100.00%	100.00%
Current Liabilities	17.28%	12.41%	9.58%	35.50%
Long-term Liabilities	0.00%	5.23%	5.38%	14.20%
Total Liabilities	17.28%	17.64%	14.96%	49.70%
Net Worth	82.72%	82.36%	85.04%	50.30%
% of Sales				
Sales	100%	100%	100%	100%
Gross Margin	72.67%	74.57%	74.64%	37.50%
Selling, General & Administrative Expenses	30.26%	44.21%	42.22%	23.50%
Advertising Expenses	2.53%	2.26%	2.06%	1.60%
Profit before Interest and Taxes	56.55%	40.65%	43.55%	2.70%
Main Ratios				
Current	5.79	8.06	10.44	2.27
Quick	5.19	7.37	9.73	1.18
Total Debt to Total Assets	17.28%	17.64%	14.96%	49.70%
Pre-Tax Return on Net Worth	128.84%	82.31%	67.33%	5.40%
Pre-Tax Return on Assets	106.58%	67.79%	57.26%	10.70%
Additional Ratios				
Net Profit Margin	42.45%	30.36%	32.24%	n/a
Return on Equity	96.73%	61.73%	50.22%	n/a

Activity Ratios				
Accounts Receivable Turnover	0.00	0.00	0.00	n/a
Collection Days	0	0	0	n/a
Inventory Turnover	12.00	6.83	6.04	n/a
Accounts Payable Turnover	6.24	9.17	9.01	n/a
Payment Days	24	30	34	n/a
Total Asset Turnover	1.89	1.67	1.32	n/a
Debt Ratios				
Debt to Net Worth	0.21	0.21	0.18	n/a
Current Liab. to Liab.	1.00	0.70	0.64	n/a
Liquidity Ratios				
Net Working Capital	$207,929	$577,888	$1,160,499	n/a
Interest Coverage	3349.66	247.94	136.25	n/a
Additional Ratios				
Assets to Sales	0.53	0.60	0.76	n/a
Current Debt/ Total Assets	17%	12%	10%	n/a
Acid Test	5.19	7.37	9.73	n/a
Sales/Net Worth	2.28	2.03	1.56	n/a
Dividend Payout	0.00	0.00	0.00	n/a

Financing Your Business

Understanding Where the Money to Start a Company Comes from

The rules for raising money are the same for any business, incorporated or not. Some types of businesses require a lot of money to get started. Think, for example, of starting your own airline. Other types of businesses require very little money to get started. Certain home-based businesses, for example, require little more than a computer and a telephone. Regardless of initial costs, nearly all new business owners invest some of their own money, and studies show that a large percentage of seed money comes directly out of the entrepreneur's pocket.

In a November 2004 Business Week story, Columbia Business School Professor Amar Bhide pointed out that roughly 80 percent of new businesses are self-financed, generally in the range of about $10,000. Startup owners may liquidate their savings accounts or borrow against the equity in their home. And they often re-invest any income from sales and services to grow the business. This prevents debt from building up but can lead to short-term cash-flow problems.

Deciding how to finance your business is a task that takes time and thoughtful planning, sometimes months or years of it. Begin early and plan carefully. In Chapter 4, we talked about making a business plan. Here, we will talk about the basic sources of financing to make your dream come true.

Financing Your Business

Your goal should be to finance your startup with as little of your own money down as possible. That way, you have money in reserve in case you underestimate your costs or need it in an emergency. Interest on most business loans is tax-deductible. Leverage allows you to build your business today so it can stand on its own two feet tomorrow.

When shopping for credit, aim for the longest terms, the lowest interest rate and the least collateral and personal liability as possible. You may choose fixed, lump sum, periodic or balloon payments. Prioritize them according to your specific needs. In the financing section of your business plan be sure to detail the interest rate, terms and conditions you desire. Carefully plan your cash flow statement as accurately as possible. Negotiate payments to coincide with both short- and long-term income projections. This requires planning and discipline. Worst-case cash flow scenarios are safer and more realistic. What is the least amount of money you will make? Time the opening of your company for approximately a month before peak season. Promote your venture well in advance. Make sure you have the right to pay off the loan before it is due without being charged a prepayment penalty, which is illegal in many states.

Other Sources of Loans

You need capital to pay for your company location and equipment, maintain supplies and operations, market and deliver your product, and recruit and keep employees. The following are several sources of financing.

Banks—For small business, look to a community bank. Build a relationship with your banker by utilizing the bank's products and soliciting advice. Today, banks are more conservative than ever with lending money, but once they do they will work with you to succeed.

Finance Companies—Easier than banks for getting loans, but usually at higher rates and with no vested interest in your success.

Credit Cards—They can help you maintain cash flow in the short term, but beware. Credit card rates and terms are volatile, and you can ruin your credit rating by overusing them.

Investors—Whether friends, family or investment firms, investors can provide you up-front cash for a share of profits down the line. They may also want to share in or at least monitor your operations. A good source for finding investors is to join trade associations in the markets you intend to sell to.

Grants—Visit the Web site of the Small Business Administration (www.sba.gov) for information on small business loans and grants. Also, check with your state and local government business development offices as well as educational, research and medical institutions.

Yourself—This is the most important financial source for two reasons.

1. Banks and investors will want to know how much of your own money you are investing in the business.

2. Accumulating your own funds slows you down, and that is a good thing when you are impatient to start getting rich. Patience allows you to accomplish vital homework, market research and planning.

Raise necessary capital by liquidating saving accounts, stocks, bonds and other investments, or selling a house or other big-ticket items.

Do-It-Yourself

Many entrepreneurs get their start by tapping into their retirement savings, personal savings and insurance policies; selling their cars; borrowing against home equity; or using their credit cards and other sources of personal cash. Some lenders, particularly credit unions, provide signature loans requiring no collateral in fairly small amounts, though rates can be considerably higher than the prime rate.

To secure a lower rate, lenders may suggest you borrow on secured savings, such as certificates of deposits. Certain bonds and securities may be used to secure loans, though in recent years that is happening less often.

Borrowing from personal assets could have tax benefits, but consult a tax advisor before you make any moves.

Credit cards are another easy source of cash. Beware, however, of high interest rates and one-time service fees.

Friends and Family

Many business owners get their start through personal loans from family and friends. Though this arrangement works well for many, it can lead to conflicts down the road. Remember, money and personal relationships do not always mix—this is why you have to be doubly careful borrowing from someone close to you. Families and friendships can be torn apart by money issues.

To help avoid misunderstandings between you and your financiers, put all agreements in writing—a standardized loan agreement may work fine or you can seek the help of an attorney.

Once you have decided who you would like to borrow money from, it is best to start with an informal discussion of the business. Your first task is to sell your business concept, which you should have outlined in your business plan. If the individual wants to know more, schedule a second meeting in a more formal atmosphere and dress professionally. Even if you have known this person all your life, you want to impress upon him or her that you are as serious about his or her role as an investor as you would be with a total stranger. Present a copy of your business plan at this time.

Once you have reached a verbal agreement on financing, seek the assistance of a business attorney to draft (or review) any written agreements.

Free Forms and Checklists

Registered readers can visit www.socrates.com/books/ready-incorporate.aspx for free forms, letters and checklists. To register, see page iv for details. Among the many items available are:

Commercial Lease • Estimated Startup Capital Worksheet • General Partnership Agreement • Minutes: First Meeting of Shareholders • Stock Ledger and Transfer Ledger • Corporate Resolutions • Personal Net Worth Worksheet • Profitability Worksheet Analysis • And more!

Financing Terms Worth Knowing

When starting a business, there are basic financial concepts you need to understand. The following are a few key terms to know:

> **Return on Investment (ROI)**—Every dime you spend in a business has to have a return beyond the amount you spent. Revenues have to cover costs and hopefully produce a profit. The equation for ROI is Profit/Assets=ROI
>
> **Working Capital**—Current assets are those short-term funds represented by cash in the bank, funds parked in near-term instruments earning interest, funds tied up in inventory, and all those accounts receivable waiting to be collected. Subtracting the company's current liabilities from these current assets shows how much working capital (your firm's truest measure of liquidity) is on hand and demonstrates your ability to pay for expansion in the short term. For example, if the firm has $500,000 in current assets and $350,000 in current liabilities, then $150,000 is free and clear as working capital, available for spending on new things as needed by the company.
>
> **Cost of Capital**—This is the true cost of securing the funds that the business uses to pay for its asset base. Some funds are from debt (less risky to the creditors, therefore a lower cost of capital to the firm), and some funds come from equity (more risky to the investors, therefore a higher cost of capital). The combination of lower cost debt capital with higher-cost equity capital produces the next item in this list.
>
> **Risk Premium**—Entrepreneurs must understand that every decision they consider has an inherent level of risk associated with it. If project A is far riskier than project B, there should be a clear risk premium that could accrue to the firm if project A is selected. But with that risk premium return, there will also be a risk premium cost to the company for the use of the funds. Business owners must continually decide whether the risk premium of additional potential return is commensurate with the additional risk costs associated with that investment project.

Borrowing from a Bank

After exhausting personal sources, the next stop for business financing is usually a bank. Securing a business loan may seem a daunting task for a sole proprietor, so learn to think like a banker before you approach a lending officer.

Various Types of Bank Financing

> **Asset-based financing**—is a general term describing a situation where the lender accepts as collateral the assets of a company in exchange for a loan. Generally, asset-based loans are collateralized against accounts receivables, inventory or equipment. Banks will only advance funds on a percentage of receivables or inventory; the typical percentages being 75 percent of receivables or 50 percent of inventory.
>
> **Line of credit**—the bank sets aside a predetermined amount of funds for the business to draw against as cash is needed. When funds are used, the credit line is reduced and when payments are made, the line is replenished.
>
> **Letter of credit**—A letter of credit is a guarantee from the bank that a specific obligation of the business will be honored. The bank generates its income by charging fees for making the guarantee.
>
> **Floor planning**—Another form of asset-based lending in which the borrower's inventory is used as collateral for the loan.

Ability to Repay/Capacity

Proof of your ability to repay the loan will top the list of most banks' requirements for loan approval. Banks want to see two sources of repayment— cash flow from the business plus a secondary source, such as collateral. To analyze the cash flow of the business, the lender will review the business's past financial statements. Generally, banks feel most comfortable dealing with a business that has been in existence for a number of years because a financial track record can be verified. If the business has consistently made a profit and that profit can cover the payment of additional debt, it is likely that the loan will be approved. If, however, the business has been operating marginally and now has a new opportunity to grow, or if that business is a startup, then it is necessary to prepare a thorough loan package with a detailed plan for repaying the loan.

Credit History

One of the first items a bank will verify when an individual or a business requests a loan is their credit worthiness. Before you apply for a loan, obtain a copy of your credit report by calling TransUnion, Equifax, or Experian, the three major credit reporting agencies. Personal credit reports may contain errors or outdated information, and you want to make sure that when the bank pulls your credit report that all the errors have been corrected and your history is up-to-date.

In many cases, people find that they paid off a bill but that it has not been recorded on their credit report. Correcting such errors can take weeks or even months, and it is your responsibility to initiate the process of correcting the error and ensuring that it was done.

Once you obtain your credit report, it is important to understand how to interpret the information and verify its accuracy. Though the reporting agency should provide a guide to help you decipher the numbers, the following is an overview of the items to review.

First, check your name, Social Security number and address at the top of the page for accuracy. Some people have found that they have credit information from another person because of mistakes in their identification information.

The remainder of your credit report will contain a list of all your past credit, including credit cards, mortgages, student loans and other consumer loans. Each credit item will be listed individually and contain your payment history. Any late or outstanding payments will be listed near the top of the list and may affect your ability to obtain a loan.

An occasional late payment may not adversely affect your credit. However, if you have any outstanding debts, a pattern of paying your debts late, a judgment against you or declared bankruptcy in the past 7 years, you may have difficulty obtaining a loan.

Oftentimes, poor credit scores are the result of divorce, a medical crisis or some other significant event. If you can show that your credit was good before and after this event and that you have tried to pay back those debts incurred in the period of bad credit, you will improve your chances of obtaining a loan. If you know there is damaging information in your credit report, prepare a written explanation of your credit problems to include in your loan application package.

Equity

Before granting business loans, financial institutions look for a certain amount of equity in a business. This equity can be in the form of retained earnings or the injection of cash from the owner or investors. Most banks want to see that the total liabilities or debt of a business is not more than four times the amount of equity. (Or stated differently, when you divide total liabilities by equity, your result should not be more than four.) In short, to secure a loan, you may need to prove that there is enough equity in the company to leverage that loan.

As indicated earlier, do not be misled into thinking that startup businesses can obtain 100 percent financing through conventional or special loan programs. A new business owner nearly always invests some of his or her own money into the business. What amount an individual must put into the business to obtain a loan depends on the type of loan, its purpose and its terms. In general, most banks want the owner to put in at least 20 to 40 percent of the total request.

Collateral

Besides equity, financial institutions usually look for a second source of loan repayment, known as collateral. Collateral consists of those personal and business assets that can be sold to pay back the loan. The value of collateral is not based on the market value. It is discounted to take into account the value that would be lost if the assets had to be liquidated.

Every loan program, including many microloan programs, requires at least some collateral to secure a loan. If a potential borrower has no collateral to secure a loan, a co-signer who has collateral to pledge is often needed. Without one, it may be difficult to obtain a loan.

Experience

New business owners should be able to prove experience in their field of business, or at least have a partner with thorough knowledge of the business, before seeking financing. Small business loans are more often granted to those owners who can prove a record of success and/or solid experience in their field.

Additional Points about Bank Financing

- Commercial banks are one of the cheapest sources of borrowing for small companies, typically charging interest rates just one to two points above prime for small business loans.

- Small firms should seek banks where small business loans are a priority, not a sideline.

- Small banks make most of their loans to small business customers.

- Small community banks are an excellent source for loans less than $1 million.

- In financing ventures, commercial banks typically seek security in the form of the business owner's personal assets.

- Be mindful that bankers will query why alternative sources of financing are not being successfully pursued.

- Most startup firms cannot attract bank loans because they cannot demonstrate sufficient assets, a healthy financial track record or, in some cases, any financial history at all.

Determining Startup Costs

To determine how much seed money you will need to start your business, begin by estimating your costs for the first several months. Every business has its own specific cash needs at various stages of development and therefore no universal formula for estimating your specific startup costs. There are basic guidelines, however, which are discussed in the following paragraphs. It may also help to consult an accountant familiar with your line of business or talk to people in your industry.

To estimate your startup costs, you must first identify the various categories of expenses that your business will incur during its startup phase. Some of these expenses will be one-time costs, such as the fee for incorporating your business or price of a sign for your building. Others will be ongoing, such as the cost of utilities, inventory and insurance. To contain costs, remember to ask yourself "Is this spending essential to the business?" Avoid unnecessary equipment purchases as well as large marketing and advertising expenditures until you have a clear idea of what this spending might return.

One-Time Startup Costs Worksheet

Many startup expenditures are one-time purchases. To estimate how much money you will need to open your doors for business, use the following worksheet to guide you through the process.

Startup Expenses	What They Are	Out-of-Pocket Cost
Advertising	Initial promotion for the business	
Starting Inventory	Amount of salable goods you will need to open	
Construction	Buildout costs for business space	
Cash	What you will need in the cash register	
Decorating	Any interior or exterior design work you will need	
Deposits	Those costs required by utilities, etc.	
Fixtures/Equipment	Total of chosen bid	
Insurance	Total of chosen bid	
Lease Payments	Fees to be paid before opening day	
Licenses/Permits	City and state totals	
Miscellaneous	Anything not in stated categories	
Professional Services	Attorneys; accountants	
Remodeling	Total of chosen bid	
Rent	Initial rent with deposit	
Services	Cleaning, security, etc.	
Signs	Total of chosen bid	
Supplies	Office supplies	
Contingencies	Estimate unexpected costs	
Other		
Other		
Total Startup Costs		$

First-Year Startup Costs

Once the doors are open, it is important to know how much it is going to cost to keep them open. This worksheet will help you estimate monthly costs of staying in business.

Expenses	Description	Amount (Monthly)
Advertising		
Bank Service Fees		
Credit Card Charges		
Delivery Fees		
Dues and Subscriptions		
Health Insurance		
Other Insurance		
Interest		
Inventory		
Lease Payments		
Loan Payments		
Miscellaneous		
Office Expenses		
Payroll Other than Owner		
Payroll Taxes		
Professional Fees		
Rent		
Repairs and Maintenance		
Sales Tax		
Supplies		
Telephone		
Utilities		
Owner's Salary (When Applicable)		
Total Ongoing Costs		

Venture Capital

Venture capital was more plentiful in the 1990s than it is today, but it can still be found. Unfortunately, it is less likely to go to startups than ever before. Those companies that receive venture capital are perceived to have excellent growth prospects but do not have access to capital markets, such as issuing stock to the public, because they are private companies. In return for venture capital, investors may receive a say in the company's management, such as a seat on the board of directors and some combination of profits, preferred shares or royalties. Sources of venture capital include wealthy individual investors, investment banks, and other financial institutions that pool investments in venture capital funds or limited partnerships. The risks and rewards of venture capital investing can be great. Venture capitalists are also called VCs.

Angel Financing

Angels are silent, private investors who provide startup firms with seed money financing in exchange for equity or a percentage of revenues. The good news for young companies is that angels usually come in at the startup phase for companies with a great idea that do not typically qualify for bank financing.

Angels typically invest in ventures involving markets and technologies with which they are familiar. They typically invest in ventures close to where they live and with trusted friends and business associates. Depending on their agreement, they may be active investors, serving on a working board of directors or providing guidance through an informal consulting or monitoring role.

Typical Angel Criteria

- The primary difference between venture capitalists and angels is that angels will accept a longer payback horizon and are willing to settle for a smaller return—20 to 25 percent a year compared to the VCs expected return on investment of 30 to 35 percent or more per year.
- Angel financing is typically between $500,000 and $1 million.
- Venture exit horizons for angels tend to be 5 to 10 years or more.
- Firms do not have to demonstrate profitability; they must demonstrate, however, strong market prospects and strong management.
- Angels often take bigger risks or accept lower rewards when they are attracted by the nonfinancial characteristics of an entrepreneur's proposal.
- Angels' investment terms and conditions tend to be briefer and more informal than those of venture capitalists.

How to Find an Angel

- The private investor angel market tends to be regional rather than local or national, which means they are a little tougher to find.

- Angel networks are typically run by nonprofit groups. Most angel networks originate from college campuses, business incubators, state economic development agencies and other nonprofit entities.

- A large number of universities have established angel networks to match entrepreneurs with investors.

- VCs can serve as a source of information for locating angels.

- Firms can join an angel network for a nominal fee. Firms provide the company's vital statistics, such as type of business, market potential and amount of funding required. The angel network distributes this information but keeps the company name anonymous. The firm's name is revealed if an investor is interested.

Strategic Alliances

Strategic alliances are an alternative to venture capital, angel or bank financing because they use consolidation as a way of pooling strengths and capital. This alliance is a relationship between affiliated companies with a common goal and shared resources. Both parties view the partnership as a joint investment.

These alliances can provide access to new markets and increase or improve manufacturing capability. Corporate partners may seek to buy into smaller companies and use them as research and development divisions. In a strategic alliance, each partner retains its own identity.

Private Market Financing Other than Angels

Private equity markets provide small amounts of money, ranging on average from $8 million to $25 million per venture. They typically take an ownership position of between 10 and 30 percent of the firm. Such markets include insurance companies, pension funds, high net worth individuals and foreign investors.

Private equity deals are often structured in the form of convertible preferred stock. Investors are allowed options to sell their stock back to the company at market price beginning after the fifth year, with a payout schedule over the next 3 successive years. These private placements are exempt from SEC registration statements and are not subject to SEC dollar amount limitations.

Factoring

Factoring is the sale and purchase of commercial accounts receivable between two parties at a discount. The factor, or purchaser of the accounts, provides cash up front to the seller and then collects on the invoices. Once the money is collected, the firm gets the balance minus a fee for the factor's services. The factor's fee ranges from 1.5 percent to five percent of the accounts receivable face value.

This financing vehicle is often used in the retail industry to raise cash quickly, often in as little as 10 days. Banks can take months. The process is particularly attractive for younger firms with few financial assets.

Vendors and Customers

For a small firm, its suppliers, customers, manufacturers and distributors are possible sources of financing as these groups have a vested interest in the firm's survival. The small firm might also seek to negotiate extended credit from suppliers. However, the firm must be able to show suppliers an ability to pay based on evidence of a large customer orders. The firm may also show the ability to negotiate advance payments from customers, to exchange equity for outside services and supplies and to pay vendors with products or services instead of cash.

Bartering

Bartering, the exchange of good and services between parties without the use of money, may be useful for startup ventures short on cash. Joining a barter network enables companies to trade goods or services with fellow members. There is usually a required cash fee per transaction.

Lease

Leasing equipment is one way to keep technology and machinery current while conserving money. You could also lease your equipment to other companies as a way to raise cash and earn tax benefits for doing so.

There are several kinds of leases. An operating lease is when the lessor owns the equipment and enjoys any tax benefits of ownership. The entity leasing the equipment, the lessee, is responsible for its maintenance and pays a fixed fee to use it for a specific period. A capital lease is backed with an asset, money in the bank or another guarantee.

Licensing

Licensing allows companies—particularly tech companies without production facilities—to finance themselves through the sale of rights for use of their technology. Licensing agreements require the help of an attorney expert in the industry to draft the legal contracts specific to it.

Small Business Administration

According to the U.S. Small Business Administration (SBA), the federal government is the largest single investor in U.S. private equity funds. The SBA's Small Business Investment Company (SBIC) program, part of the U.S. Small Business Administration, was created in 1958 to fill the gap between the availability of venture capital and the needs of small businesses in startup and growth situations. For more information, go to www.sba.gov.

The government itself does not make direct investments or target specific industries. Essentially, the SBIC program is a fund of funds, meaning that portfolio management and investment decisions are left to qualified private fund managers.

As a result, the SBA has minimal direct involvement in an SBIC's portfolio management operations.

The SBA also offers the following loan options for businesses:

Basic 7(a) Loan Guaranty–This program is the SBA's primary business loan program to help qualified small businesses obtain financing when they might not be eligible for business loans through normal lending channels. It is also the agency's most flexible business loan program, as financing under this program can be guaranteed for a variety of general business purposes, including working capital, machinery and equipment, furniture and fixtures, land and building (including purchase, renovation and new construction), leasehold improvements and debt refinancing (under special conditions). Loan maturity is up to 10 years for working capital and generally up to 25 years for fixed assets. For more information, visit www.sba.gov/financing/sbaloan/7a.htm.

Certified Development Company (CDC), a 504 Loan Program– This program provides long-term, fixed-rate financing to small businesses to acquire real estate or machinery or equipment for expansion or modernization. Typically, a 504 project includes a loan secured from a private-sector lender with a senior lien, a loan secured from a CDC (funded by a 100 percent SBA-guaranteed debenture) with a junior lien covering up to 40 percent of the total cost and a contribution of at least 10 percent equity from the borrower. The maximum SBA debenture generally is $1 million and up to $1.3 million in some cases. For more information, visit www.sba.gov/financing/sbaloan/cdc504.htm.

Microloan, a 7(m) Loan Program–This program provides short-term loans of up to $35,000 to small businesses and not-for-profit child-care centers for working capital or the purchase of inventory, supplies, furniture, fixtures, machinery and/or equipment. Proceeds cannot be used to pay existing debts or to purchase real estate. The SBA makes or guarantees a loan to an intermediary who in turn makes the microloan to the applicant. These organizations also provide management and technical assistance. The loans are not guaranteed by the SBA. The microloan program is available in selected locations in most states. For more information, visit www.sba.gov/financing/sbaloan/microloans.htm.

Loan Prequalification–Like prequalifying for a mortgage, this program allows business applicants to have their loan applications for $250,000 or less analyzed and potentially approved by the SBA before they are taken to lenders for consideration. The program focuses on the applicant's character, credit, experience and reliability rather than assets. An SBA-designated intermediary works with the business owner to review and strengthen the loan application. The review is based on key financial ratios, credit and business history and the loan-request terms. The program is administered by the SBA's Office of Field Operations and by SBA district offices.

US Government Departments

www.business.gov
The official link to the U.S. Government Includes information about:

- Business Statistics
- Trade Statistics
- Country Data
- Business Publications
- Employment Data
- Market Research
- Publications by Agency
- Environment

www.firstgov.gov
The Government's Official Web Portal

www.irs.gov/businesses/small
Small Business and Self-Employed One-Stop Resource

www.sba.gov
Small Business Association

www.sba.gov/library/pubs.html#fm-8
Small Business Association Publications Library

Associations

SCORE
www.score.org

The Service Corps of Retired Executives, more commonly known as SCORE, is a nonprofit group of mostly retired businesspeople who volunteer to provide counseling to small businesses at no charge. A program of the SBA, SCORE has been around since 1964 and has helped more than 3 million entrepreneurs and aspiring entrepreneurs. SCORE is a source for all kinds of business advice, from how to write a business plan to investigating marketing potential and managing cash flow. SCORE counselors work out of nearly 400 local chapters throughout the United States. You can obtain a referral to a counselor in your local chapter by contacting the national office.

www.nbia.org
National Business Incubation Association (NBIA)

The NBIA is the national organization for business incubators, which are organizations specially set up to nurture young firms and help them survive and grow. Incubators provide leased office facilities on flexible terms, shared business services, management assistance, help in obtaining financing, and technical support. NBIA says there are nearly 600 incubators in North America. Its services include providing a directory to local incubators and their services.

<u>www.uschamber.org</u>
U.S. Chamber of Commerce

The many chambers of commerce throughout the United States are organizations devoted to providing networking, lobbying, training and more. If you think chambers are all about having lunch with a bunch of community boosters, think again. Among the services the U.S. Chamber of Commerce offers is a Web-based business solutions program that provides online help with specific small-business needs, including planning, marketing and other tasks such as creating a press release, collecting a bad debt, recruiting employees or creating a retirement plan.

The U.S. Chamber of Commerce is the umbrella organization for local chambers, of which there are more than 1,000 in the United States. If you plan on doing business overseas, don't forget to check for an American Chamber of Commerce in the countries where you hope to have a presence. They are set up to provide information and assistance to U.S. firms seeking to do business there. Many, but not all, countries have American Chambers.

SBA Development Centers

Anchorage, AK District Office
510 L Street, Suite 310
Anchorage, AK 99501
1.907.271.4022

Alabama District Office
801 Tom Martin Drive, Suite 201
Birmingham, AL 35211
1.205.290.7101
Fax 1.205.290.7404

Arkansas District Office
2120 Riverfront Drive, Suite 250
Little Rock, AR 72202
1.501.324.5871
Fax 1.501.324.5199

Arizona District Office
2828 N. Central Avenue, Suite 800
Phoenix, AZ 85004
1.602.745.7200
Fax 1.602.745.7210

Fresno District Office
2719 N. Air Fresno Drive,
Suite 200
Fresno, CA 93727
1.559.487.5791
Fax: 1.559.487.5636

Los Angeles District Office
330 N. Brand, Suite 1200
Glendale, CA 91203
1.818.552.3215

Sacramento District Office
650 Capitol Mall, Suite 7-500
Sacramento, CA 95814
1.916.930.3700
Fax 1.916.930.3737

San Diego District Office
550 W. C Street, Suite 550
San Diego, CA 92101
1.619.557.7250
Fax 1.619.557.5894
TTY 1.619.557.6998

San Francisco District Office
455 Market Street, Sixth Floor
San Francisco, CA 94105
1.415.744.6820

Santa Ana District Office
200 W. Santa Ana Boulevard,
Suite 700
Santa Ana, CA 92701
1.714.550.7420
TTY/TDD 1.714.550.0655

Colorado District Office
721 19th Street, Suite 426
Denver, CO 80202
1.303.844.2607

Connecticut District Office
330 Main Street, Second Floor
Hartford, CT 06106
1.860.240.4700

Washington, DC District Office
1110 Vermont Avenue, N.W.,
Ninth Floor
Washington, D.C. 20005
1.202.606.4000

Wilmington, DE District Office
824 N. Market Street, Suite 610
Wilmington, DE 19801
1.302.573.6294

North Florida District Office
7825 Baymeadows Way, Suite 100B
Jacksonville, FL 32256
1.904.443.1900

South Florida District Office
100 S. Biscayne Boulevard
Seventh Floor
Miami, FL 33131
1.305.536.5521
Fax 1.305.536.5058

Georgia District Office
233 Peachtree Street, N.E., Suite 1900
Atlanta, GA 30303
1.404.331.0100

Guam Branch Office
400 Route 8, Suite 302
First Hawaiian Bank Building
Mongmong, GU 96927
1.671.472.7419
Fax 1.671.472.7365

Hawaii District Office
300 Ala Moana Boulevard,
Room 2-235
Box 50207
Honolulu, HI 96850
1.808.541.2990
Fax 1.808.541.2976

Des Moines Office
210 Walnut Street, Room 749
Des Moines, IA 50309
1.515.284.4422

Cedar Rapids Office
215 4th Avenue S.E., Suite 200
Cedar Rapids, IA 52401
1.319.362.6405

Boise District Office
380 E. Parkcenter Boulevard
Suite 330
Boise, ID 83706
1.208.334.1696
Fax 1.208.334.9353

Illinois District Office
500 W. Madison Street, Suite 1250
Chicago, IL 60661
1.312.353.4528

Indiana District Office
429 N. Pennsylvania Street,
Suite 100
Indianapolis, IN 46204
1.317.226.7272

Kansas District Office
271 W. 3rd Street, N. Suite 2500
Wichita, KS 67202
1.316.269.6616

Kentucky District Office
600 Dr. MLK Jr. Place
Louisville, KY 40202
1.502.582.5971

New Orleans District Office
365 Canal Street, Suite 2820
New Orleans, LA 70130
1.504.589.6685

Massachusetts District Office
10 Causeway Street, Room 265
Boston, MA 02222
1.617.565.5590

Maryland District Office
City Crescent Building, Sixth Floor
10 South Howard Street
Baltimore, MD 21201
1.410.962.4392

Maine District Office
Edmund S. Muskie Federal Building,
Room 512
68 Sewall Street
Augusta, ME 04330
1.207.622.8274

Michigan District Office
477 Michigan Avenue
Suite 515, McNamara Building
Detroit, MI 48226
1.313.226.6075

Minneapolis, MN District Office
100 N. Sixth Street
Suite 210-C Butler Square
Minneapolis, MN 55403
1.612.370.2324
Fax:1.612.370.2303

Kansas City District Office
323 W. 8th Street, Suite 501
Kansas City, MO 64105
1.816.374.6701

Mississippi District Office
AmSouth Bank Plaza
210 E. Capitol Street, Suite 900
Jackson, MS 39201
1.601.965.4378
Fax 1.601.965.5629
or 1.601.965.4294

Gulfport Branch Office
Hancock Bank Plaza
2510 14th Street, Suite 101
Gulfport, MS 39501
1.228.863.4449
Fax 1.228.864.0179

Montana District Office
10 W. 15th Street, Suite 1100
Helena, MT 59626
1.406.441.1081
Fax 1.406.441.1090

North Carolina District Office
6302 Fairview Road, Suite 300
Charlotte, NC 28210
1.704.344.6563
Fax 1.704.344.6769

North Dakota District Office
657 Second Avenue North,
Room 219
Fargo, ND 58102
1.701.239.5131

Nebraska District Office
11145 Mill Valley Road
Omaha, NE 68154
1.402.221.4691

New Hampshire District Office
JC Cleveland Federal Building
55 Pleasant Street, Suite 3101
Concord, NH 03301
1.603.225.1400
Fax 1.603.225.1409

New Jersey District Office
Two Gateway Center, 15th Floor
Newark, NJ 07102
1.973.645.2434

Albuquerque District Office
625 Silver S.W., Suite 320
Albuquerque, NM 87102
1.505.346.7909
Fax 1.505.346.6711

Nevada District Office
400 S. 4th Street, Suite 250
Las Vegas, NV 89101
1.702.388.6611
Fax 1.702.388.6469

Buffalo District Office
111 W. Huron Street, Suite 1311
Buffalo, NY 14202
1.716.551.4301
Fax 1.716.551.4418

New York District Office
26 Federal Plaza, Suite 3100
New York, NY 10278
1.212.264.4354
Fax 1.212.264.4963

Syracuse District Office
401 S. Salina Street, Fifth Floor
Syracuse, NY 13202
1.315.471.9393
Fax 1.315.471.9288

Cleveland, OH District Office
1350 Euclid Avenue, Suite 211
Cleveland, OH 44115
1.216.522.4180
Fax 1.216.522.2038
TDD 1.216.522.8350

Columbus, OH District Office
Two Nationwide Plaza, Suite 1400
Columbus, OH 43215
1.614.469.6860

Oklahoma City District Office
Federal Building
301 NW Sixth Street
Oklahoma City, OK 73102
1.405.609.8000

Portland, OR District Office
601 SW Second Avenue, Suite 950
Portland, OR 97204
1.503.326.2682
Fax 1.503.326.2808

Philadelphia District Office
Robert N.C. Nix Federal Building
900 Market Street, Fifth Floor
Philadelphia, PA 19107
1.215.580.2SBA

Pittsburgh District Office
411 Seventh Avenue, Suite 1450
Pittsburgh, PA 15219
1.412.395.6560

Puerto Rico and US Virgin Islands
District Office
252 Ponce de Leon Ave.
Citibank Tower, Suite 201
Hato Rey, PR 00918
1.787.766.5572 or 1.800.669.8049
Fax 1.787.766.5309

Rhode Island District Office
380 Westminster Street, Room 511
Providence, RI 02903
1.401.528.4561

South Carolina District Office
1835 Assembly Street, Room 1425
Columbia, SC 29201
1.803.765.5377
Fax 1.803.765.5962

South Dakota District Office2329
N. Career Avenue, Suite 105
Sioux Falls, SD 57107
1.605.330.4243
Fax 1.605.330.4215
TTY/TDD 1.605.331.3527

Tennessee District Office
50 Vantage Way, Suite 201
Nashville, TN 37228
1.615.736.5881
Fax 1.615.736.7232
TTY/TDD 1.615.736.2499

Dallas District Office
4300 Amon Carter Boulevard,
Suite 114
Fort Worth, TX 76155
1.817.684.5500
Fax 1.817.684.5516

El Paso District Office
10737 Gateway West
El Paso, TX 79935
1.915.633.7001
Fax 1.915.633.7005

Dallas District Office
4300 Amon Carter Bouldevard,
Suite 114
Fort Worth, TX 76155
1.817.684.5500
Fax 1.817.684.5516

Harlingen District Office
222 E. Van Buren Street, Suite 500
Harlingen, TX 78550
1.956.427.8533

Corpus Christi Branch Office
3649 Leopard Street, Suite 411
Corpus Christi, TX 78408
1.361.879.0017

Houston District Office
8701 S. Gessner Drive, Suite 1200
Houston, TX 77074
1.713.773.6500
Fax 1.713.773.6550

Lubbock District Office
1205 Texas Avenue, Room 408
Lubbock, TX 79401
1.806.472.7462
Fax: 1.806.472.7487

San Antonio District Office
17319 San Pedro, Suite 200
San Antonio, TX 78232
1.210.403.5900
Fax: 1.210.403.5936
TDD: 1.210.403.5933

Utah District Office
125 S. State Street, Room 2231
Salt Lake City, UT 84138
1.801.524.3209

Richmond District Office
400 N. 8th Street
Federal Bldg., Suite 1150
Richmond, VA 23240
1.804.771.2400
Fax 1.804.771.2764

Vermont District Office
87 State Street, Room 205
Montpelier, VT 05601
1.802.828.4422

Seattle District Office
1200 Sixth Avenue, Suite 1700
Seattle, WA 98101
1.206.553.7310

Spokane Branch Office
801 W. Riverside Avenue, Suite 200
Spokane, WA 99201
1.509.353.2811

Wisconsin District Office
740 Regent Street, Suite 100
Madison, WI 53715
1.608.441.5263
Fax 1.608.441.5541

or

Wisconsin District Office
310 W. Wisconsin Ave. Room 400
Milwaukee, WI 53203
1.414.297.3941
Fax 1.414.297.1377

West Virginia District Office
320 W. Pike Street, Suite 330
Clarksburg, WV 26301
1.304.623.5631

Wyoming District Office
100 E. B Street
Federal Building
P.O. Box 44001
Casper, WY 82602
1.307.261.6500

State Agencies

Check with your state government for specific programs that offer aid to small businesses. Many states have their own venture capital funds willing to work with companies in their early stages of development. Also, state business agencies are always able to refer women and minorities to specific funding resources available locally.

Going Public

All corporations issue stock, but selling it on the public market changes a company profoundly. Selling stock to the public provides a great source of funding but subjects your company to far more intense scrutiny. Going public requires extensive legal and accounting help, publicity (to make your company known to the investment public) and possible management reorganization that addresses the new governance climate. The process of taking a company public is a book in itself, so begin by consulting experts in your field to start your education.

Summary

Financing a business, no matter how small, should never be an afterthought, even if you are starting in your attic. Estimating your capital needs at startup and afterward is critical, and assessing your own personal finance needs is essential. When you start a business, your business and personal finances should be kept separate.

6 Advice Worth Paying for

How to Best Use Attorneys and Accountants at the Start of the Process

When you hire an attorney or an accountant, you are paying for guidance and expertise in an area you presumably have limited knowledge in. In business, the challenge is to manage your advisory help as you would your business—with respect for their skills but with an eye towards the bottom line.

Most Americans need legal and accounting assistance at some point in their lives—putting agreements in writing, documenting business transactions and filing complex tax returns are just a few of the reasons. But too often these basic but important legal matters are neglected because of the cost. The fact is, most legal services are expensive.

Yet when you start your business, hiring professional legal and accounting help may be the most cost-effective step you take in the planning process. Once your business is up and running and you have a better sense of the paperwork involved, you may be able to handle some of the tasks associated with incorporation yourself.

Most new business owners acknowledge the need for hiring an accountant. Setting up a chart of accounts, reviewing financial figures, and preparing necessary federal, state and local tax returns on a personal and business basis are tasks with which most owners would welcome assistance. The complexity of tax and finance work requires the help of an expert in the field.

The benefits of an attorney may not be as obvious at first, but an attorney can prove a valuable resource when drafting agreements with vendors, contractors, and even staff. An attorney is also essential for issues relating to shareholders and the board of directors. Perhaps most important, however, is an attorney's advice and direction on matters of legal compliance on the federal and state level for your corporation.

Finding the Right Attorney

Once you have made the decision to search for legal help, you may need some guidance in choosing one. Look for the following skill sets indicative of a good business attorney.

Business Setup

Look for an attorney well-versed in various business structures who can help you decide whether a corporation, partnership or limited liability company (LLC) is the best way to organize your business. He or she should be able to prepare the necessary paperwork and be up-front about how much you can do yourself to save on fees.

Contracts Expertise

Many online services can file the necessary incorporation papers for you, but an attorney familiar with your industry and perhaps your local business environment will be best equipped to offer your business an added value the online companies cannot. Your industry, your liability exposure and whether you employ people are factors to take into account when choosing legal help. An attorney with the right legal experience can help protect you in all these areas and may help you find opportunities you would not find otherwise.

Real Estate

Leasing commercial space—offices, storefronts and warehouses—are potential landmines for business owners because most commercial contracts favor the landlord. Your attorney should be skilled in negotiating business leases with terms that benefit you.

Taxes and Licenses

Although your accountant will prepare and file your business tax returns each year, your attorney should know how to register your business for federal and state tax identification numbers and understand the tax consequences of the more basic business transactions in which your business will engage. There may come a time when your attorney needs to talk to your accountant and vice versa. You need to make sure that can happen in an efficient and timely manner.

Intellectual Property

If you are in a media, design or other creative business, it is important to hire an attorney who can help you register products for federal trademark and copyright protection as well as offer other services that will help you protect and develop your work. Most general business counsel can advise on filing matters, but for complicated content issues, you will need an attorney who specializes in intellectual property issues. If this is your line of work, make sure there are qualified intellectual property experts in the firm you hire.

Liability Exposure

If you are in a business where you face potential legal liability—and most business do face some liability issues—a lawyer can help you evaluate your exposure and recommend solutions, such as purchasing liability insurance. The evaluation of your exposure is important, of course, in determining whether to incorporate in the first place so that you can protect your personal assets, but it is also important in protecting your business assets moving forward.

Interviewing a Potential Attorney

Remember that an attorney or accountant work works for you—not the other way around. So when you interview attorneys for the first time, it makes sense to prepare a list of questions relative to your needs and their experience. Important questions to ask might include:

• What is your business experience?
If you want an attorney to help you with incorporation, it is logical to ask how many incorporations they have handled and whether they handle both in-state and out-of-state incorporation. If you have a business that may cross state lines someday, choose an attorney with skills in both areas.

• How good are your diagnostic skills?
Good attorneys are a bit like doctors; they can identify the minor symptoms that might turn into big problems later. No attorney can possibly know everything about every area of law, but ask them about your industry, what legal expertise they can provide in that area and if they can speak in general terms about the casework they have accomplished in that area. You may also want to glance around the attorney's office for books and magazines in the specialty you are seeking.

• Can you explain complex legal matters to me in a way I can understand?
Like good doctors, good attorneys can explain complicated topics simply. Attorneys who can provide straightforward explanations and access to written materials to educate their clients on topics relevant to their business are invaluable.

• Will you personally be handling my work?
In many firms, the attorney who brings you in as a client is not necessarily the one you will be working with in the long run. It may be a less experienced associate without the skills needed to manage your business. Make sure the attorney who sells you on the firm is the attorney who is going to be handling your work.

• How do you handle billing?
Most attorneys will charge a flat one-time fee for routine matters, such as forming a corporation or LLC, but may not volunteer that fact unless you ask about it. Also, be sure to ask if the flat fee includes disbursements (the attorney's out-of-pocket expenses, such as filing fees and overnight courier charges) and when the fee is due. Many attorneys require payment of a flat fee up front so that they can cover their out-of-pocket expenses. You should always ask to hold back 10 to 20 percent of a flat fee, though, in the event the attorney does not do the job well. Once you are satisfied with the work, pay the remainder promptly.

> • **Can we communicate?**
> A good attorney should take the time to explain to you all issues and possible options. If they are encouraging or discouraging you from doing something, they should be able to provide a reasoned and complete explanation.
>
> • **Are you easy to reach?**
> This is a question about service and geography. Any attorney you bring on to serve your business should be accessible for necessary requests over the phone and in person. As a client, you should of course reserve your requests to urgent matters and try to consolidate issues during phone calls or visits whenever possible.
>
> • **Are we on the same page?**
> How well you like your attorney on a personal level may be a secondary concern, but it is important that you think alike when it comes to business matters.

How to Manage Fees

When paying for advice that affects your future, remember that short-term costs often reap long-term benefits. At the same time, remember that higher fees do not necessarily mean better service. Make sure you are getting your money's worth when hiring professionals to assist you in the process of incorporation.

If you have some knowledge of the legal processes involved in incorporation, you might choose to hire an attorney as a type of editor—someone who can read over and approve your work before it is submitted. In this way, you can substantially reduce your legal expenses and still benefit from the expertise of a professional.

Regardless of the level of service you require, all attorneys have standard fee arrangements. The following are the most common:

• **Hourly or per diem rate**—Most attorneys bill by the hour. If travel is involved, they may bill by the day. You might ask if you can negotiate a fixed number of hours of service.

• **Flat fee**—Some attorneys suggest a flat fee for certain routine matters, such as reviewing a contract or closing a loan. See if this works for you.

• **Monthly retainer**—If you anticipate heavy contact with your attorney, you may benefit from paying a monthly fee that entitles you to all the routine legal advice you need.

• **Contingent fee**—For lawsuits or other complex matters, attorneys often work on a contingency basis. This means that if they succeed, they receive a percentage of the proceeds—usually between 25 percent and 40 percent. If they fail, they receive only out-of-pocket expenses. This is not a fee arrangement that applies for routine business law matters, but it makes sense to discuss all possible fee structures for issues headed to court.

The following is another, somewhat controversial, method of billing and one that you should explore in detail with your attorney before agreeing to:

- **Value billing**. Some law firms bill at a higher rate on business matters if the attorneys obtain a favorable result, such as negotiating a large, money-saving contract for your company. It is often difficult to know if you are truly receiving a higher level of service with this type of arrangement. If you have doubts, ask for a different billing arrangement.

The Following Are Further Steps You Can Take to Control Legal Costs

- **Have the attorney estimate the cost of each matter in writing.**
  If the bill comes in over the estimate, ask why. Some attorneys also offer caps, guaranteeing in writing the maximum cost of a particular service. This helps you budget and provides more certainty than an estimate.

- **Learn what increments of time the firm uses to calculate its bill.**
  Attorneys keep track of their time in increments as short as 6 minutes or as long as half an hour. You have a right to this information.

- **Ask for monthly, itemized bills.**
  Some attorneys wait until a bill gets large before sending an invoice. Ask for monthly invoices instead, and review them. The most obvious red flag is excessive fees; this means too many people—or the wrong people—are working on your file. Check also to make sure that work billed to other clients does not show up on your bill.

- **Ask for a prompt payment discount.**
  Some firms offers as much as a five percent discount on invoices paid within 30 days. Such an arrangement can add thousands of dollars to your yearly bottom line.

- **Be prepared.**
  Before you meet with or call your attorney, have the necessary documents with you and know exactly what you want to discuss. Fax needed documents in advance so that your attorney is prepared for your discussion.

- **Limit phone calls.**
  This is self-explanatory; too many phone calls increase your bill and can tax the resources of a busy attorney.

How to Find a Good Attorney

- **Talk to People You Trust**
  Good attorneys develop good reputations—try to gather names from businesspeople you trust.

- **Directories**
  The Yellow Pages and the Martindale-Hubbell Law Directory (in your local library and at www.martindale.com/xp/Martindale/home/xml can help you locate an attorney with the right education, background and expertise for your case.

- **Databases**
  A paralegal should be able to run a quick computer search of local attorneys for you by using legal databases.

- **City and State Bar Associations**
  Bar associations are listed in phone books. Along with attorney referrals, your bar association can direct you to low-cost legal clinics or specialists in your area.

- **Law Schools**
  For simple items, you might be able to contact your local law school's legal clinic.

The Law Firm Visit

Trust your first impressions when you visit a potential attorney's office for the first time. Take a look around and note the following:

- The decor and general appearance of the office. Though the firm need not have lavish furnishings, it should look clean and organized.

- Up-to-date computer equipment and support personnel. Outdated computers and overtaxed assistants can mean lost files and poor record-keeping.

- How the attorney presents himself or herself. Look for a neat, tailored appearance and a professional demeanor. Ask yourself "Would I feel comfortable having this person represent me in court?"

- Whether the attorney is attentive to your concerns. Does he or she take notes during the conversation and ask relevant questions?

- Availability of references. First-rate attorneys will not hesitate to provide you a list of satisfied clients.

Summary

Professional legal and accounting advice are crucial to your business at various points in its life cycle. Be prepared to ask tough questions when choosing an attorney and accountant, and consider handling some of the paperwork yourself to keep fees at a minimum.

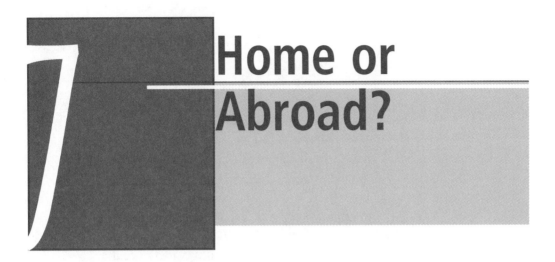

Home or Abroad?

Incorporating in Your Home State or Elsewhere

For most companies, the question of where to incorporate is simple—they incorporate in their home state because that is where they will be conducting business and housing their operations.

However, the ultimate question of where to incorporate depends on the corporation's industry, where its customers are and what types of employees and functions it will need to make the business grow. It also requires some willingness to ask the question "Where is this corporation going to be 5, 10 or 15 years from now?"

The fact that we are now in a global economy has serious implications for many companies, even small ones. Perhaps you are a company founder based on the East Coast and do much of your manufacturing business in Asia. Would it be best to incorporate where you live, or might it be best to incorporate in a state on the West Coast where your shipments come in, which might, in the long-term, make more sense from a tax, regulatory and fee standpoint?

The answers are as unique as your business, and these critical questions call for expertise. Some suggestions:

- As always, any effort to incorporate should involve a discussion with an attorney or certified public accountant. Where to incorporate is a vital part of that discussion and should take place with experts in corporate law and taxation.
- Trade groups in your chosen industry might be able to provide detailed information and advice on business structures.
- The Small Business Administration provides in-depth data on corporate startups, including the process of deciding where to incorporate. To learn more visit www.sba.gov/starting_business/index.htm.

Business owners are free to incorporate in all 50 states and the District of Columbia. Some businesses do business in states other than where they are incorporated. If a corporation is transacting business in a state where it is not incorporated, it must register for a certificate of authority to transact such business in the other state as a foreign corporation.

What you should consider in your decision to pick a state for incorporation:

- Where will your physical facilities be located?
- How much does it cost to apply for incorporation in that state, and how much does it cost annually to continue as a corporation?
- How much does it cost to live there? Calculate your cost of living as well as that of your employees.
- Does the state charge an annual franchise tax—typically an annual tax paid by all businesses incorporated in a particular state?
- Are you free to register your name in that state? If you are free to use your business name in your home state but not in another target state, it may pose problems with marketing.
- What will you pay in state and local business income taxes in that target state? Is it worth the expense?

What States Are Most Appealing?

The state of Delaware has long been a favorite for corporations. More than half a million business entities have their legal home in Delaware, including more than 50 percent of all publicly traded U.S. companies and 58 percent of the Fortune 500 companies. To compete with Delaware, many other states have rewritten their corporate laws. However, most state laws favoring corporations appeal to large corporations. Small companies, particularly those not planning to go public, gain few benefits.

If your business is, for example, a retail store in New York City, it would be more advisable to set up a New York corporation. If you were to set up a Delaware corporation and operate a store in New York City, you would still have to qualify to do business in the state of New York, which would require the following steps:

- Filing an application to do business as a foreign or out-of-state corporation.
- Paying franchise taxes as a foreign corporation in New York.
- Reporting and paying annual taxes in New York as well as Delaware.

It is important to make sure that where you incorporate is the state best suited for your business.

Because a number of other states have revised their own corporation laws, that the advantages once available only in Delaware are now available in many states. Nevada and Wyoming are two such states. In fact, Nevada offers lower taxes, no corporate franchise fees and more protection and privacy for corporate officers, directors and stockholders than does Delaware.

Consider Nevada or Wyoming only when your corporation will not regularly do business elsewhere or remains a passive operating entity. The one reported downside of Nevada corporations is that they draw the most frequent IRS audits of any state in the country. Wyoming offers the same corporate advantages as Nevada and reportedly has fewer IRS audits.

In the end, the best location for you is the one most beneficial for your business. Discuss your options with your accountant or attorney.

Foreign Corporations

If you need to transact business outside your state of formation, you will need to file papers to qualify as a foreign corporation or foreign LLC. Corporations are considered domestic only in the state where they are formed, so any decision to take business across state lines, particularly with offices and facilities, needs to be considered carefully. Filing to become a foreign corporation in one or more states exponentially increases your fees, taxes and other related expenses.

To find out more about state laws, refer to Appendix A for a comprehensive listing of incorporation rules in each state. State Web sites typically contain legal language, so ask your attorney for assistance if you need help making sense of any information. Another resource is the Martindale-Hubbell Law Directory, found in public and law libraries and online at www.martindale.com/xp/Martindale/home.xml.

Appointment of a Registered Agent

States generally require that their corporations maintain a registered agent in the state in which they incorporate to receive communications and summonses in the event of a lawsuit. A registered agent may be an officer of the company or a company designated by the corporation as its designated agent. All registered agent contact information needs to be filed with the states in which the corporation does business.

Keeping Interstate Records

Each state has rules on what business can be conducted inside its borders. Therefore, if you do business only within the state you are registered in, there should be no problems. However, if you are running a business that sells goods across state lines as a corporation, make sure you are operating within the other state's laws. Failure to do so could result in the piercing of the corporate veil, meaning that the liability protections afforded to corporation officers could be voided in court. This a compelling reason to check the laws of every state before you open for business, particularly if you sell through a catalog or the Internet.

Engaging in interstate commerce does not always constitute doing business within a state. However, if you engage in such interstate commerce and have a registered office, address or agent in a state other than the one in which you are incorporated, you need to register in that state as a foreign corporation.

Other principal business activities that are considered doing business include:

- soliciting and receiving orders by mail within that state
- soliciting orders within that state through an agent, sales representative or independent contractor
- shipping orders from a warehouse within that state
- paying state taxes
- accepting service of process

The Model Corporation Act

The Model Corporation Act, drafted by a group of lawyers and law professors, lists activities that, in and of themselves, do not constitute doing business. Because this act is the basis for the laws in many states, it is a good guide to what activities you can do without having to qualify as a business in another state. The language reads as follows:

A foreign corporation shall not be considered to be transacting business in this state, for the purposes of this Act, by reason of carrying on in this state any one or more of the following activities:

- Maintaining or defending any action or suit or any administrative or arbitration proceeding or effecting the settlement thereof or the settlement of claims or disputes.
- Holding meetings of its directors or shareholders or carrying on other activities concerning its internal affairs.
- Maintaining bank accounts.
- Maintaining offices or agencies for the transfer, exchange and registration of its securities or appointing and maintaining trustees or depositories with relation to its securities.
- Effecting sales through independent contractors.
- Soliciting or procuring orders, whether by mail or through employees or agents or otherwise, where such orders require acceptance without this state before becoming binding contracts.
- Creating as borrower or lender, or acquiring indebtedness or mortgages or other security interests in real or personal property.
- Securing or collecting debts or enforcing any rights in property securing the same.
- Transacting any business in interstate commerce.
- Conducting an isolated transaction completed within a period of 30 days and not in the course of a number of repeated transactions of like nature.

Summary

Small startup companies filing for incorporation should look first to their home state when choosing a location. Do take into account, however, your industry, your growth prospects and other factors and consult an attorney or tax advisor before making a final decision.

8 Documents, Documents, Documents

Managing the Paperwork of Incorporation

All businesses involve paperwork—record keeping required by the government for tax and reporting purposes as well as that used for internal accounting. And though all business structures require scrupulous record keeping, if you are changing from a sole proprietorship or a partnership to a corporation, be prepared for an increase in the amount of documentation required for your business activities. Business officers of a corporation must comply with rigorous state and federal reporting requirements and deadlines that make incorporation the most complicated business structure overall.

But not all corporations face the same reporting obligations. As discussed in previous chapters, there are several different categories of corporations. C corporations—the traditional structure for most public companies—often require the most complex and work-intensive record keeping. S corporations and close corporations have fewer reporting requirements.

Companies also now face the added responsibility of the Sarbanes-Oxley Act (SOA), legislation passed in 2002 to create more stringent rules for corporate documentation and penalties for wrongdoing. Though the new law applies only to publicly held companies, nonprofit and smaller corporations are starting to adopt SOA practices as a way to bolster confidence in their financial data and IT processes.

Establishing a Records Area

For easy, reliable access to your company's records, it is best to set up a single area where documents can be placed and stored securely. For new, small corporations, this may be as simple as organizing a binder containing essential items for the routine maintenance and administration of a corporation. The file should include sample minutes, resolutions and bylaws, stock certificates, a corporate seal and a stock ledger. You should also keep a file containing the company's official articles of incorporation, bylaws, initial and subsequent minutes of directors and shareholders meetings and a stock register to track current shareholder statistics.

Bookkeeping

A corporation is viewed in the eyes of the law as a legal entity separate and apart from the owners. Therefore, the IRS requires you to maintain two separate sets of records, one for your personal affairs and one for the affairs of the corporation.

Accounting and Bookkeeping

Few entrepreneurs are trained accountants, but the successful ones let the numbers lead them. Before you devise marketing or financial strategies, of make most everyday decision, always ask "What is the bottom line?" Answers will surface if you maintain accurate and complete financial records. To keep good financial records, you do not need an accounting degree. You just need to be organized, diligent and accurate with mathematical calculations.

Start by opening a separate checking account for your business with your company's name, address and phone number printed on the checks. To open a company bank account, you need to obtain an Employer Identification Number for your company. To obtain this, simply file Form SS-4 with the Internal Revenue Service. If you are a corporation, you may be required to produce a corporate resolution duly signed, often with the corporate seal, as an official corporate indication of authorization to open such an account. Write checks for every business-related purchase, and deposit all income into your business checking account. Balance your account at least monthly, and keep all canceled checks on file for at least 3 years—required for IRS tax audits. To keep track of expenditures, never write checks to cash.

Hint
There is a distinction between accounting and bookkeeping procedures.
Accounting is a beginning-to-end process of collecting financial data, generating financial statement and preparing tax forms.
Bookkeeping is the function of collecting financial data only.

Most small business owners are not knowledgeable in bookkeeping and accounting procedures and this is usually the first area that is outsourced.

The two basic accounting methods are cash and accrual.

Cash Method

This is the accounting method used by individuals and many small businesses. Due to its simplicity, it may be appropriate for your small business. Determining gross income with the cash method is merely a matter of adding up the cash, checks, and fair market value of property and services you receive during the year. In other words, you record income at the time cash is received and record the expense when you make the payment. Using this method, your income for the year includes all checks you receive, regardless of when you cash the checks or withdraw the money. You cannot avoid paying tax by not depositing checks or credit card charge slips.

Using the cash method, your business expenses are usually deducted in the year you pay them. For example, you order some office supplies from a mail order catalog in November 2004, and they arrive in December. You send a check to pay for them in January 2005. Under the cash method, that business deduction should be claimed on your 2005 tax return because that is the year you pay for the supplies.

Certain businesses cannot use the cash method. The IRS requires you to declare the accounting method you will use and if your corporation's annual average gross receipts exceed $5 million you must use the accrual method. Smaller businesses with few credit accounts most often use the cash method of accounting. Special rules apply for the accounting of inventory. See IRS Publication 538 Accounting Periods and Methods.

Accrual Method

This method of accounting is more precise than the cash method. Its main purpose is to match income and expenses in the correct year. With the accrual method, you record a transaction at the time it is made regardless of when the payment occurs. For example, the accrual method calls for you to report income for the year when you perform a service for a customer. It does not matter that your customer does not pay you until the following year. Again, if you keep sales inventory, it is generally preferable to use accrual accounting.

Similarly, you generally deduct your business expenses in the year you become liable for them, regardless of when you actually paid them. Let us look at the office supply example again. Under the accrual method, you can deduct the business expenses for supplies on your 2003 taxes, for the year you ordered the supplies and they were delivered. You sent a check to pay for them in January 2005. You can deduct the expenses in 2004, because that is the year when you became liable for the expense.

Once you decide which accounting method is the right one for your business, you must follow it consistently. Generally, you cannot change your method of accounting unless you get special permission from the IRS to change.

As a rule, however, it is not necessary to maintain an elaborate bookkeeping system. A separate bank account and bookkeeping that clearly shows what you and the corporation separately earn and pay out is usually sufficient. A local bookkeeper or accountant can set up a convenient accounting and tax system for your business or you can buy an accounting program, such as Quicken or QuickBooks, to track your business finances.

To open a corporate bank account, you will need an employer identification number (EIN) for your corporation, even if you do not have employees. This bank account must be used exclusively for corporate needs. The bank will probably also require a corporate resolution, duly signed with the corporate seal, as an official corporate indication of authorization to open a bank account.

TIN's and EIN's

An EIN is also known as a Federal Taxpayer Identification Number (TIN), and is used to identify a business entity. An EIN is for use in connection with your business activities only. Do not use your EIN in place of your Social Security number (SSN).

You can apply for an EIN online at www.irs.gov. Type the letters EIN in the IRS search box and select Employer ID Numbers (EIN). Or, if you would rather apply by phone, contact the IRS Business and Specialty Tax Line.

When applying for an EIN, complete Form SS-4. This form is available online at the IRS Web site, local IRS offices and at all Social Security offices.

Purpose of Form

Use Form SS-4 to apply for an EIN. An EIN is a nine-digit number (for example, 12-3456789) assigned to sole proprietors, corporations, partnerships, estates, trusts, and other entities for tax filing and reporting purposes. The information you provide on this form will establish your business tax account.

After accessing the online SS-4 application, do not press the Back button to return to instructions or other Web pages. Doing so will result in a loss of all information entered and will require you to input the information again. We suggest you print the instructions for easy reference prior to completing your online Form SS-4 application.

Hint
An EIN is for use in connection with your business activities only. Do NOT use your EIN in place of your Social Security number.

Who Must Obtain an EIN

You must complete and submit Form SS-4 if you have not been assigned an EIN before, and:

- You pay wages to one or more employees, including household employees.
- You are required to have an EIN to use on any return, statement, or other document, even if you are not an employer.
- You are a withholding agent required to withhold taxes on income, other than wages, paid to a nonresident alien (individual, corporation, partnership, etc.). A withholding agent may be an agent, broker, fiduciary, manager, tenant, or spouse, and is required to file Form 1042, Annual Withholding Tax Return for U.S. Source Income of Foreign Persons.
- You file Schedule C, Profit or Loss From Business, Schedule C-EZ, Net Profit From Business, or Schedule F, Profit or Loss From Farming, or Form 1040, U.S. Individual Income Tax Return, and have a Keogh plan or are required to file excise, employment, or alcohol, tobacco or firearms returns.

You should apply for your EIN early so that you have it when you need to file a tax return or make a deposit. You can get an EIN quickly by calling the Tele-TIN phone number for your state. If you prefer, you can fax a completed Form SS-4 to the IRS Service Center, and they will respond with a return fax in about 1 week. If you apply by mail, send your completed Form SS-4 at least 4 to 5 weeks before you need your EIN to file a return or make a deposit.

How To Apply for an EIN

You can apply for an EIN online, by telephone, by fax, or by mail depending on how soon you need to use the EIN. Use only one method for each entity so you do not receive more than one EIN for an entity.

Online—You can receive your EIN by Internet and use it immediately to file a return or make a payment. Go to the IRS website at www.irs.gov/businesses and click on Employer ID Numbers under topics. Generally, a sole proprietor should file only one Form SS-4 and needs only one EIN, regardless of the number of businesses operated as a sole proprietorship or trade names under which a business operates. However, if the proprietorship incorporates or enters into a partnership, a new EIN is required. Also, each corporation in an affiliated group must have its own EIN.

Note: Not all businesses may use this method. An EIN will be issued after the successful submission of the completed Form SS-4 online. For more information or to see if your business can apply online, visit www.irs.gov/businesses/small.

Mail—If requested by an IRS representative, mail or fax the signed Form SS-4 (including any third party designee authorization) within 24 hours to the IRS address provided by the IRS representative.

Telephone—You can receive your EIN by telephone and use it immediately to file a return or make a payment. Call the IRS at 800.829.4933. (International applicants must call 215.516.6999.) The hours of operation are 7:00 a.m. to 10:00 p.m. The person making the call must be authorized to sign the form or be an authorized designee. If you are applying by telephone, it will be helpful to complete Form SS-4 before contacting the IRS. An IRS representative will use the information from the Form SS-4 to establish your account and assign you an EIN. Write the number you are given on the upper right corner of the form and sign and date it. Keep this copy for your records.

Delayed EIN Information—If you do not have an EIN by the time a return is due, write "Applied For" and the date you applied in the space shown for the number. Do not show your SSN as an EIN on returns. If you do not have an EIN by the time a tax deposit is due, send your payment to the Internal Revenue Service Center for your filing area as shown in the instructions for the form that you are filing. Make your check or money order payable to the United States Treasury and show your name (as shown on Form SS-4), address, type of tax, period covered and date you applied for an EIN.

Note

Taxpayer representatives can apply for an EIN on behalf of their client and request that the EIN be faxed to their client on the same day. By using this procedure, you are authorizing the IRS to fax the EIN without a cover sheet. Call 800.829.4933 to verify a number or to ask about the status of an application by mail.

How to Obtain Forms and Publications

Phone—You can order forms, instructions, and publications by phone 24 hours a day, 7 days a week. Call 800.TAX.FORM (800.829.3676). You should receive your order or notification of its status within 10 workdays.

Personal computer—With your personal computer and modem, you can get the forms and information you need using the IRS Web site www.irs.gov or File Transfer Protocol at ftp.irs.gov.

CD—For small businesses, return preparers, or others who may frequently need tax forms or publications, a CD containing over 2,000 tax products (including many prior year forms) can be purchased from the National

Technical Information Service (NTIS)—To order Pub. 1796, Federal Tax Products on CD, call 877.CDFORMS or 877.233.6767 toll free or visit www.irs.gov/cdorders.

Form **SS-4**	**Application for Employer Identification Number**	EIN

Form **SS-4**
(Rev. December 2001)
Department of the Treasury
Internal Revenue Service

Application for Employer Identification Number
(For use by employers, corporations, partnerships, trusts, estates, churches, government agencies, Indian tribal entities, certain individuals, and others.)
▶ See separate instructions for each line.   ▶ Keep a copy for your records.

EIN

OMB No. 1545-0003

Type or print clearly.

1 Legal name of entity (or individual) for whom the EIN is being requested

2 Trade name of business (if different from name on line 1)

3 Executor, trustee, "care of" name

4a Mailing address (room, apt., suite no. and street, or P.O. box)

5a Street address (if different) (Do not enter a P.O. box.)

4b City, state, and ZIP code

5b City, state, and ZIP code

6 County and state where principal business is located

7a Name of principal officer, general partner, grantor, owner, or trustor

7b SSN, ITIN, or EIN

8a **Type of entity** (check only one box)
☐ Sole proprietor (SSN) _____
☐ Partnership
☐ Corporation (enter form number to be filed) ▶ _____
☐ Personal service corp.
☐ Church or church-controlled organization
☐ Other nonprofit organization (specify) ▶ _____
☐ Other (specify) ▶

☐ Estate (SSN of decedent) _____
☐ Plan administrator (SSN) _____
☐ Trust (SSN of grantor) _____
☐ National Guard   ☐ State/local government
☐ Farmers' cooperative ☐ Federal government/military
☐ REMIC   ☐ Indian tribal governments/enterprises
Group Exemption Number (GEN) ▶ _____

8b If a corporation, name the state or foreign country (if applicable) where incorporated

State

Foreign country

9 **Reason for applying** (check only one box)
☐ Started new business (specify type) ▶_____
☐ Hired employees (Check the box and see line 12.)
☐ Compliance with IRS withholding regulations
☐ Other (specify) ▶

☐ Banking purpose (specify purpose) ▶ _____
☐ Changed type of organization (specify new type) ▶ _____
☐ Purchased going business
☐ Created a trust (specify type) ▶ _____
☐ Created a pension plan (specify type) ▶ _____

10 Date business started or acquired (month, day, year)

11 Closing month of accounting year

12 First date wages or annuities were paid or will be paid (month, day, year). **Note:** *If applicant is a withholding agent, enter date income will first be paid to nonresident alien. (month, day, year)* . . . . ▶

13 Highest number of employees expected in the next 12 months. **Note:** *If the applicant does not expect to have any employees during the period, enter "-0-."* . . . . ▶

Agricultural	Household	Other

14 Check **one** box that best describes the principal activity of your business.
☐ Construction ☐ Rental & leasing ☐ Transportation & warehousing ☐ Health care & social assistance ☐ Wholesale–agent/broker
☐ Real estate   ☐ Manufacturing   ☐ Finance & insurance   ☐ Accommodation & food service ☐ Wholesale–other ☐ Retail
☐ Other (specify)

15 Indicate principal line of merchandise sold; specific construction work done; products produced; or services provided.

16a Has the applicant ever applied for an employer identification number for this or any other business? . . . . . ☐ Yes   ☐ No
Note: *If "Yes," please complete lines 16b and 16c.*

16b If you checked "Yes" on line 16a, give applicant's legal name and trade name shown on prior application if different from line 1 or 2 above.
Legal name ▶   Trade name ▶

16c Approximate date when, and city and state where, the application was filed. Enter previous employer identification number if known.
Approximate date when filed (mo., day, year)   City and state where filed   Previous EIN

Third Party Designee	Complete this section **only** if you want to authorize the named individual to receive the entity's EIN and answer questions about the completion of this form.	
	Designee's name	Designee's telephone number (include area code) ( )
	Address and ZIP code	Designee's fax number (include area code) ( )

Under penalties of perjury, I declare that I have examined this application, and to the best of my knowledge and belief, it is true, correct, and complete.

Applicant's telephone number (include area code) ( )

Name and title (type or print clearly) ▶

Signature ▶   Date ▶

Applicant's fax number (include area code) ( )

For Privacy Act and Paperwork Reduction Act Notice, see separate instructions.   Cat. No. 16055N   Form **SS-4** (Rev. 12-2001)

Do I Need an EIN?

File Form SS-4 if the applicant entity does not already have an EIN but is required to show an EIN on any return, statement, or other document.[1] **See also the separate instructions for each line on Form SS-4.**

IF the applicant...	AND...	THEN...
Started a new business	Does not currently have (nor expect to have) employees	Complete lines 1, 2, 4a–6, 8a, and 9–16c.
Hired (or will hire) employees, including household employees	Does not already have an EIN	Complete lines 1, 2, 4a–6, 7a–b (if applicable), 8a, 8b (if applicable), and 9–16c.
Opened a bank account	Needs an EIN for banking purposes only	Complete lines 1–5b, 7a–b (if applicable), 8a, 9, and 16a–c.
Changed type of organization	Either the legal character of the organization or its ownership changed (e.g., you incorporate a sole proprietorship or form a partnership)[2]	Complete lines 1–16c (as applicable).
Purchased a going business[3]	Does not already have an EIN	Complete lines 1–16c (as applicable).
Created a trust	The trust is other than a grantor trust or an IRA trust[4]	Complete lines 1–16c (as applicable).
Created a pension plan as a plan administrator[5]	Needs an EIN for reporting purposes	Complete lines 1, 2, 4a–6, 8a, 9, and 16a–c.
Is a foreign person needing an EIN to comply with IRS withholding regulations	Needs an EIN to complete a Form W-8 (other than Form W-8ECI), avoid withholding on portfolio assets, or claim tax treaty benefits[6]	Complete lines 1–5b, 7a–b (SSN or ITIN optional), 8a–9, and 16a–c.
Is administering an estate	Needs an EIN to report estate income on Form 1041	Complete lines 1, 3, 4a–b, 8a, 9, and 16a–c.
Is a withholding agent for taxes on non-wage income paid to an alien (i.e., individual, corporation, or partnership, etc.)	Is an agent, broker, fiduciary, manager, tenant, or spouse who is required to file **Form 1042,** Annual Withholding Tax Return for U.S. Source Income of Foreign Persons	Complete lines 1, 2, 3 (if applicable), 4a–5b, 7a–b (if applicable), 8a, 9, and 16a–c.
Is a state or local agency	Serves as a tax reporting agent for public assistance recipients under Rev. Proc. 80-4, 1980-1 C.B. 581[7]	Complete lines 1, 2, 4a–5b, 8a, 9, and 16a–c.
Is a single-member LLC	Needs an EIN to file **Form 8832,** Classification Election, for filing employment tax returns, **or** for state reporting purposes[8]	Complete lines 1–16c (as applicable).
Is an S corporation	Needs an EIN to file **Form 2553,** Election by a Small Business Corporation[9]	Complete lines 1–16c (as applicable).

[1] For example, a sole proprietorship or self-employed farmer who establishes a qualified retirement plan, or is required to file excise, employment, alcohol, tobacco, or firearms returns, must have an EIN. **A partnership, corporation, REMIC (real estate mortgage investment conduit), nonprofit organization (church, club, etc.), or farmers' cooperative must use an EIN for any tax-related purpose even if the entity does not have employees.**

[2] However, **do not** apply for a new EIN if the existing entity only **(a)** changed its business name, **(b)** elected on Form 8832 to change the way it is taxed (or is covered by the default rules), or **(c)** terminated its partnership status because at least 50% of the total interests in partnership capital and profits were sold or exchanged within a 12-month period. (The EIN of the terminated partnership should continue to be used. See Regulations section 301.6109-1(d)(2)(iii).)

[3] Do not use the EIN of the prior business unless you became the "owner" of a corporation by acquiring its stock.

[4] However, IRA trusts that are required to file **Form 990-T,** Exempt Organization Business Income Tax Return, must have an EIN.

[5] A plan administrator is the person or group of persons specified as the administrator by the instrument under which the plan is operated.

[6] Entities applying to be a Qualified Intermediary (QI) need a QI-EIN even if they already have an EIN. **See Rev. Proc. 2000-12.**

[7] See also *Household employer* on page 4. (**Note:** State or local agencies may need an EIN for other reasons, e.g., hired employees.)

[8] Most LLCs **do not** need to file Form 8832. See **Limited liability company (LLC)** on page 4 for details on completing Form SS-4 for an LLC.

[9] An existing corporation that is electing or revoking S corporation status should use its previously-assigned EIN.

✪

Where to Send Your Completed Form

If your principal business, office or agency, or legal residence in the case of an individual, is located in:	Call the Fax-TIN number shown or file with the Internal Revenue Service Center at:
Connecticut, Delaware, District of Columbia, Florida, Georgia, Maine, Maryland, Massachusetts, New Hampshire, New Jersey, New York, North Carolina, Ohio, Pennsylvania, Rhode Island, South Carolina, Vermont, Virginia, West Virginia	Attn: EIN Operation P. O. Box 9003 Holtsville, NY 11742 Fax-TIN 1.631.447.8960
Illinois, Indiana, Kentucky, Michigan	Attn: EIN Operation Cincinnati, OH 45999 Fax-TIN 1.859.669.5760
Alabama, Alaska, Arizona, Arkansas, California, Colorado, Hawaii, Idaho, Iowa, Kansas, Louisiana, Minnesota, Mississippi, Missouri, Montana, Nebraska, Nevada, New Mexico, North Dakota, Oklahoma, Oregon, Puerto Rico, South Dakota, Tennessee, Texas, Utah, Washington, Wisconsin, Wyoming	Attn: EIN Operation Philadelphia, PA 19255 Fax-TIN 1.215.516.3990
If you have no legal residence, principal place of business, or principal office or agency in any state:	Attn: EIN Operation Philadelphia, PA 19255 Telephone 1.215.516.6999 Fax-TIN 1.215.516.3990

Once the Corporation Gets Started

Once organized, the corporation must maintain a continuous record of all authorized actions approved by its stockholders or directors. Resolutions record all major decisions made by the corporation's board. Though not always required, it is a good idea to record your actions in the form of resolutions. Doing so provides documentation that the actions were taken by and on behalf of the corporation.

Detailed minutes of each meeting are also required, and necessary for the following reasons:

- Parties dealing with the corporation may want evidence that the corporate action was approved.
- Officers and employees within the corporation are entitled to protection if their acts were approved.
- Accurate minutes are frequently necessary to preserve certain tax benefits or to avoid tax liabilities and penalties.
- Minutes are often necessary to prove that the corporation is operated as a separate entity independent of its principals.

Any changes to the corporation's certificate or articles of incorporation must be approved by both the stockholders and directors. In addition to amendments, some states also require corporations to file a notarized affidavit that verifies the number of outstanding shares at the time of the vote. Stockholders must also vote to dissolve the corporation or to file for bankruptcy or reorganization.

Resolutions

Resolutions adopted by the board of directors that generally do not require stockholder approval involve everyday operations of the corporation, including but not limited to leasing; major purchases; hiring; banking; borrowing; investing; and the paying of dividends, salaries and bonuses. Amendments to the certificate or articles of incorporation must be filed with the secretary of state in the state of incorporation for the amendments to become effective.

Generally, you need only complete the resolution form that conforms to the corporate action voted upon. Occasionally, however, you may need to modify the form to suit your particular needs. Always be certain the resolution accurately states the corporate action approved. In some cases, particularly on more important transactions, you may find it necessary to have an attorney decide what the resolution should contain.

Though prepared forms can greatly simplify your record-keeping requirements, they are not a substitute for your good judgment in deciding how you should document the actions of your corporation.

Records of Stockholder Actions

Stockholders can usually vote in person or by proxy on the broadest issues relating to the corporation, which typically include changes of corporate name, address, purpose, the amount or type of shares, and other matters involving the corporate structure. Stockholders' action may also be needed on major legal or financial issues, such as whether to mortgage, encumber, pledge or lease all or substantially all of the corporate assets or to file bankruptcy, merge or consolidate.

For more information on how shareholder meetings need to be conducted, turn to Chapter 9.

Summary

Record-keeping is a particularly significant issue for corporations. Failure to properly document separation of corporate and personal funds as well as major governance decisions can lead to an end of legal protections for individuals who incorporate.

Remember to Register

In order to gain access to free forms, dictionaries, checklists and updates, readers must register their book purchase at Socrates.com. An eight-digit Registration Code is provided on the enclosed CD. See page iv for further details.

Meetings & Formalities

How Formal Do the Formalities of Incorporation Have to Be?

For most small corporations, particularly those that are not publicly traded, meetings and reports tend to be fairly simple affairs. Because the primary purpose of these tasks is to inform—rather than impress—the officers and shareholders, all that is required is adherence to the guidelines and deadlines set forth by their state of incorporation.

Annual meetings and reports sponsored by major corporations are a different matter entirely. If you have ever been to a large company's annual meeting as a stockholder, you may have witnessed just such a dog-and-pony show. Though some corporations take a no-frills approach, you are more likely to see multimedia presentations, executives on parade, free product samples and a shareholder question-and-answer period that can sometimes leave executives sweating.

Why all the fuss? Because the annual meeting is both a bane and a boon to a corporation. Though it sometimes provides for uncomfortable public scrutiny, particularly if the operating results are not that impressive, it is also an important promotional opportunity for the firm. It is a way to bring the faithful back to the fold and to secure new investors.

Even if you are starting small, you may one day be hosting a large annual meeting for your firm. With this in mind, the following sections discuss how to prepare for, conduct and report on an annual meeting for a corporation, regardless of size.

Point One: Take Required Meetings Seriously

For small corporations, an annual meeting may consist of no more than a group of owner/shareholders in work clothes gathering in the coffee room for donuts and a short meeting agenda. If you adhere to the laws of your state (for contact information on your state, refer to Appendix A), such a meeting is entirely appropriate. What matters is the detail of your agenda, your preparation for it and the minutes you keep for the company's records.

Point Two: How to Prepare for an Annual Meeting

The primary function of the stockholders is to elect the board of directors—everything else is largely window dressing, but even window dressing takes preparation.

Your articles of incorporation or bylaws will specify where and when a stockholder meeting can legally be held. The book of minutes should show the time and place of each meeting so that you can prove that the meeting complied with the legal requirements.

For any annual meeting, whether the corporation is large or small, public or private, it is important to prepare. The degree of preparation depends on the complexity of your agenda and how many shareholders and other guests you will be hosting.

The first task is to appoint someone to chair the organization of the meeting. Keep in mind that the primary goal of the meeting is to ensure that shareholders leave the meeting well informed and perhaps entertained—it is not terribly different from inviting guests to your home. You want to make a good impression.

Complete the following tasks before setting the date of the meeting:

- Check your state's specific meeting requirements.
- Set up a meeting planning file—some people call it a control book. This can be a binder, a computer file or a file cabinet, but create a central repository so you and others working on the meeting have easy access to the information at all times. Such as file will also make planning next year's meeting easier.
- List the goals you need to accomplish at this meeting. You do not need to limit the meeting to the state-required subjects. The annual meeting is a selling and promotional opportunity for any issues you feel are important. Select a major theme for the meeting as a framework.
- Delegate scriptwriting (or outline creation) for all executives' presentations. That is, know what you and others plan to say before taking the podium. There is nothing worse than a speech without focus.
- Assign tasks to various executives and staff for the meeting. Gathering and organizing information, particularly in a multiperson company, should involve everyone.
- Select, brief and rehearse your presenters. The right presenters can ensure a meeting's success, while the wrong presenters can torpedo a meeting. Make sure that all speakers can clearly communicate what needs to be said—briefly and to the point.
- Prepare your presenters for the shareholder and press Q & A session, if applicable. There is no controlling for what stockholders or reporters may ask, and presenters should be capable of handling difficult questions without harming the company's reputation.

- Make a list of everything that could possibly go wrong, and then plan contingencies. This means finding alternate meeting space, understudies, backup A/V assistance—anything that fits your list.

- Do not underestimate security. Anytime you welcome outsiders into your company or put them in touch with executives, there are risks. In this post 9/11 world, it makes sense to keep lists of possible attendees and in extreme cases, consult with experts on how to best keep everyone safe.

- After the meeting, solicit feedback on what went right and wrong and what you can do better next year. Prepare a summary, along with a list of suggestions for next year's meeting, and include this information in your meeting file.

Point Three: What Happens at a Shareholder Meeting

Shareholders must adhere to certain rules and procedures when conducting any official stockholder meeting, not just the annual meeting. The following are some of these rules:

- Every stockholder must be properly notified in advance about the time and place of the meeting, who is calling the meeting and any matters that will be considered there, subject to your incorporated state's requirements.

- It is common in small corporations for the stockholders to do without a formal notice, especially when the bylaws set the time and place of the regular annual meeting of stockholders, which can be done by having all stockholders sign a waiver of notice at the meeting. Unscheduled or special meetings of stockholders may require notice, although a signed waiver of notice can also be used.

- No business can be transacted at a stockholders' meeting unless a quorum is present. Therefore, it is essential that the book of minutes reflect the quorum, which is usually set in the bylaws.

- Stockholder meetings must have a chairperson to preside over the meeting. They must also have a secretary to record what happens. The bylaws will ordinarily designate these officials by specifying that the president serve as chairperson and the secretary act as secretary. However, substitutes are usually allowable.

- The first item of business at every stockholder meeting should be to approve the minutes of the previous meeting. Once the minutes are approved, they formally and legally record what occurred and become part of official corporate records.

- Even though small company meetings may be the most informal, parliamentary procedure is standard conduct for meetings. It is important to document exactly who proposed, seconded and voted on major initiatives, given the heightened demand for detailed record-keeping.

Corporate Stock in a Nutshell

> **Common stock**—Holders of common stock have the primary voice in selecting directors. There are voting rights attached to each share of stock—typically one vote per share. Shareholders are entitled to share in the profits and in final distribution of the corporate assets on dissolution of the corporation.
>
> **Preferred stock**—Holders of preferred stock are usually entitled to preference over the holders of common stock with respect to receipt of dividends and distribution of assets on dissolution of the corporation.

Types of Stock Value

> **No-Par Value Stock**—Stock with no par value is stock for which no fixed price is set. In small corporations, the owners issue themselves a number of shares and simply infuse money in the corporation when needed.
>
> **Par Value Stock**—Par value stock is stock with a specified value. For example, a share of stock with a par value of $100 is the value of the stock at the time it was issued. The current market value may be more or less than the par value.

Corporations issue no-par stock for flexibility. If the corporation's stock has no par value, there is no set price for the stock. In this case, the directors can raise the price of the stock when the corporation becomes more valuable.

Point Four: What Happens at a Board Meeting

Most of the rules and procedures that apply to stockholder meetings apply equally to meetings of the board of directors, with the following exceptions:

- Directors should meet more often than shareholders. The board's job is to supervise the executives and to act as the shareholders' advocate. Even in a small company, inside (executive) and outside (nonexecutive) board members have the ultimate goal of protecting shareholders, which means constant vigilance over company operations.

- Meetings and their schedules should be set in the bylaws.

- Minutes from the meeting provide essential documentation for all authorized corporate actions. The minutes should therefore be kept meticulously, and the board must be particularly careful to document not only its actions but why the action was taken. Many of the recent corporate scandals (WorldCom, Enron) were the result of poor board oversight.

Summary

Regardless of the size of your corporation, all meetings and related documentation should be handled in accordance with the rules and procedures required by federal and state guidelines. Failure to observe these laws could void your corporate status in the event of a legal challenge.

10 The Ongoing Role of Directors, Officers & Shareholders

Why Managing These Relationships Is Critical

Appointing a first-rate board of directors is a vital step in ensuring the integrity and accountability of your company. The board acts as trustees for the shareholders, safeguarding the stockholders' interest in the company by overseeing the actions of management. This checks-and-balances system is required by law for all corporations. During recent years, we have all witnessed the fallout resulting from boards not properly overseeing company operations— Enron and WorldCom are prime examples.

Many C corporations that plan to stay closely held for a generation and never go public retain the same board of directors for many years, or perhaps the life of the company. Other, larger corporations establish limits on the number of years a board member may serve.

Who Really Runs the Company?

The answer might surprise you. In a corporate structure, it is the board, not the president or CEO, that has the ultimate responsibility to the shareholders. The board appoints senior management and oversees their performance. The board also oversees the flow of accurate and timely information to stockholders and works to enhance company profit. Corporate governance is what quality boards, working with quality corporate officers, are entrusted with providing for shareholders.

In small corporations with multiple board members, you might find officers who are board members as well as shareholders. There is potential for abuse when this happens, though it is often covered up.

Note
Some states require only one or two board members. For more information, check the state-by-state incorporation listings starting in Appendix A.

Composition of a Corporate Board

A member of a board is called a director. There are two types of directors who serve on corporate boards—inside directors and outside directors. Inside directors work for the company; outside directors do not work for the company but have been asked to join because they have a certain expertise in the business that might benefit the board.

Recent moves to toughen corporate board oversight have also instilled a philosophy that top managers, such as company president, chief executive officer or chief operating officer should never be the board chairman. Though in small corporations it might be a necessity, in larger corporations, those dual titles allow one person too much power.

Too often in recent years we have seen major corporate boards bring on celebrities, former politicians or world leaders to add prestige to their list of directors. And though many of these people may take their responsibilities seriously, a good board should seek out the most knowledgeable board members who are willing to ask hard questions and force changes in management if company performance warrants it.

Of course, if you are a small company, you are unlikely to extend a board invitation to a former president or prime minister. But for all companies, big and small, board members face the same dilemma—finding high-quality directors with knowledge, experience and dedication to their job.

Sarbanes-Oxley and Today's Boards

Without a doubt, the Sarbanes-Oxley Act (SOA) of 2002 is the single most important piece of legislation affecting corporate governance, financial disclosure and the practice of public accounting since the U.S. securities laws of the early 1930s. And though it now affects only public companies, most good business accountants and attorneys will encourage you to start organizing your tax, record-keeping and board operations along SOA lines if you ever hope to go public. The new restrictions cover everything from board member content and terms to technology and new record-keeping requirements that affect the way officers work with auditors and attorneys.

For a full listing of SOA provisions, visit the American Institute of Certified Public Accountants' Web site at www.aicapa.org/indo/sarbanes_oxley_summary.htm.

A 2004 study by the management recruiting firm Spencer Stuart noted that SOA has made it a lot tougher to recruit directors. The reason, of course, is that boards now have a lot more work to do and the directors face a higher likelihood of being found personally responsible for missteps that occur on their watch. The firm points out that demand for quality board directors is skyrocketing, but candidates who would normally jump at the chance are now having second thoughts because SOA is making compliance a lot tougher at their own companies. While there is still prestige in being asked to serve on a corporate board, most talented managers today wonder if their time would not be better spent keeping their own companies out of trouble.

The following questions are where most executives start when considering their first board or expanding an existing one.

Where Do I Find Good Board Members?

Small corporate owners, especially those that are family owned and managed, often look to family members to serve on their board of directors. Family or otherwise, the individuals you are considering for the board should be capable, experienced and able to offer your company their unique expertise.

Larger or quickly expanding companies may benefit from the influence of outside directors. Carefully chosen, these people can provide insight that executives close to the company cannot.

How Many Board Members Do I Need?

Most states require a minimum number of board members. This does not mean that the minimum number required is ideal for your company or that you should populate your boardroom with a football team. Boards can only act if a quorum (a minimum number or percentage of directors specified in the corporate bylaws) is present at a meeting or if they consent to actions in writing. The more individuals you have weighing in on each item of business, the tougher it may be to get things done. Your advisors can help you decide the right number of board members to fit your firm, but a good target for a small to midsize firm is between five and seven members.

When choosing outside board members, it is generally not a good idea to put direct competitors on your board for obvious reasons. Good outside directors may include accountants, bankers, lawyers, marketing experts, insurance agents or presidents of other businesses. You do not want outside directors who are already on the company payroll because they may be less likely to speak their mind, though it is legal in most states to appoint them.

Big companies often have a system in place to attract and appoint board members, usually in the form of outside firms that screen for certain talent and skills the current board is lacking. Small companies typically do not have these resources. Therefore, small business owners may find the following suggestions effective in their search for quality board members:

- Keep an eye out for talented executives and experts who might be good board candidates in the future. Do not rule out retired executives who still have a lot to give.
- Recognize those investors who may want a seat on the board. It is a good idea to screen investors for suitability as board members.

- Create a primer on the company for potential directors and have them sign a confidentiality agreement. Most savvy directors ask for this information before making a decision.

- Develop a training program for new directors. This can be as basic as a notebook containing information on how meetings are conducted, upcoming agenda issues and anything you consider worthy of their knowledge. No matter how experienced, new directors should be given some background on the company and how the board works. Make every effort to help them acclimate to your corporate environment.

- Determine the best way to indemnify directors. Since the Enron scandal, directors and officers' insurance has gotten so expensive that many directors expect the company to provide this insurance. Talk to your attorneys about the costs and implications of various options.

- Keep accurate and detailed records of what goes on in all board meetings, including subcommittee meetings.

What Is the Right Personality Mix and Workload?

First-rate board members will display not only clear leadership and analytical qualities but understand the dynamic of working as an equal member of a team. Big egos may work well at the top of some corporations but may be divisive in a board situation.

Board members—like juries—have to work together to take decisive actions. Devising an effective board requires managing personalities and putting the right mix together. Most boards have director recruitment committees of their own, which generally work without the influence of company management. The overarching goal is to have a mix of people who will look dispassionately at the business and provide sound advice, action and guidance when warranted.

Do Board Members Get Paid?

Most companies offer some compensation to board members because of the time and effort required of them. To determine a fair salary, discuss with your advisory team what companies of your size and industry are paying board members.

Some companies also provide shares of stock and/or stock options to their directors as an employment incentive. The theory behind this practice is that profit-sharing is a bigger motivator than salary alone.

What If Your Board Makes Mistakes?

Underperforming boards or directors are a liability for your company and its shareholders. It is therefore important to have a legal system in place to remove them, and adequate indemnification procedures to protect them against shareholder litigation. Though indemnification is an attractive feature of the corporate structure, a judgment against your directors can bankrupt your company. Research the true cost of your proposed board of directors before you incorporate. A good board can help your company grow, but like everything else, it comes at a price.

How Do You and Your Board Resolve Conflicts?

Boards of directors and company executives may sometimes disagree on their roles in managing the company. If, as an owner, you feel you are being micromanaged by your board, review with your board their roles and responsibilities. Boards should not be involved in day-to-day management issues unless the company is in serious trouble. At the same time, remember that the advantage of having a board is that it can offer you and your company a wider variety of perspectives and skills that may benefit your business. The disadvantage is that the board can become overbearing and intrusive where it is not warranted. Maintain a healthy balance between the two and your board will serve as a vital business asset.

Building a Board of Advisors

A Board of Advisors serves a different function than a Board of Directors. A board of advisors provides essential guidance, information and services to your new venture. Often the board will play devil's advocate, pointing out potential markets and flaws in what you're doing. It's a tremendous think-tank resource to keep you on track and find the resources you need to succeed. Advisors usually serve as unpaid advisors and do not have voting power when it comes to major company decisions and the hiring and firing of executives and officers. Advisors are usually reimbursed travel expenses for their dedication of time and service. Most advisors anticipate and expect additional phone calls seeking advice in-between scheduled meetings. Advisory committees usually meet two to four times a year to review finances, ideas, proposed product developments and sales and marketing strategies. Advisory members are generally professionals with expertise and contacts you need to fill a gap in your own management team. Your advisors will have a strong belief in what you're doing and want to be a part of your new business.

There is a distinct difference between a Board of Advisors and a Board of Directors. A Board of Directors has a greater level of influence over the management team and is capable of taking control from the founders if the board disagrees with the plans and direction the team is making.

Forming an Advisory Board

Building an advisory board with a variety of talents will provide you with varied opinions about your business. For example, to blend together the best talents for your business, invite a banker, lawyer, industry expert, accountant or CFO, business consultant, one or two successful business owners and technology expert to join your advisory board. The diverse professional skills of your board will help you view your business from many different angles. The length of time an advisor serves may be as short as 1 year or as long as 5 years. Some companies design their terms to be 1 year with renewal options. That way, if an advisor becomes too busy to serve, he or she may be replaced with minimal disruption.

Summary

Board composition, like all issues related to corporations, should be given careful consideration. All board members should be evaluated on their ability to grow the business.

11 Incorporating in Canada

The Basics

The basic steps involved in establishing a corporation in Canada are similar to those in the United States. Businesses are formed under the following structures:

- Sole proprietorship
- Corporations
- Franchises
- Partnership
- Cooperatives
- Joint ventures

Where to Start

Each province and territory in Canada has its own rules about business formation, fees and other information, so be sure and check with your local government before beginning the process. To find the latest information online, visit the main Canadian government Web site at http://canada.gc.ca.

Corporations

Your first decision is which province you plan to organize the corporation. As in the United States, most businesses in Canada incorporate in the province where they are located.

If you carry on business in more than one province, it is necessary to register your corporation as an extraprovincial corporation in other provinces.

In Canada, in addition to registering your corporation in a province, you also have the choice to register as a federal corporation. If you have a federal corporation, you then register as an extraprovincial corporation in each province where you conduct business. The fees for this range from $75 to nearly $5,000 (Canadian) for each province.

The main advantage to having a federal corporation is that there is no need to register as an extraprovincial corporation. The main disadvantage is that there are stringent federal financial reporting rules, even for private companies.

Subsidiaries and branches of a business are treated differently in terms of taxes, the ability to raise capital and the extent of the parent company's liability. Generally, a Canadian subsidiary may not be consolidated with other operations for foreign tax purposes. Establishing a branch operation may be beneficial to offset initial losses.

Also, to federally incorporate, the company's board of directors must meet the requirements of the Canada Business Corporation Act. Under this act, a majority of the directors of a federally incorporated company must be resident Canadians. However, only one-third of the directors of a holding corporation need be resident Canadians if the holding corporation in combination with its subsidiaries earns less than five percent of its gross revenues in Canada.

Types of Corporations

Private Corporation: A private corporation can be formed by one or more people. A majority of its directors must be Canadian residents. If none of the directors reside in the province in which it does business, the corporation must appoint a power of attorney who resides in the province. A private corporation cannot sell shares or securities to the general public.

Public Corporation: Generally, a public corporation is one that offers its securities to the public.

Federal Corporation: Businesses may be incorporated as private and public corporations federally under the Canada Business Corporation Act, which can be found at http://laws.justice.gc.ca/en/C-44. A federally incorporated corporation can conduct business throughout Canada, though it may be required to register or obtain a license in a province in which it does business.

All forms can be found at http://strategis.ic.gc.ca/sc_mrksv/corpdir/corpFiling/engdoc/index.htm.

Federal/Provincial Overview

Federal Incorporation

Advantages:

- Allows the corporation to conduct business in any province or territory in which it is registered.
- Allows the corporation to use the same business name in each province or territory.

Disadvantages:

- Higher setup costs.
- More annual paperwork, including provincial filings.
- Increased financial disclosure.

Provincial Incorporation

Advantages:

- Relatively low-cost incorporation as long as you operate within a particular province.

Disadvantages:

- Higher costs if you plan to incorporate in another province later.

16 Steps in the Incorporation Process

1. Decide whether to incorporate.

2. Decide where to incorporate.

3. Select a corporate name.

4. Select a registered agent, if necessary.

5. Draft a certificate of incorporation.

6. Sign a certificate of incorporation and file it with the appropriate office.

7. Hold the incorporators' initial meeting to elect directors.

8. Hold an organizational meeting of the initial board of directors.

9. Select a corporate seal and stock certificates and issue shares.

10. Receive a tax identification number.

11. Choose a fiscal year.

12. File a doing business as certificate, if necessary.

13. Apply for authorization to do business in other provinces, if necessary.

14. Obtain necessary province and local licenses and permits.

15. Hold regular, official meetings of directors and stockholders.

16. Document actions and maintain accurate corporate records.

Choose a Corporate Name

To choose an effective corporate name, consider one with the following attributes:

- A distinctive portion that identifies the particular corporation.
- A descriptive portion that identifies the particular activities of the corporation.
- A legal element, identifying the company as a corporation, such as Limited, Incorporated or Corporation.
- No similarity to other existing company names.

All corporate names in Canada can be in English or French, in both English and French, or in a combined English-French version.

Search and reserve that name. All provinces have access to search features on their respective Web sites.

Have Your Corporate Name Searched and Reserved

Regardless of where you incorporate your business in Canada, you will need to have a name search done to determine the suitability of the corporate name you have chosen. Various provinces and territories have specific rules for conducting this search.

Prepare Documents

Generally, to incorporate your business, you will need to prepare the following three incorporation documents:

---

1. The Memorandum
Sets out the rules for the conduct of the company.

2. Articles of Corporation
The rules and regulations that will govern the conduct of the company members and directors.

3. The Notice of Offices
States the location of the two required offices for your corporation: the registered office and the records office.

Federal incorporators need to prepare a Notice of Directors and submit a federally based NUANS report. If you are filing provincially, be sure you check the document requirements for your specific province before you proceed to the next step of filing documents.

Summary

Like the United States, the incorporation process in Canada usually begins in the province or territory where the company was born. Canadians, however, have the opportunity to file federal incorporation papers that allow them to freely operate in all provinces and territories provided they adhere to regular requirements and filings required in each province or territory.

Section ■ Three

Getting the Right Ongoing Advice

12 Corporate Taxation

An Overview for First-Time Filers

We have the Europeans to thank for the earliest corporations. Before the seventeenth century, corporations were an invention that allowed nonprofit entities to build hospitals and universities for the public good. By the colonial era, they had become a privilege extended by the monarchy to a group of investors to finance trade expeditions—and then the money started rolling in.

Incorporation gave the world the East India Company, which led to the British colonization of India. The Hudson's Bay Company became the settling force for Canada. It helped that the Crown decided to put military might behind a business concept that changed the world.

Today, there are not necessarily armies behind modern expeditions—though some might disagree. But tax law is now the force that gives corporations their world-changing muscle—and occasionally their Achilles' heel. This chapter covers the generalities of tax law that affect today's corporations.

U.S. Tax Information

Overview

Like a small business owner, the IRS never rests. They have created an increasingly complex and ever-changing labyrinth of tax forms for even the smallest mom-and-pop operations. Tax time is a lot less hectic when your books are accurate, organized and up-to-date year-round. Completing IRS forms can be largely a matter of plugging in figures from your profit and loss statement and income and expense ledgers. It may pay to hire an accountant to make sure you not only comply with legal requirements but also maximize your deductions. This chapter will help you better plan for tax time.

> **Hint**
>
> If you area a sole proprietor with no employees, pay no excise tax and did not inherit the business you may be able to use your Social Security number for tax purposes. All other cases require an EIN.

Separating a Business from a Hobby

It is generally accepted that people prefer to make a living doing something they like. A hobby is an activity for which you do not expect to make a profit. If you do not carry on your business or investment activity to make a profit, there is a limit on the deductions you can take.

You must include on your return income from an activity from which you do not expect to make a profit. An example of this type of activity is a hobby or a farm you operate mostly for recreation and pleasure. You cannot use a loss from the activity to offset other income. Activities you do as a hobby, or mainly for sport or recreation, come under this limit. So does an investment activity intended only to produce tax losses for the investors.

The limit on not-for-profit losses applies to individuals, partnerships, estates trusts and S corporations. It does not apply to corporations other than S corporations.

In determining whether you are carrying on an activity for profit, all the facts are taken into account. No one factor alone is decisive. Among the factors to consider are whether:

- You carry on the activity in a businesslike manner;
- The time and effort you put into the activity indicate you intend to make it profitable;
- You depend on income from the activity for your livelihood;
- Your losses are due to circumstances beyond your control (or are normal in the startup phase of your type of business);
- You change your methods of operation in an attempt to improve profitability;
- You, or your advisors, have the knowledge needed to carry on the activity as a successful business;
- You were successful in making a profit in similar activities in the past;
- The activity makes a profit in some years and the amount of profit it makes; and
- You can expect to make a future profit from the appreciation of the assets used in the activity.

Calendar Year vs. Fiscal Year

When you apply for an EIN, you will note that the IRS asks you to declare a fiscal year start and end. In some states, even the Certificate of Incorporation requires the fiscal year to be given. Of course, it is easiest to choose the calendar year as your corporation's fiscal year. However, if that is impossible, a second choice would be July 1 to June 30. In that case, for your first year of incorporation, you would have to file two sets of income tax forms: For the first half of the year you would file as a sole proprietor (individual return) using Schedule C and any other appropriate schedules. For the second half of the year, you would file a corporate return (form 1120, or Form 1120S if you make a Subchapter S election) and an individual return—because you are now an employee of your corporation.

Similarly, if you choose April 1 to October 1 as the beginning of your fiscal year, you will have to file the same two sets of tax returns. If you choose April 1, you would file as a sole proprietor for the first quarter (January 1 to March 31), and you would file corporate and individual returns for the past three quarters (April 1 to December 31). If you choose October 1, you would file as a sole proprietor for the first three quarters (January 1 to September 30) and corporate and individual returns for the last quarter (October 1 to December 31).

The advantage of a separate fiscal year is that it allows flexibility in tax planning. By having two tax years to work with, you and your accountant have more flexibility in tax planning. And the tax savings, corporate and personal, can be significant. You may want to choose a fiscal year on the advice of your accountant, who can determine the fiscal year most advantageous to you. If you choose the calendar year as your fiscal year, you will have fewer tax forms to file. However, there may be advantages to choosing a different fiscal year.

Tax Information from the IRS

Advice from an IRS agent is not always reliable. However, you can obtain surprisingly clear and helpful information from several IRS publications, including: Starting a Business and Keeping Records (IRS Publication 583), Tax Guide for Small Business (Publication 334), Employer's Tax Guide (Circular E), Tax Calendar (Publication 509) and Tax Withholding and Estimated Tax (Publication 505).

Self-Employment Tax

Many people are not aware of the self-employment tax, also known as SECA (Self-Employment Contributions Act). Sole proprietorships, partners and active owners in LLCs must pay tax on business income if they earn more than $400 in a given year.

If you operate at a loss, you own no income tax on the business. You can also apply this Net Operating Loss (NOL) to other taxable personal income or allow the credit to carry over to other years. If you are unable to generate a profit over several years, the IRS may rule your venture is a hobby and disallow any tax benefits.

Hint

It is advisable to earmark a portion of your income and financial assets for taxes—20 to 25 percent is a good start. Anything left over can be used as a capital investment fund or bonus. This is especially important for sole proprietors who have to pay self-employment tax, which makes up your share of Social Security and Medicare payments.

Employee and Payroll Taxes

If you hire employees, prepared to devote about 30 percent of your payroll to taxes and paperwork. You are responsible for withholding all of your (full- or part-time) employees' federal and state income tax, Social Security and Medicare taxes from paychecks, remitting them with your overall tax bill. You also must pay your portion of Social Security and Medicare benefit funds. On employee salaries up to $87,922 you are taxed 6.2 percent for Social Security and 1.45 percent for Medicare.

Payroll taxes—including withholding—are due quarterly on these dates:

- April 30 for wages paid January—March
- July 31 for April—June
- October 31 for July—September
- January 31 for October—December

If owed taxes exceed $500, the due date becomes the fifteenth day of the next month.

Independent Contractors

You may be able to save paperwork and expenses by hiring independent contractors. These workers are in business for themselves, pay their own taxes and insurance, use their own equipment and facilities, require little or no supervision and are typically paid per project. To avoid threat of tax fraud and liability charges, make sure the above factors apply, and make these points clear to the workers. A written Independent Contractor's Agreement is the best protection against potentially expensive or damaging misunderstandings. When hiring an independent contractor, be sure to record his or her full name, address and Social Security or EIN number.

An employer does not generally have to withhold or pay any taxes on payments to independent contractors. The general rule is that an individual is an independent contractor if: the person for whom the services are performed has the right to control or direct only the result of the work, and not what will be done and how it will be done or the method of accomplishing the result.

People such as lawyers, contractors, subcontractors, public stenographers, and auctioneers who follow an independent trade, business or profession in which they offer their services to the public are generally not employees. However, whether such people are employees or independent contractors depends on the facts in each case. The earnings of a person who is working as an independent contractor are subject to Self-Employment (SE) tax.

The employer however, is responsible for asking all independent contractors to complete a FDIC Substitute For W-9 Request for Taxpayer Identification Number and Certification. This form is provides the independent contractor's correction TIN to the company who in turn must report any income paid above $600 to an independent contractor.

Business Expenses

To qualify as a deduction from your taxable income, expenses must be business related, ordinary, necessary and reasonable. Keep accurate tabs on expenses by paying from your business account, entering expenses in the appropriate expense ledger category, and keeping all receipts. Expenses must be recorded as what you actually paid out—not market value. Interest charges for purchases are not deductible. Barter economy is treated like any other business income based on fair market value.

Deducting startup costs may be complicated and may require the help of an accountant. Business-related startup expenses may be deducted in one of two ways: capitalized at the time you quit or sell your business or amortized monthly over a 60-month period.

The IRS also frequently denies deductions until the business actually makes a sale, although tax courts contend that as long as they are in business. In either case, it is a good idea to put off as many expenses as possible until you are in business.

To be eligible for business deductions, your business must be an activity undertaken with the intent of making a profit. It is presumed you meet this requirement if your business makes a profit in any 2 years of a 5-year period.

Once you this far along, you can deduct business expenses such as supplies, subscriptions to professional journals, and an allowance for the business use of your car or truck. You can also claim deductions for home-related business expenses such as utilities, and in some cases, even a new paint job on your home. The IRS is going to treat the part of your home you use for business as thought it were a separate piece of property. This means that you will have to keep good records and take care not to mix business and personal matters. No specific method of record keeping is required, but your records must clearly justify any deductions you claim. Before making any tax deduction for your home office or any other home office expense be sure to consult with your tax advisor.

Depreciation

Over time, business equipment ages, deteriorates or becomes obsolete. You can get back a portion of your cost for certain property by taking deductions for depreciation. Items you acquire before starting your operation may be depreciated based on their market value at the time you began using them for business. Major repairs and improvements may also be depreciated.

Generally, to depreciate your assets, the property must be used in your business or income-producing activity. You stop depreciating the property when you have recovered its cost (or other basis), or when you retire it from service, whichever comes first. The kind of property you own affects how you can claim a depreciation deduction. Property falls into two categories: tangible and intangible.

Tangible Property

This type of property can be seen or touched, such as building, cars, machinery or equipment. If you own tangible property that you use for both personal and business purposes, you may take deductions based only on the business use portion of the property. Certain types of property can never be depreciated. For example, you cannot depreciate the cost of land because it does not wear out or become obsolete. The cost of inventory does not qualify for the depreciation deduction, either.

Intangible property

Intangible property generally refers to any property that cannot be seen or touched, such as copyrights, franchises, or patents. Certain types of intangible property cannot be depreciated, but must be amortized instead. To see if you can claim depreciation deductions, view Form 4562 Depreciation and Amortization for instructions.

You may be able to deduct all or part of the cost of certain qualifying property used in your business in the year you placed it in service by claiming a section 179 deduction ("Election to Expense Certain Business Assets"). The advantage of claiming the section 179 deduction is that you get to deduct more up front. Like depreciation deductions, you can claim the section 179 deduction only when your property is ready to be used in your business or income-producing activity.

There are limitations. For example, if the cost of all qualifying property in 2004 is $400,000 or more, the maximum section 179 deduction you can take is reduced by the amount over $400,000. When the cost of all qualifying property in 2004 exceeds $500,000, then no section 179 deduction is allowed. The maximum section 179 deduction for 2004 is $100,000. You cannot deduct costs in excess of your taxable income, which includes your trade and business income, plus your wages and salaries for the year. You use form 4562 to make the election to claim a section 179 deduction or carryover.

If you decide taxable profits at year's end are too small to warrant immediate deduction, you may choose to write the costs according to depreciation of any or all items with a life of over 1 year. This means you deduct the cost of an item divided over several years. Length of depreciation ranges form 3 to 39 years depending on the type of goods.

The U.S. Tax System

During the tax year all businesses must adhere to all reporting and payment schedules. Not all reporting dates are the same and are dependent on the type of legal structure you have selected for your business.

Each organization type has different reporting and filing dates. To locate filing dates, find the legal structure that best describes your organization to review your company's key filing dates.

Sole Proprietor Calendar Worksheet

January 15	Estimated tax filing	Form 1040ES
April 15	Estimated tax filing	Form 1040ES
June 15	Estimated tax filing	Form 1040ES
September 15	Estimated tax filing	Form 1040ES
January 31	Social Security (FICA) tax and income tax withholding	Forms 941, 941E, 942 and 943

April 30	Social Security (FICA) tax and income tax withholding	Forms 941, 941E, 942 and 943
July 31	Social Security (FICA) tax and income tax withholding	Forms 941, 941E, 942 and 943
October 31	Social Security (FICA) tax and income tax withholding	Forms 941, 941E, 942 and 943
January 31	Providing information on Social Security (FICA) tax and the withholding of income tax to employee	Form W-2
January 31	Federal Unemployment Tax (FUTA)	Form 940-EZ or 940
January 31	Federal Unemployment Tax (FUTA) (only if liability for unpaid taxes exceeds $100)	Form 8109 to make deposits
April 15	Federal Unemployment Tax (FUTA) (only if liability for unpaid taxes exceeds $100)	Form 8109 to make deposits
July 31	Federal Unemployment Tax (FUTA) (only if liability for unpaid taxes exceeds $100)	Form 8109 to make deposits
October 31	Federal Unemployment Tax (FUTA) (only if liability for unpaid taxes exceeds $100)	Form 8109 to make deposits
January 31	Statement returns to nonemployees and transactions with other or independent contractors	Form 1099 to individuals
February 28	Statement returns to nonemployees and transactions with other or independent contractors	Form 1099 to IRS
April 15	Income tax filing	Schedule C (Form 1040)
April 15	Self-employment tax filing	Schedule SE (Form 1040)

If your tax year is not January 1 through December 31:

Schedule C (Form 1040) is due on the fifteenth day of the fourth month after the end of your tax year.

Schedule SE is due the same day as income tax (Form 1040).

Estimated Tax (1040ES) is due on the fifteenth day of the fourth, sixth and ninth months of the tax year and the fifteenth day of the first month after the end of your tax year.

Partnership Calendar Worksheet

January 15	Estimated tax filing by individual who is a partner	Form 1040ES
April 15	Estimated tax filing by individual who is a partner	Form 1040ES
June 15	Estimated tax filing by individual who is a partner	Form 1040ES
September 15	Estimated tax filing by individual who is a partner	Form 1040ES
January 31	Social Security (FICA) tax and income tax withholding	Forms 941, 941E, 942 and 943
April 30	Social Security (FICA) tax and income tax withholding	Forms 941, 941E, 942 and 943
July 31	Social Security (FICA) tax and income tax withholding	Forms 941, 941E, 942 and 943
October 31	Social Security (FICA) tax and income tax withholding	Forms 941, 941E, 942 and 943
January 31	Providing information on Social Security (FICA) tax and the withholding of income tax to employee	Form W-2
January 31	Federal Unemployment Tax (FUTA)	Form 940-EZ or 940
January 31	Federal Unemployment Tax (FUTA) (only if liability for unpaid taxes exceeds $100)	Form 8109 to make deposits
April 15	Federal Unemployment Tax (FUTA) (only if liability for unpaid taxes exceeds $100)	Form 8109 to make deposits
July 31	Federal Unemployment Tax (FUTA) (only if liability for unpaid taxes exceeds $100)	Form 8109 to make deposits
October 31	Federal Unemployment Tax (FUTA) (only if liability for unpaid taxes exceeds $100)	Form 8109 to make deposits
January 31	Statement returns to nonemployees and transactions with other or independent contractors	Form 1099 to individuals
February 28	Statement returns to nonemployees and transactions with other or independent contractors	Form 1099 to IRS
February 28	Providing information on Social Security (FICA) tax and the withholding of income tax to employee	Forms W-2 and W-3 to SSA
April 15	Income tax filing	Schedule C (Form 1040)
April 15	Annual return of income	Form 1065
April 15	Self-employment tax filing (by individual who is a partner)	Schedule SE (Form 1040)

If your tax year is not January 1 through December 31:

Income tax is due on the fifteenth day of the fourth month after the end of your tax year.

Schedule SE is due the same day as income tax (Form 1040.)

Estimated Tax (1040ES) is due on the fifteenth day of the fourth, sixth, and ninth months of the tax year, and the fifteenth day of the first month after the end of your tax year.

S Corporation Calendar Worksheet

January 15	Estimated tax filing (by individual S corporation shareholder)	Form 1040ES
April 15	Estimated tax filing (by individual S corporation shareholder)	Form 1040ES
June 15	Estimated tax filing (by individual S corporation shareholder)	Form 1040ES
September 15	Estimated tax filing (by individual S corporation shareholder)	Form 1040ES
January 31	Social Security (FICA) tax and income tax withholding	Forms 941, 941E, 942 and 943
April 30	Social Security (FICA) tax and income tax withholding	Forms 941, 941E, 942 and 943
July 31	Social Security (FICA) tax and income tax withholding	Forms 941, 941E, 942 and 943
October 31	Social Security (FICA) tax and income tax withholding	Forms 941, 941E, 942 and 943
January 31	Providing information on Social Security (FICA) tax and the withholding of income tax to employee	Form W-2
January 31	Federal Unemployment Tax (FUTA)	Form 940-EZ or 940
January 31	Federal Unemployment Tax (FUTA) (only if liability for unpaid taxes exceeds $100)	Form 8109 to make deposits
April 15	Federal Unemployment Tax (FUTA) (only if liability for unpaid taxes exceeds $100)	Form 8109 to make deposits
July 31	Federal Unemployment Tax (FUTA) (only if liability for unpaid taxes exceeds $100)	Form 8109 to make deposits
October 31	Federal Unemployment Tax (FUTA) (only if liability for unpaid taxes exceeds $100)	Form 8109 to make deposits
January 31	Statement returns to nonemployees and transactions with other or independent contractors	Form 1099 to individuals
February 28	Statement returns to nonemployees and transactions with other or independent contractors	Form 1099 to IRS

February 28	Providing information on Social Security (FICA) tax and the withholding of income tax to employee	Forms W-2 and W-3 to SSA
April 15	Income tax filing	Form 1120S
April 15	Income tax filing (individual S corporation shareholder)	Form 1040

If your tax year is not January 1 through December 31:

Income Tax (Form 1120 or 1120-A) is due on the fifteenth day of the third month after the end of your tax year.

Estimated Tax (1120-W) is due on the fifteenth day of the fourth, sixth, ninth and twelfth months of the tax year.

Corporation Calendar Worksheet

April 15	Estimated tax filing by individual who is a partner	Form 1120W
June 15	Estimated tax filing by individual who is a partner	Form 1120W
September 15	Estimated tax filing by individual who is a partner	Form 1120W
December 15	Estimated tax filing by individual who is a partner	Form 1120W
January 31	Social Security (FICA) tax and income tax withholding	Forms 941, 941E, 942 and 943
April 30	Social Security (FICA) tax and income tax withholding	Forms 941, 941E, 942 and 943
July 31	Social Security (FICA) tax and income tax withholding	Forms 941, 941E, 942 and 943
October 31	Social Security (FICA) tax and income tax withholding	Forms 941, 941E, 942 and 943
January 31	Providing information on Social Security (FICA) tax and the withholding of income tax to employee	Form W-2
January 31	Federal Unemployment Tax (FUTA)	Form 940-EZ or 940
January 31	Federal Unemployment Tax (FUTA) (only if liability for unpaid taxes exceeds $100)	Form 8109 to make deposits
April 15	Federal Unemployment Tax (FUTA) (only if liability for unpaid taxes exceeds $100)	Form 8109 to make deposits
July 31	Federal Unemployment Tax (FUTA) (only if liability for unpaid taxes exceeds $100)	Form 8109 to make deposits
October 31	Federal Unemployment Tax (FUTA) (only if liability for unpaid taxes exceeds $100)	Form 8109 to make deposits

January 31	Statement returns to nonemployees and transactions with other or independent contractors	Form 1099 to individuals
February 28	Statement returns to nonemployees and transactions with other or independent contractors	Form 1099 to IRS
March 15	Income tax filing	Form 1120 or 1120-A

If your tax year is not January 1 through December 31:

Income tax is due on the fifteenth day of the fourth month after the end of your tax year.

Schedule SE is due the same day as income tax (Form 1040.)

Estimated Tax (1040ES) is due on the fifteenth day of the fourth, sixth, and ninth months of the tax year, and the fifteenth day of the first month after the end of your tax year.

Employment Taxes

Small business owners often have great responsibilities while operating and managing a business. Before you become an employer and hire employees, you need a EIN.

If you have employees, you are responsible for several federal, state, and local taxes. As an employer, you must withhold certain taxes from your employees pay checks. Employment taxes include the following:

- Federal income tax withholding
- Social Security and Medicare taxes
- Federal Unemployment Tax Act (FUTA).
- Federal Income Taxes/Social Security and Medicare Taxes

You generally must withhold federal income tax from your employee's wages. To figure how much to withhold from each wage payment, use the employee's Form W-4 and the methods described in Publication 15, Employers Tax Guide and Publication 15-A, Employers Supplemental Tax Guide.

Social Security and Medicare taxes pay for benefits that workers and families receive under the Federal Insurance Contributions Act (FICA). Social Security tax pays for benefits under the old age, survivors and disability insurance part of FICA. Medicare tax pays for benefits under the hospital insurance part of FICA. You withhold part of these taxes from your employee's wages and you pay a matching amount yourself.

To report federal income taxes, Social Security, and Medicare taxes use Form 941, Employer's Quarterly Federal Tax Return or Form 943, Employer's Annual Federal Tax Return for Agriculture Employees, if you are a farmer who employs employees.

Federal Unemployment (FUTA) Tax

The federal unemployment tax is part of the federal and state program under the Federal Unemployment Tax Act (FUTA) that pays unemployment compensation to workers who lose their jobs. You report and pay FUTA tax separately form social security and Medicare taxes and withheld income tax. You pay FUTA tax only from your own funds. Employees do not pay this tax or have it withheld from their pay. Report FUTA taxes on Form 940, Employer's Annual Federal Unemployment (FUTA) Tax Return or if you qualify, you can use the simpler Form 940-EZ instead.

Depositing Taxes

In general, you must deposit income tax withheld and both the employer and employee Social Security and Medicare taxes (minus any advance EIC payments) by mailing or delivering a check, money order, or cash to a financial institution that is an authorized depositary for Federal taxes. However, some taxpayers are required to deposit using the Electronic Federal Tax Deposit System (EFTPS). For additional information, call the IRS or visit www.irs.gov and go to the IRS Employment Taxes for Small Businesses page.

Independent Contractors vs. Employees

Before you can determine how to treat payments you make for services, you must first know the business relationship that exists between you and the person performing the services. The person performing the services may be:

- An independent contractor
- A common-law employee (Employee)
- A statutory employee
- A statutory nonemployee

In determining whether the person providing service is an employee or an independent contractor, all information that provides evidence of the degree of control and independence must be considered.

It is critical that you, the employer, correctly determine whether the individuals providing services are employees or independent contractors. Generally, you must withhold income taxes, withhold and pay Social Security and Medicare taxes, and pay unemployment tax on wages paid to an employee. You do not generally have to withhold or pay any taxes on payments to independent contractors.

> **Caution**
>
> If you incorrectly classify an employee as an independent contractor, you can be held liable for employment taxes for that worker, plus a penalty.

Determining Who Is an Independent Contractor

A general rule is that you, the payer, have the right to control or direct only the result of the work done by an independent contractor, and not the means and methods of accomplishing the result.

> **Example**
> Suzy Smith, a marketing consultant, submitted a job estimate to a
> company for marketing work at $40 per hour for 400 hours. She is to
> receive $1,600 every week for the next 10 weeks. This is not considered
> payment by the hour. Even if she works more or less than 400 hours
> to complete the work, Suzy will receive $16,000. She also performs
> additional marketing projects under contracts with other companies. Suzy
> is an independent contractor.

Reporting Payments Made to Independent Contractors

You may be required to file information returns to report certain types of
payments made to independent contractors during the year. For example, you
must file Form 1099-MISC, Miscellaneous Income, to report payments of $600
or more to persons not treated as employees (e.g., independent contractors) for
services performed for your trade or business. For details about filing Form 1099
and for information about required electronic or magnetic media filing, refer to
information returns.

What is a Common-Law Employee?

Under common-law rules, anyone who performs services for you is your employee
if you can control what will be done and how it will be done. This is so even when
you give the employee freedom of action. What matters is that you have the right
to control the details of how the services are performed.

To determine whether an individual is an employee or independent contractor
under the common law, the relationship of the worker and the business must
be examined. All evidence of control and independence must be considered.
In an employee-independent contractor determination, all information that
provides evidence of the degree of control and degree of independence must be
considered.

Facts that provide evidence of the degree of control and independence fall into
three categories: behavioral control, financial control and the type of relationship
of the parties. Refer to Publication 15-A, Employer's Supplemental Tax Guide for
Additional Information.

Defining Who Is an Employee

A general rule is that anyone who performs services for you is your employee if
you can control what will be done and how it will be done.

> **Example**
> Donna Lee is a salesperson employed on a full-time basis by Bob Blue, an auto dealer. She works 6 days a week, and is on duty in Bob's showroom on certain assigned days and times. She appraises trade-ins, but her appraisals are subject to the sales manager's approval. Lists of prospective customers belong to the dealer. She has to develop leads and report results to the sales manager. Because of her experience, she requires only minimal assistance in closing and financing sales and in other phases of her work. She is paid a commission and is eligible for prizes and bonuses offered by Bob. Bob also pays the cost of health insurance and group-term life insurance for Donna. Donna is an employee of Bob Blue.

What is a Statutory Employee?

If workers are independent contractors under the common law rules, such workers may nevertheless be treated as employees by statute (statutory employees) for certain employment tax purposes if they fall within any one of the following four categories and meet the three conditions described under Social Security and Medicare taxes.

1. A driver who distributes beverages (other than milk) or meat, vegetable, fruit, or bakery products; or who picks up and delivers laundry or dry cleaning, if the driver is your agent or is paid on commission.

2. A full-time life insurance sales agent whose principal business activity is selling life insurance or annuity contracts, or both, primarily for one life insurance company.

3. An individual who works at home on materials or goods that you supply and that must be returned to you or to a person you name, if you also furnish specifications for the work to be done.

4. A full-time traveling or city salesperson who works on your behalf and turns in orders to you from wholesalers, retailers, contractors, or operators of hotels, restaurants, or other similar establishments. The goods sold must be merchandise for resale or supplies for use in the buyer s business operation. The work performed for you must be the salesperson's principal business activity. Refer to the Salesperson section located in Publication 15-A, Employer s Supplemental Tax Guide for additional information.

Statutory NonEmployees

There are two categories of statutory non-employees: direct sellers and licensed real estate agents. They are treated as self-employed for all federal tax purposes, including income and employment taxes, if:

- Substantially all payments for their services as direct sellers or real estate agents are directly related to sales or other output, rather than to the number of hours worked and

- Their services are performed under a written contract providing that they will not be treated as employees for Federal tax purposes.

- Refer to information on Direct Sellers located in Publication 15-A, Employer s Supplemental Tax Guide for additional information.

Misclassification of Employees

Consequences of treating an employee as an independent contractor. If you classify an employee as an independent contractor and you have no reasonable basis for doing so, you may be held liable for employment taxes for that worker. See Internal Revenue Code section 3509 for additional information.

Most businesses start out small. As a new business owner you need to know your federal tax responsibilities. This page provides links to basic federal tax information for people who are starting a business. It also provides information to assist in making basic business decisions. The list should not be construed as all-inclusive. Other steps may be appropriate for your specific type of business.

Business Taxes

The form of business you operate determines what taxes you must pay and how you pay them. The following are the four general types of business taxes.

- Income Tax
- Employment Taxes
- Self-Employment Tax
- Excise Tax

All business except partnerships must file an annual income tax return. Partnerships file an information return. The form you use depends on how your business is organized.

The federal income tax is a pay-as-you-go tax. You must pay the tax as you earn or receive income during the year. An employee usually has income tax withheld from his or her pay. If you do no pay your tax through withholding, or do not pay enough tax that way, you might have to pay estimated tax. If you are not required to make estimated tax payments, you may pay any tax due when you file your return. For additional information refer to Publication 583, Starting a Business and Keeping Records.

Self-Employment Tax

Self-employment tax (SE tax) is a Social Security and Medicare tax primarily for individuals who work for themselves. Your payments of SE tax contribute to your coverage under the social security system. Social Security coverage provides you with retirement benefits, disability benefits, survivor benefits, and hospital insurance (Medicare) benefits.

You must pay SE tax and file Schedule SE (Form 1040) if either of the following applies.

- Your net earnings from self-employment were $400 or more
- You had church employee income of $108.28 or more

For additional information, refer to Self-Employment Tax

Employment Taxes

When you have employees, you as the employer have certain employment tax responsibilities that you must pay and forms you must file. Employment taxes include the following:

- Social Security and Medicare taxes
- Federal income tax withholding
- Federal unemployment (FUTA) tax

Excise Tax

Excise taxes are taxes paid when purchases are made on a specific good, such as gasoline. Excise taxes are often included in the price of the product. There are also excise taxes on activities, such as on wagering or on highway usage by trucks. Excise Tax has several general excise tax programs. One of the major components of the excise program is motor fuel.

The Importance of Good Record-keeping

Everyone in business must keep records. Keeping good records is very important to your business. Good records will help you do the following:

- Monitor the progress of your business
- Prepare your financial statements
- Identify source of receipts
- Keep track of deductible expenses
- Prepare your tax returns
- Support items reported on tax returns
- Monitor the progress of your business

You need good records to monitor the progress of your business. Records can show whether your business is improving, which items are selling, or what changes you need to make. Good records can increase the likelihood of business success.

Prepare your Financial Statements

You need good records to prepare accurate financial statements. These include income (profit and loss) statements and balance sheets. These statements can help you in dealing with your bank or creditors and help you manage your business.

- An income statement shows the income and expenses of the business for a given period of time.
- A balance sheet shows the assets, liabilities, and your equity in the business on a given date.

Identify Source of Receipts

You will receive money or property from many sources. Your records can identify the source of your receipts. You need this information to separate business form nonbusiness receipts and taxable form nontaxable income.

Keep Track of Deductible Expenses

You may forget expenses when you prepare your tax return, unless you record them when they occur.

Prepare your Tax Return

You need good records to prepare your tax returns. These records must support the income, expenses and credits you report. Generally, these are the same records you use to monitor your business and prepare your financial statement.

Support Items Reported on Tax Returns

You must keep your business records available at all times for inspection by the IRS. If the IRS examines any of your tax returns, you may be asked to explain the items reported. A complete set of records will speed up the examination.

You may choose any record-keeping system suited to your business that clearly shows your income. Except in a few cases, the law does not require any special kind of records. However, the business you are in affects the type of records you need to keep for federal tax purposes. Your record-keeping system should also include a summary of your business transactions. This summary is ordinarily made in your business books (for example, accounting journals and ledgers). Your books must show your gross income, as well as your deductions and credits. For most small businesses, the business checkbook is the main source for entries in the business books.

Supporting Business Documents

Purchases, sales, payroll, and other transactions you have in your business will generate supporting documents such as invoices and receipts. Supporting documents include sales slips, paid bills, invoices, receipts, deposit slips and canceled checks. These documents contain the information you need to record in your books. It is important to keep these documents because they support the entries in your books and on your tax return. You should keep them in an orderly fashion and in a safe place. For instance, organize them by year and type of income or expense. For more detailed information refer to Publication 583, Starting a Business and Keeping Records.

The following are some of the types of records you should keep:

Gross Receipts

This is the income you receive from your business. You should keep supporting documents that show the amounts and sources of your gross receipts. Documents for gross receipts include the following:

• Cash register tapes	• Bank deposit slips
• Receipt books	• Invoices
• Credit card charge slips	• Forms 1099-MISC

Purchases

Refers to the items you buy and resell to customers. If you are a manufacturer or producer, this includes the cost of all raw materials or parts purchased for manufacture into finished products. Your supporting documents should show the amount paid and that the amount was for purchases. Documents for purchases include the following:

• Canceled checks	• Cash register tape receipts
• Credit card sales slips	• Invoices

Expenses

Refers to the costs you incur (other than purchases) to carry on your business. Your supporting documents should show the amount paid and that the amount was for a business expense. Documents for expenses include the following:

• Canceled checks	• Cash register tapes
• Account statements	• Credit card sales slips
• Invoices	• Petty cash slips for small cash payments

Travel, Transportation, Entertainment and Gift Expenses

If you deduct travel, entertainment, gift or transportation expenses, you must be able to prove (substantiate) certain elements of expenses. For additional information on how to prove certain business expenses, refer to Publication 463, Travel, Entertainment, Gift and Car Expenses.

> **Hint**
>
> Assets are the property, such as machinery and furniture that you own and use in your business. You must keep records to verify certain information about your business assets. You need records to compute the annual depreciation and the gain or loss when you sell the assets.

Recording Business Transactions

A good record-keeping system includes a summary of your business transactions. Business transactions are ordinarily summarized in books called journals and ledgers. You can buy them at your local stationery or office supply store. A journal is a book where you record each business transaction shown on your supporting documents. You may have to keep separate journals for transactions that occur frequently.

There are specific employment tax records you must keep. Keep all records of employment for at least 4 years. A ledger is a book that contains the totals from all of your journals. It is organized into different accounts.

Whether you keep journals and ledgers and how you keep them depends on the type of business you are in. For example, a record-keeping system for a small business might include the following items:

- Business checkbook
- Monthly summary of cash receipts
- Depreciation worksheet
- Daily summary of cash receipts
- Check disbursements journal
- Employee compensation records

Note

The system you use to record business transactions will be more effective as you follow good record-keeping practices. For example, record expenses when they occur, and identify the source of recorded receipts. Generally, it is best to record transactions on a daily basis.

Keep all records of employment taxes for at least 4 years. These should be available for IRS review. Records should include:

- Your EIN
- Amounts and dates of all wage, annuity, and pension payments
- Amounts of tips reported
- The fair market value of in-kind wages paid
- Names, addresses, social security numbers, and occupations of employees and recipients
- Any employee copies of Form W-2 that were returned to you as undeliverable
- Dates of employment
- Periods for which employees and recipients were paid while absent due to sickness or injury and the amount and weekly rate of payments you or third-party payers made to them
- Copies of employees' and recipients' income tax withholding allowance certificates (Forms W-4, W-4P, W-4S, and W-4V)
- Dates and amounts of tax deposits you made
- Copies of returns filed
- Records of allocated tips
- Records of fringe benefits provided, including substantiation
- Occupational Safety and Health Administration (OSHA)

Every employer covered by OSHA who has more than 10 employees, except for employers in certain low-hazard industries such as retail, finance, insurance, real estate, and some service industries, must maintain OSHA-specified records of job-related injuries and illnesses.

Burden of Proof

The responsibility to prove entries, deductions, and statements made on your tax returns is known as the burden of proof. You must be able to prove (substantiate) certain elements of expenses to deduct them. Generally, taxpayers meet their burden of proof by having the information and receipts (where needed) for the expenses. You should keep adequate records to prove your expenses or have sufficient evidence that will support your own statement. You generally must have documentary evidence, such as receipts, canceled checks, or bills, to support your expenses.

The length of time you should keep a document depends on the action, expense, or event the document records. Generally, you must keep your records that support an item of income or deductions on a tax return until the period of limitations for that return runs out.

The time you are required to keep records includes the period of time during which you can amend your tax return to claim a credit or refund, or that the IRS can assess more tax. You should also keep copies of your filed tax returns in the following situations:

- You owe additional tax and situations (2), (3), and (4), below, do not apply to you; keep records for 3 years.
- You do not report income that you should report, and it is more than 25 percent of the gross income shown on your return; keep records for 6 years.
- You file a fraudulent income tax return; keep records indefinitely.
- You do not file a return; keep records indefinitely.
- You file a claim for credit or refund after you file your return; keep records the later of 3 years or 2 years after tax was paid.
- Your claim is due to a bad debt deduction; keep records for 7 years.
- Your claim is due to a loss from worthless securities; keep records for 7 years.
- Keep information on an asset for the life of the asset, even when you dispose of the asset; keep records indefinitely.
- Keep all employment tax records for at least 4 years after the date that the tax becomes due or is paid, whichever is later.
- The following questions should be applied to each record as you decide whether to keep a document or throw it away.

Keep records relating to property until the period of limitations expires for the year in which you dispose of the property in a taxable disposition. You must keep these records to figure any depreciation, amortization, or depletion deduction and to figure the gain or loss when you sell or otherwise dispose of the property.

When your records are no longer needed for tax purposes, do not discard them until you check to see if you have to keep them longer for other purposes. For example, your insurance company or creditors may require you to keep them longer than the IRS does.

Resources

Free Publications available from the IRS:

Publication 535, Business Expenses

Publication 536, Net Operating Losses

Publication 547, Casualties, Disasters, and Thefts (Business and Nonbusiness)

Publication 594, IRS Collection Process (PDF)

Publication 583, Starting a Business and Keeping Records

Publication 334, Tax Guide for Small Business

Tax Topic 762, Basic Information

To determine whether a worker is an independent contractor or an employee, you must examine the relationship between the worker and the business. All evidence of control and independence in this relationship should be considered. The facts that provide this evidence fall into three categories behavioral control, financial control, and the type of relationship itself.

Publication 1976, Section 530 Employment Tax Relief Requirements (PDF)

Section 530 provides businesses with relief from Federal employment tax obligations if certain requirements are met.

IRS Internal Training, Employee/Independent Contractor

This manual provides you with the tools to make correct determinations of worker classifications. It discusses facts that may indicate the existence of an independent contractor or an employer-employee relationship. This training manual is a guide and is not legally binding. If you would like the IRS to make the determination of worker status, file IRS Form SS-8.

Form SS-8 (PDF)

Determination of Worker Status for Purposes of Federal Employment Taxes and Income Tax Withholding

Publication 15-A

The Employer's Supplemental Tax Guide has detailed guidance including information for specific industries.

Publication 15-B

The Employer's Tax Guide to Fringe Benefits: Supplements Circular E (Pub. 15), Employer's Tax Guide, and Publication 15-A, Employer's Supplemental Tax Guide. It contains specialized and detailed information on the employment tax treatment of fringe benefits.

The original C corporation is a unique animal among business structures. A corporation is the only type of business that must pay its own income taxes on profits, which makes sense to the degree that a corporation is treated as a person under the law. Whatever risks, liabilities and rewards are created by the human elements of a business, the buck stops at the corporate level.

Dual Taxation—A Reprise

We have already talked about dual (or double) taxation, but we should define it again. C corporations are treated as separate legal taxable entities for income tax purposes. As such, corporations pay tax on their earnings. If corporate earnings are distributed to shareholders in the form of dividends, the corporation does not receive the reasonable business expense deduction, and dividend income is taxed as regular income to the shareholders. Thus, to the extent that earnings are distributed to shareholders as dividends, there is a double tax on earnings at the corporate and shareholder level.

S corporations and limited liability companies are pass-through entities that are not subject to the double tax.

What a Corporate Tax Filing Looks Like

The corporation must file a corporate tax return, IRS Form 1120, and pay taxes at a corporate income tax rate on any profits. If a corporation owes taxes, it must estimate the amount of tax due for the year and make payments to the IRS on a quarterly basis in April, June, September and January.

What Are Tax-Deductible Expenses?

To cut taxable profits, a corporation can deduct its business expenses—basically, any money the corporation spends in the legitimate pursuit of profit. In addition to startup costs, operating expenses, and product and advertising outlays, a corporation can deduct the salaries and bonuses it pays and all of the costs associated with medical and retirement plans for employees.

Shareholder Tax Payments

The corporation's owners, if they work for the corporation, pay individual income taxes on their salaries and bonuses, just as regular employees of any company. Salaries and bonuses are deductible business expenses, so the corporation deducts those costs and does not pay taxes on them.

Tax on Dividends

If a corporation distributes dividends to the owners—which seldom happens at small corporations where the owners work—the owners must report and pay personal income tax on these amounts. Because dividends, unlike salaries and bonuses, are not tax deductible, the corporation must also pay taxes on them. This means that dividends are taxed twice—once to the corporation and again to the shareholders.

What Are the Benefits of Corporate Income Tax?

There are many important benefits (and several critical disadvantages) to becoming a C corporation and paying taxes under its rules. You may need a tax advisor to help you figure out the cost-benefit factors for your company.

The following are advantages to a C corporation:

Retained Earnings

Often, a profitable corporation will want or need to retain some of profits in the business at the end of the year, particularly if it needs to fund expansion. If it does, that money will be taxed to the corporation at corporate income tax rates. Because initial corporate income tax rates (15 to 25 percent on profits up to the first $75,000) are lower than most owners' marginal income tax rates for the same amount of income, a corporation's owners can save money by keeping some profits in the company. It is important to note that this does not apply to professional corporations (e.g., those conducting business in the field of law, medicine or engineering); they are taxed at a flat 35 percent rate. As we have mentioned, sole proprietorships, partnerships and LLCs must pay taxes on all business profits at their individual income tax rates, regardless of whether the profits are reinvested in the business. Most corporations can safely keep a total of $250,000 in the corporation at any one time without facing tax penalties. Some professional corporations may not retain more than $150,000.

Deductibility of Benefits

C corporations can deduct the full cost of employee benefits provided to staff. This includes the business' owners who are not taxed on these benefits. Other business entities can deduct the cost of benefits as a business expense, but owners who receive these benefits will ordinarily be taxed on their value.

Summary

When considering the implications of corporate tax law on your business, be sure to have an experienced accountant available. Though there are significant tax advantages exclusive to C corporations, the type of business you own and your long-term goals will impact the benefits available to you. Make sure those benefits more than offset the expense of staying incorporated.

Buying Benefits

Options Available to Corporations

Employee benefits are an important part of attracting talent to a growing corporation. To determine the best selection of benefits for your employees, along with appropriate tax advice, we suggest you consult with an accountant as well as a benefits advisor who specializes in your type of business.

Health Care

C corporations, despite their initial expense and complexity, are the most flexible business structure in terms of employee benefits. C corporations can deduct 100 percent of their health insurance costs for employees, including employees who are shareholders in the corporation. The costs of any medical reimbursement plans are also fully deductible.

Salaries/Bonuses

A corporation may deduct reasonable salaries paid to employees and businesses. Any amount the IRS finds unreasonable is treated as a taxable dividend.

Retirement Plans

Corporations may deduct payments made on behalf of employees to qualified retirement plans. Contributions and accumulated earnings under such plans are not taxed until the employee starts drawing on those plans.

Generally, a retirement plan can be either a defined benefit plan or a defined contribution plan. A defined benefit plan starts with a specific monthly benefit that the participant will receive at retirement and then calculates the amount needed to produce that benefit. A defined contribution plan provides an individual account for each participant and makes no promises as to how much the participant will receive at retirement. The benefits received at retirement are determined by how much is contributed and how well the fund performs while the contributions accumulate. Many years ago, virtually all employer-provided retirement plans were defined benefit plans. Today, virtually all employer-provided retirement plans are some form of defined contribution plan.

With the help of qualified benefits advisors, companies can set up the following retirement plans:

401(k) Plan

A 401(k) plan is a defined contribution plan offered by a corporation to its employees. These plans allow employees to set aside tax-deferred income for retirement purposes. In some cases, employers will match their contribution dollar for dollar. Taking a distribution of the funds before a specified age will trigger a penalty tax. The name 401(k) comes from the tax code section describing the program.

SIMPLE Plan

A Savings Incentive Match Plan for Employees (SIMPLE) plan is a retirement plan sponsored by employers that requires less paperwork and fees than conventional 401(k) plans. Employees may elect to contribute to these plans through salary deferrals, and employers benefit from the tax-deductible contributions made to the plan. The employer has the option of matching a certain portion of the employee's deferrals or making nonelective contributions to all eligible employees. An annual limit applies in both cases. A minimum compensation eligibility requirement exists for employees who want to join this plan. Employees cannot establish any other qualified retirement plans at the same time.

Money Purchase Pension Plan

A money purchase pension plan is a defined contribution plan in which the amount of contributions each employee receives from the employer is in proportion to that employee's wages. Unlike profit-sharing plans, these contributions are mandatory every year, regardless of profits.

Profit-Sharing Plan

A profit-sharing plan is an arrangement in which an employer shares some of its profits with its employees. The compensation can be stocks, bonds, or cash and can be immediate or deferred until retirement. Profit sharing allows for changing contributions each year. Contributions are determined by a formula to allocate the overall contribution and distribution of accumulated funds after the retirement age. Unless the plans are defined as elective deferral plans, the contributions are not tax deductible, but contributions and earnings grow tax-deferred until withdrawal.

Targeted Benefit Plan

A targeted benefit plan is a blend of defined contribution and defined benefit plans. A targeted plan allows contributions to employee accounts so that employees can reach a targeted amount at retirement.

Employee Stock Ownership Plan (ESOP)

An ESOP is a trust established by a corporation that acts as a tax-qualified, defined- contribution retirement plan by making the corporation's employees partial owners. Contributions are made by the sponsoring employer and can grow tax-deferred, just as with an IRA or 401(k). But unlike other retirement plans, the contributions must be invested in the company's stock. The benefits for the company include increased cash flow, some tax savings and increased productivity from highly motivated workers. The main benefit for the employees is the ability to share in the company's success. Due to the tax benefits, the administration of ESOPs is regulated, and numerous restrictions apply. An ESOP is also called a stock purchase plan.

The IRS provides complete information on starting retirement plans for small business on their Web site. The address is www.irs.gov/retirement/article/0,,id=108975,00.html.

Insurance

Corporations may deduct amounts paid for a variety of insurance products purchased on behalf of employees, including:

- term life insurance
- accident and health insurance
- disability insurance
- health insurance

Corporations are also allowed to deduct amounts paid by the corporation to repay the medical expenses of employees, their spouses and dependents. These amounts are not included in the employee's income for tax purposes.

Stock Options

Stock options can be granted in private or public corporations. There are two types of stock options: nonqualified stock options (NSOs) and qualified (incentive), stock options (ISOs). ISOs qualify for special tax treatment. For example, gains may be taxed at capital gains rates instead of higher, ordinary income rates.

ISO holders typically pay lower capital gains taxes when they sell shares purchased under this plan. For more information on these types of plans, consult a tax professional.

Employee Stock Purchase Plans

An employee stock purchase plan (ESPP) is a type of broad-based stock plan that allows employees to use after-tax payroll deductions to acquire their company's stock, usually at a discount of up to 15 percent.

Under U.S. tax law, a qualified 423 employee stock purchase plan allows employees to purchase stock at a discount (from fair market value) without any taxes owed on the discount at the time of purchase. In some cases, a holding period will be required for the purchased stock in order to receive favorable long-term capital gains tax treatment on a portion of the gains when the shares are sold.

A nonqualified employee stock purchase plan is usually similar to a qualified 423 plan but without the preferred tax treatment for employees. Most corporations establish these plans with investment companies, so ask for guidance from your attorney and tax advisor before you select a plan.

Summary

All corporations qualify for certain benefits offerings for owners and workers, though C corporations allow for the broadest range of options. It is important to discuss this issue with an attorney and a tax and benefits advisor before you select a corporate structure for your business. Because benefits are an essential draw for talent at most companies, select the best possible package for your corporation.

14 Lawyers & Accountants

When It Pays to Keep Them on Board

In Chapter 6, we discussed economical ways to hire advisors at the preliminary phase of a corporation. Under certain conditions, it may make sense to consider continuing the relationship. The following are areas in which professional tax and legal advice may be useful.

Corporate Governance

Laws change and so do rules about what constitutes a corporation. Qualified attorneys can help you keep pace with new requirements as well as old ones. An attorney can also keep you informed about changing rules and restrictions on record-keeping, meetings and board appointments. Failure to adhere to these requirements could pierce the corporate veil in the event of a lawsuit or other legal action, exposing corporate officers to personal liability or other legal problems.

Intellectual Property

As your business grows, so does your storehouse of intellectual property—ideas, proprietary marks, trademarks and product designs. Since the dawn of the computer age, intellectual property has been one of the hottest areas of the law and the most subject to change. A qualified intellectual property attorney can help you protect the critical items that give you a competitive edge.

Employment Agreements

Many companies, especially technology companies, count the knowledge of their employees among their most important assets. To prevent those assets from walking out the door with your best ideas and processes, you will need well-written nondisclosure and noncompete agreements that protect the company without scaring potential new employees away.

Exit Strategies

Though much thought and energy is spent on establishing a business, little attention is paid to the thought of selling it or shutting it down. A good attorney and accountant can guide you through what could be a complicated process. To safeguard what you have built, hire professionals to assist.

Summary

Review Chapter 6 for tips on hiring first-rate staff, then consider the many reasons why a continuing relationship with an attorney and a tax expert is a smart investment for your business.

Free Forms and Checklists

Registered readers can visit www.socrates.com/books/ready-incorporate.aspx for free forms, letters and checklists. To register, see page iv for details. Among the many items available are:

Commercial Lease • Estimated Startup Capital Worksheet • General Partnership Agreement • Minutes: First Meeting of Shareholders • Stock Ledger and Transfer Ledger • Corporate Resolutions • Personal Net Worth Worksheet • Profitability Worksheet Analysis • And more!

Planning for Change

How to Dissolve a Corporation and Other Change-Related Matters

As painful as it may be, you should think about your corporation's dissolution even before forming it. Though it is only natural to assume that your corporation will continue forever, it is nevertheless wise to plan ahead in order to give yourself maximum flexibility should the end ever come.

Dissolution, of course, is not the only change your corporation could undergo. During the course of its life, your business could merge, consolidate or be sold, and each possible event should be considered. To prepare for such an event, first place a value on your business. Valuation is based on several factors, including the sales or fees earned and the market value of corporate assets.

An accountant can best help you determine your corporation's worth, or you can value it yourself.

Once you have established an approximate value for your company, you can then make the decision to either sell the assets or the stock of the company. All companies, even those publicly traded, have a par value on their shares that is much lower than the current valuation of the stock.

Another factor to consider is the relationship of your corporation to your estate planning. Remember, C corporations can live forever if there is no end date placed on them. You may want to discuss estate issues now with your accountant related to the closure or sale of the business later.

The following are 10 ways to plan for your company's dissolution:

1. Expiration
The corporation will end at the time you specify in the corporate charter (certificate of incorporation) if you have set an expiration date.

2. Surrender of the charter
When shareholders of a corporation elect by majority vote to surrender the corporate charter to the state and it is formally accepted, the corporation ends.

3. Filing a certificate of dissolution
The corporation may file a certificate of dissolution with the secretary of state in the state of incorporation.

4. Consolidation
When two corporations unite to form a new C corporation, the merging corporations have been dissolved by consolidation. The new C corporation assumes all the assets, property rights, privileges and liabilities of the consolidating corporations.

5. Merger
When a corporation merges into a second corporation, the second corporation survives. The surviving corporation absorbs all the assets, property rights, privileges and often the liabilities of the absorbed corporation, but continues its own separate corporate existence thereafter.

6. The occurrence of a condition
A corporation may be dissolved when a condition (a specific event) clearly specified in the corporate charter occurs, such as the death of a principal. This provision is rare, however, as corporations have a perpetual life independent of their principals.

7.Legislative repeal
Under the inherent rights reserved by most states to alter, amend or repeal the charter granted to a corporation, a legislature may, for some reason, find it necessary to revoke a corporate charter, thereby terminating the corporate existence. This is more commonly exercised with nonprofit corporations.

8. Action by the attorney general
The state (and only the state) can sue to terminate the existence of a corporation. If it is satisfied that the state has proven its case, the court may revoke the corporate charter. For example, the court may terminate the existence of a corporation if it finds that the corporation has not filed required taxes or documents or that it has abused or neglected to use its powers.

> ## 9. Directors' or shareholders' petition
> Statutes may permit the majority of the board of directors to petition for the dissolution of the corporation. They may do this, for example, if the assets of the corporation are not sufficient to discharge its liabilities. The stockholders of a majority of all outstanding shares entitled to vote on the issue may also be empowered by statute to petition the court for dissolution on similar grounds.
>
> ## 10. Shareholders' petition under deadlock statutes
> A typical so-called deadlock statute commonly provides: Unless otherwise provided in the certificate of incorporation, the holders of one-half of all outstanding shares of a corporation entitled to vote in an election of directors may present a petition for dissolution on one or more of the following grounds:
>
> 1. That the directors are so divided respecting the management of the corporation's affairs that the votes required for action by the board cannot be obtained.
>
> 2. That the shareholders are so divided that the votes required for the election of directors cannot be obtained.
>
> 3. That there is internal dissension and two or more factions of shareholders are so divided that dissolution would be beneficial to the shareholders.

Keep in mind that corporate dissolution is not the same as revocation of S corporation status. Even if S corporation status is revoked, the corporation continues to exist as a C corporation. If the corporation is dissolved, however, it reverts to proprietorship or partnership status.

Summary

Planning for the beginning, middle and end of a corporation is important. Make sure you get the right legal and financial advice to do it properly.

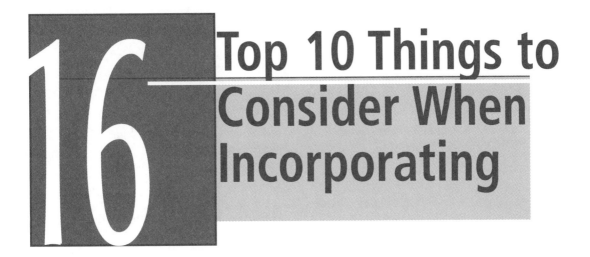

16 Top 10 Things to Consider When Incorporating

Though the items on the following list relate to incorporating, they also apply to any business or career plan you have. Consult the items on this list before you make a move.

1. Do not go it alone
The simplest corporations might be able to guide themselves through the incorporation process and beyond, but foregoing the advice of an attorney or accountant over the life of your business can be foolhardy from a tax and growth standpoint.

2. Do not jump in without a plan
Incorporating might be the right business fit, but have you taken the time to plan out the business itself? Have you drafted a business plan that looks at your potential market and, most importantly, your financing options? Many people start businesses and after a few months wonder why they are there. Incorporation will not help you decide whether your business idea is viable, but a good business plan might.

3. Do not forget the worst-case scenario
People starting new businesses may fail to ask themselves some very basic questions about possible disasters—business related and otherwise—that could affect their future. Business plans may help you focus on success, but contingency plans help you focus on the things most new business owners do not like to think about—unexpected competitors, protecting assets, lawsuits and dealing with sickness or injury and its effect on the business. As you are writing your business plan, consider writing a second-draft contingency plan for your own use, incorporating possible problems and a plan to deal with them.

4. Borrow carefully

Though friends and family are often the first source for seed money after entrepreneurs empty their own pockets, borrowing from those you know can also lead to problems down the road. Make sure you put all financial agreements in writing so that you do not endanger relationships. At the same time, it makes sense to learn everything you can about the broad range of business financing options before you start your business plan. A business plan without potential funding sources is futile.

5. Avoid excessive overhead

Restrict initial purchases for office equipment and other startup items to the essentials. Buy everything you need, not everything you want, especially if your offices are not viewed by the public. You can always upgrade later.

6. Avoid hiring for convenience

Though the startup phase of a business can be extremely busy, avoid hiring full-time administrative help or other paid assistance until you have a better idea of what your long-term needs will be. Employees cost money, and you may find that you do not have enough work to keep them busy. Outsource as much work as you safely can at the start until you get a better idea of your business cycle.

7. Do not bring in board members before you need to

Many states will allow incorporations with a single board member at the start, but some people are too easily tempted to offer directors' slots to early financers or family and friends. Board slots should be reserved for those qualified to hold them. If they cannot offer solid advice and leadership to grow the business, do not consider them.

8. Do not get stuck on minutiae

In the early days of business, owners may waste too much time in areas that are not likely to produce results. Focus your energy on the big picture and your long-term goals.

9. Focus on profit

Decide which areas of your business are likely to produce the most profit and focus your energies there. The wait-and-see approach is rarely effective.

10. Prepare an exit strategy

Is there a certain point at which you can see yourself leaving the business? Too many people dream about getting into business but do not plan for ending things in a tidy way. Consider when and how you might imagine leaving the business: Selling to another owner? Consolidating with a similar business? Closing? Thinking ahead will help you plan along the way for various scenarios.

Section ■ Four

Incorporation Rules: State by State

The following listings provide basic requirements for corporations and limited liability companies in each of the 50 states and district of Columbia. Domestic filings are filed by businesses or individuals residing in the state they wish to file in. Foreign corporations refer to businesses whose owners are based in another state. Though LLCs are not corporations, their filing fees are listed because they are an increasingly popular business structure option.

We encourage you to investigate all the state and federal Web sites listed below because each state provides more detail on procedure and provisions than space allows. Also, laws and fees might change at any time.

Alabama

Alabama Secretary of State
Attn: Corporations Division
11 S. Union Street, Suite 207
Montgomery, AL 36104
1.334.242.5324
www.sos.state.al.us

Where to Get Forms and Background

www.sos.state.al.us/business/corporations.cfm

State Filing Fees

(Does not include processing fees specific to counties or types of industries):

• Domestic profit corporation	$40
• Foreign corporation	$175
• Domestic LLCs	$40

Additional fees may be required at the county level.

Naming Procedures for Corporations

The corporate name must include the word Corporation or Incorporated or an abbreviation of one of these words (Inc. or Corp.). The original and two copies of the Articles of Incorporation and the Certificate of Name Reservation must be filed in the county where the corporation's registered office is located. Names can be reserved for 120 days at $10.

Names can be reserved for corporations, but not for LLCs.

Director Information

- Corporations require one or more directors
- No residency requirement
- No age requirement
- Directors need to be listed in the articles of incorporation

Report Filing Requirements

Alabama corporations and qualified foreign corporations must file an Alabama Business Privilege Tax Return, which also serves as an annual report. Most corporations' annual reports are due March 15.

Detailed Tax Information

Alabama Department of Revenue:
www.ador.state.al.us

State and Federal Tax Forms

www.irs.ustreas.gov/formspubs/index.htm

Securities Registration Information

http://asc.state.al.us

Alaska

Department of Commerce
Corporations Section
PO Box 110808
Juneau, AK 99811
1.907.465.2530
www.commerce.state.ak.us/occ/home.htm

Where to Get Forms and Background

www.commerce.state.ak.us/bsc/cforms.htm

State Filing Fees

(Does not include processing fees specific to counties or types of industries)

• Domestic profit corporation	$250
• Foreign corporation	$350
• Domestic LLCs	$250

Naming Procedures for Corporations

Alaskan businesses pay a $25 name reservation fee to reserve a corporate name as well as a name for an LLC.

Director Information

- Corporations require one or more directors
- No residency requirement
- Directors must be at least 19 years old
- Directors are not required to be listed in articles of incorporation

Record-Keeping

A list of shareholders, books and records of account, and the minutes of shareholders' and directors' meetings must be kept at the registered office or principal place of business.

Report Filing Requirements

Alaska corporations and qualified foreign corporations must file a biennial report in January of each alternate year with the Corporations Section. The biennial corporation tax is $100 for domestic profit corporations and $200 for foreign corporations. LLCs must file a biennial report by January 2 with the Corporations Section.

Detailed Tax Information

Alaska Department of Revenue
www.revenue.state.ak.us

State and Federal Tax Forms

www.irs.ustreas.gov/formspubs/index.htm

Securities Registration Information

www.commerce.state.ak.us/bsc/secur.htm

Arizona

Arizona Corporation Commission
1300 W. Washington
Phoenix, AZ 85007
1.602.542.3026

or

Arizona Corporation Commission
400 W. Congress, Suite 221
Tucson, AZ 85701
1.520.628.6560
www.cc.state.az.us/corp/index.htm

Where to Get Forms and Background

www.cc.state.az.us/corp/filings/forms/index.htm

State Filing Fees

(Does not include processing fees specific to counties or types of industries)

• Domestic profit corporation	$60
• Foreign corporation	$175
• Domestic LLCs	$50

Naming Procedures for Corporations

The name must be distinguishable from all preexisting names in the corporate database. The name cannot be too similar to an existing corporation, limited liability company, trade name or mark, limited partnership, business trust or any form of business entity regulated by the Arizona Corporation Commission or secretary of state 1.Arizona Revised Statutes §§10.401 or 29.602). The naming fee is $10.

Director Information

- Corporations require one or more directors
- No residency requirement
- No age requirement
- Directors must be listed in articles of incorporation

Report Filing Requirements

Arizona corporations are required to file an annual report with the Arizona Corporation Commission with a filing fee of $45.

LLCs are not required to file periodic reports.

Detailed Tax Information

Arizona Department of Revenue
www.revenue.state.az.us

State and Federal Tax Forms

www.irs.ustreas.gov/formspubs/index.htm

Securities Registration Information

www.ccsd.cc.state.az.us

Arkansas

Secretary of State/Business and Commercial Services Division
1401 W. Capitol Avenue
Victory Building, Suite 250
Little Rock, AR 72201
1.501.682.3409
www.ark.org/sos/ofs/docs/index.php

Where to Get Forms and Background

www.ark.org/sos/ofs/docs/index.php

State Filing Fees

(Does not include processing fees specific to counties or types of industries)

• Domestic profit corporation	$50
• Foreign corporation	$282
• Domestic LLCs	$50

Naming Procedures for Corporations

Incorporators may reserve a corporate name by filing a name reservation application with the secretary of state, along with a $25 name reservation fee. That reservation is effective for 120 days. The same rules apply to LLCs.

Director Information

- Minimum number: not less than three. However, if there are only one or two shareholders of record, the number of directors may be less than three but not less than the number of shareholders
- Residence requirements: no provision
- Age requirements: none
- Directors are not required to be listed in the articles of incorporation

Report Filing Requirements

Arkansas corporations are required to file an Arkansas Corporation Franchise Tax Report with the secretary of state by May 1.

Detailed Tax Information

Arkansas Department of Revenue
www.accessarkansas.org/dfa

State and Federal Tax Forms

www.irs.ustreas.gov/formspubs/index.htm

Securities Registration Information

www.state.ar.us/arsec

California

California Secretary of State
Corporations Unit
1500 11th Street
Sacramento, CA 95814
1.916.657.5448
www.ss.ca.gov/business/business.htm

Where to Get Forms and Background

www.ss.ca.gov/business/business.htm

State Filing Fees

(Does not include processing fees specific to counties or types of industries)

• Domestic profit corporation	$100
• Foreign corporation	$100
• Domestic LLCs	$70

Naming Procedures for Corporations

The name must not be likely to mislead the public, be the same as, or resemble so closely as to lead to deception, the name of a domestic or qualified foreign corporation, a name under reservation or the registered or assumed name of a foreign corporation. The name needs the Superintendent of Bank's approval if it contained the words Bank, Trust or Trustee. Filers pay a $10 fee to reserve a name, and the registration stays active for 60 days.

Director Information

- Minimum number: not less than three, unless there are only one or two shareholders of record. If there are only one or two shareholders of record, the number of directors may be less than three but not less than the number of shareholders

- Residence requirements: no provision

- Age requirements: none

- Directors are not required to be listed in the articles of incorporation

Report Filing Requirements

Every domestic stock corporation must file a Statement of Information 1.Form SI.200 C or Form SI.200 N/C.with the secretary of state within 90 days after filing the original articles of incorporation and annually thereafter during the applicable filing period, which is the calendar month during which its original articles of incorporation were filed and the immediately preceding 5 calendar months. If the name or address of the agent for service of process has changed, a corporation must file a complete statement. A corporation is required to file a statement even though it may not be actively engaged in business at the time this statement is due.

Detailed Tax Information

California Department of Revenue
www.ftb.ca.gov

State and Federal Tax Forms

www.irs.ustreas.gov/formspubs/index.html

Securities Registration Information

www.corp.ca.gov/srd/security.htm

Colorado

Colorado Department of State
Business Division
1560 Broadway, Suite 200
Denver, CO 80202
1.303.894.2200
www.sos.state.co.us (Select Business Center)

Where to Get Forms and Background

www.sos.state.co.us/pubs/business/main.htm

State Filing Fees

(Does not include processing fees specific to counties or types of industries)

• Domestic profit corporation	$50/$0.99 if filed online
• Foreign corporation	$50/no online option
• Domestic LLCs	$50/$0.99 if filed online

The domestic profit corporation fees were introduced in early 2005.

Naming Procedures for Corporations

The name of a business corporation must contain the word Corporation, Company, Incorporated, Limited or an abbreviation thereof. The name must not imply it is organized for any purpose not stated in its charter, bylaws or articles of incorporation. The name must be distinguishable upon the records from the name of any domestic or foreign corporation, limited liability company, limited partnership, and other business entities formed in Colorado.

The statement for reservation of a name costs $10 in person or by mail or $0.99 online.

Director Information

- • Minimum number: one or more
- • Residence requirements: no provision
- • Age requirements: directors must be at least 18 years of age
- • Directors are not required to be listed in the articles of incorporation

Report Filing Requirements

As of January 1, 2002, reports are now due annually by the end of the second month in which the report is mailed to the corporation. The same rules apply to LLCs.

Business Licensing

Certain types of businesses in the state are required to obtain a license and pay a fee. These businesses include architects, brokers, chiropractors, dentists, engineers, family, therapists, geologists, optometrists, pharmacists, physical therapists and veterinarians.

Detailed Tax Information

Colorado Department of Revenue
www.revenue.state.co.us/TPS_Dir/wrap.asp?ind=business

State and Federal Tax Forms

www.irs.ustreas.gov/formspubs/index.html

Securities Registration Information

www.dora.state.co.us/securities

Connecticut

State of Connecticut Corporations Division
30 Trinity Street
Hartford, CT 06106
1.860.509.6001
www.sots.state.ct.us

Where to Get Forms and Background

www.sots.state.ct.us/CommercialRecording/crdform.html

State Filing Fees

(Does not include processing fees specific to counties or types of industries)

• Domestic profit corporation	$50 plus a franchise fee
• Foreign corporation	$300
• Domestic LLCs	$60

Naming Procedures for Corporations

The name of the corporation must be in English letters or numbers and must contain one of the following words: Corporation, Company, Incorporated, Limited, Societa per Azioni, or contain the abbreviation Corp., Inc., Co., Ltd., or S.p.A. The name may not imply it is organized for any purpose not permitted in its certificate. The name must be distinguishable from the name of a domestic profit corporation, a reserved or registered corporate name, the fictitious name of a foreign corporation, the name of a nonprofit corporation, the name of any domestic or foreign nonstock corporation, or other business entities filed with the state. The fee to reserve a name is $30.

Director Information

- Minimum number: one or more
- Residence requirements: no provision
- Age requirements: none
- Directors are not required to be listed in the articles of incorporation

Report Filing Requirements

Connecticut corporations and qualified foreign corporations must file annual reports by the last day of the month in which the entity originally filed in the state. The annual report fee is $75.

Detailed Tax Information

Connecticut Department of Revenue Services
www.ct.gov/drs/site/default.asp

State and Federal Tax Forms

www.irs.ustreas.gov/formspubs/index.html

Securities Registration Information

www.state.ct.us/dob/pages/secdiv.htm

Delaware

Division of Corporations
P.O. Box 898
Dover, DE 19903
1.302.739.3073 (Press 2)
www.delaware.gov

Where to Get Forms and Background

www.state.de.us/corp/default.shtml

www.state.de.us/corp/newfee.pdf

State Filing Fees

(Does not include processing fees specific to counties or types of industries)

• Domestic profit corporation	$89
• Foreign corporation	$160
• Domestic LLCs	$90

Naming Procedures for Corporations

The name of the corporation: (i) shall contain one of the words Association, Company, Corporation, Club, Foundation, Fund, Incorporated, Institute, Society, Union, Syndicate or Limited (or abbreviations thereof, with or without punctuation), or words (or abbreviations thereof, with or without punctuation) of like import of foreign countries or jurisdictions (provided they are written in roman characters or letters); (ii) shall be such as to distinguish it upon the records in the office of the Division of Corporations in the Department of State from the names on such records of other corporations, partnerships, limited partnerships, limited liability companies or statutory trusts organized, reserved or registered as a foreign corporation, partnership, limited partnership, limited liability company or statutory trust under the laws of this state, except with the written consent of such other foreign corporation or domestic or foreign partnership, limited partnership, limited liability company or statutory trust executed, acknowledged and filed with the secretary of state in accordance with §103 of this title and (iii) shall not contain the word bank or any variation thereof except for the name of a bank reporting to and under the supervision of the state bank commissioner of this state or a subsidiary of a bank or savings association (as those terms are defined in the Federal Deposit Insurance Act, as amended, at 12 U.S.C. §1813), or a corporation regulated under the Bank Holding Company Act of 1956, as amended, 12 U.S.C. §1841 et seq., or the Home Owners' Loan Act, as amended, 12 U.S.C. §1461 et seq.; provided, however, that this section shall not be construed to prevent the use of the word bank or any variation thereof in a context clearly not purporting to refer to a banking business or otherwise likely to mislead the public about the nature of the business of the corporation or to lead to a pattern and practice of abuse that might cause harm to the interests of the public or the state as determined by the Division of Corporations in the Department of State; the word trust is also prohibited unless approved by the state bank commissioner. You can reserve a corporate name for $10 per name or a limited liability company, limited partnership, statutory trust, general partnership and limited liability partnership name for a fee of $75 per name.

Director Information

- Minimum number: one or more
- Residence requirements: no provision
- Age requirements: none
- Directors are not required to be listed in the articles of incorporation

Report Filing Requirements

A domestic profit corporation must file an Annual Franchise Tax Report by March 1 of each year for the previous calendar year. The reports are mailed to the Delaware Registered Agent in January. The filing fee to place the reports on file is $25. The corporation must also pay an annual franchise tax due which is based on the number of shares the corporation has authorized.

Detailed Tax Information

Delaware Division of Revenue
www.state.de.us/revenue/default.shtml

State and Federal Tax Forms

www.irs.ustreas.gov/formspubs/index.html

Securities Registration Information

www.state.de.us/securities

District Of Columbia

Department of Consumer and Regulatory Affairs
941 N. Capitol Street N.E.
Washington, DC 20002
1.202.442.4400
www.brc.dc.gov

Where to Get Forms and Background

http://dcra.dc.gov/dcra/cwp/view,a,1342,Q,600904,dcraNav,|33408|.asp

State Filing Fees

(Does not include processing fees specific to counties or types of industries)

• Domestic profit corporation	$150
• Foreign corporation	$200
• Domestic LLCs	$150

Naming Procedures for Corporations

The name must contain the word Corporation, Company, Incorporated, Limited or an abbreviation thereof. The name shall not be the same as or deceptively similar to name of a domestic profit corporation, authorized foreign corporation or reserved name already existing in the district. Naming fees are $35 for corporations and LLCs.

Director Information

- Minimum number: one or more
- Residence requirements: no provision
- Age requirements: none
- Directors are required to be listed in the articles of incorporation

Report Filing Requirements

District of Columbia corporations and qualified foreign corporations must file an annual report no later than April 15. The filing fee is $100. LLCs must file 2.year reports due on or before June 16 following the LLC's registration and on or before June 16 every 2 years thereafter.

Detailed Tax Information

District of Columbia Office of Tax and Revenue
http://cfo.dc.gov/otr/site/default.asp?otrNAV_GID

State and Federal Tax Forms

www.irs.ustreas.gov/formspubs/index.html

Securities Registration Information

www.disb.dc.gov/disr/site/default.asp

Florida

Florida Department of State Division of Corporations
Corporate Filings
P.O. Box 6327
Tallahassee, FL 32314
1.850.245.6052
www.sunbiz.org/index.html

Where to Get Forms and Background

www.dos.state.fl.us/doc/form_download.html

State Filing Fees

(Does not include processing fees specific to counties or types of industries)

• Domestic profit corporation	$78.75
• Foreign corporation	$78.75
• Domestic LLCs	$125

Naming Procedures for Corporations

The name must contain the word Corporation, Company, Incorporated or an abbreviation thereof. The name may not contain language stating or implying that the corporation is organized for purposes other than that permitted by Florida law or the articles of incorporation. The name must be such as will distinguish it from another corporation formed in the state. Fictitious name fee is $50.

Director Information

- Minimum number: one or more
- Residence requirements: no provision
- Age requirements: directors must be at least 18 years of age
- Directors are not required to be listed in the articles of incorporation

Report Filing Requirements

Florida corporations must file an annual report by May 1, with a filing fee of $150.

Detailed Tax Information

State of Florida Department of Revenue
www.state.fl.us/dor

State and Federal Tax Forms

www.irs.ustreas.gov/formspubs/index.htm

Securities Registration Information

www.dbf.state.fl.us

Georgia

Office of Secretary of State Corporations Division
2 MLK Jr. Drive S.E.
Suite 315, West Tower
Atlanta, GA 30334
1.404.656.2817
www.sos.state.ga.us/corporations/filing

Where to Get Forms and Background

www.sos.state.ga.us/corporations

State Filing Fees

(Does not include processing fees specific to counties or types of industries)

• Domestic profit corporation	$100
• Foreign corporation	$100
• Domestic LLCs	$100

Naming Procedures for Corporations

The name shall include the word Corporation, Company, Incorporated, Limited or an abbreviation thereof. The name shall not exceed 80 characters, including spaces and punctuation. The name may not contain language stating or implying the corporation is organized for a purpose other than that permitted by Georgia law or the articles of incorporation. The name may not contain anything that, in the reasonable judgment of the secretary of state, is obscene. The name must be distinguishable from the other corporation names in the state. Name reservation fee for corporations and LLCs is $25.

Director Information

- Minimum number: one or more
- Residence requirements: no provision
- Age requirements: directors must be at least 18 years of age
- Directors are not required to be listed in the articles of incorporation

Report Filing Requirements

Annual reports are due by April 1 of each year. Corporations also must make an original report within 90 days of incorporation. The annual registration fee is $15.

Detailed Tax Information

Georgia Department of Revenue
www.etax.dor.ga.gov

State and Federal Tax Forms

www.irs.ustreas.gov/formspubs.index.htm

Securities Registration Information

www.sos.state.ga.us/securities

Hawaii

State of Hawaii
Department of Commerce and Consumer Affairs
Business Registration Division
1010 Richards Street
P.O. Box 40
Honolulu, HI 96810
1.808.586.2744
www.businessregistrations.com

Where to Get Forms and Background

www.hawaii.gov/dcca/areas/breg/registration

State Filing Fees

(Does not include processing fees specific to counties or types of industries)

• Domestic profit corporation	$50
• Foreign corporation	$50
• Domestic LLCs	$50

Naming Procedures for Corporations

The name shall contain the word Corporation, Incorporated, Limited or an abbreviation thereof. The name shall not be the same as or substantially identical to the name of any other corporation, partnership or foreign corporation or partnership existing or authorized to transact business within the state. The naming fee for corporations and LLCs is $10.

Director Information

- Minimum number: not less than three, unless there are only one or two shareholders of record; then the number of directors may be fewer than three but not fewer than the number of shareholders
- Residency requirements: none
- Age requirements: none
- Directors are not required to be listed in the articles of incorporation

Report Filing Requirements

Hawaii corporations and qualified foreign corporations must file an annual report by March 31. Filing fee is $25. Legislation pending in 2005 will lower the filing fee to $10.

Detailed Tax Information

Hawaii Department of Taxation
www.state.hi.us/tax/tax.htm

State and Federal Tax Forms

www.irs.ustreas.gov/formspubs/index.htm

Securities Registration Information

www.hawaii.gov/dcca/areas/sec

Idaho

Office of the Secretary of State
700 West Jefferson
Boise, ID 83720
1.208.334.2300
www.idsos.state.id.us/corp/corindex.htm

Where to Get Forms and Background

www.idsos.state.id.us/corp/corindex.htm

State Filing Fees

(Does not include processing fees specific to counties or types of industries)

• Domestic profit corporation	$100 (untyped, $120)
• Foreign corporation	$100 (untyped, $120)
• Domestic LLCs	$100 (untyped, $120)

Naming Procedures for Corporations

The corporation name must contain the word Corporation, Company, Incorporated, Limited or an abbreviation thereof, provided that if Company or Co. is used, it may not be immediately preceded by the word and or the symbol &. The name may not contain any word or phrase indicating or implying the corporation is organized for any purpose other than one or more of the purposes contained in its articles of incorporation. The name may not be the same as or deceptively similar to that of a domestic corporation or a qualified foreign corporation or a reserved name, with qualified exceptions. The limited liability company must contain the words limited liability company or limited company or any of the following abbreviations: L.L.C., L.C., LLC or LC. The naming fee for corporations is $25.

Director/Manager.Member Information

- Minimum number: one or more
- Residence requirements: no provision (registered agents must be Idaho residents)
- Age requirements: none
- Directors are not required to be listed in the articles of incorporation
- Manager.members are required to be listed in the articles of organization for the LLCs

Report Filing Requirements

Idaho corporations, qualified foreign corporations, Idaho limited liability companies and qualified foreign limited liability companies must file an annual corporate report, which is due the last day of the month in the anniversary month of incorporation or organization. If on time, there is no filing fee. The secretary of state's office mails the form 2 months before its due date.

Detailed Tax Information

Idaho State Tax Commission
http://tax.idaho.gov

State and Federal Tax Forms

www.irs.ustreas.gov/formspubs/index.htm

Securities Registration Information

http://finance.idaho.gov

Illinois

Kenneth V. Buzbee, Director
Illinois Secretary of State/Business Services
Michael J. Howlett Building
501 S. 2nd Street, Room 328
Springfield, IL 62756
1.217.782.6961

or

69 West Washington Street
Suite 1240
Chicago, IL 60602
1.312.793.3380
www.cyberdriveillinois.com/departments/business_services/home.html

Where to Get Forms and Background

www.cyberdriveillinois.com/departments/business_services/publications_and_forms/home.htm

State Filing Fees

(Does not include processing fees specific to counties or types of industries)

• Domestic profit corporation	$150
• Foreign corporation	$150
• Domestic LLCs	$300

Naming Procedures for Corporations

The name shall contain the word Corporation, Company, Incorporated, Limited or an abbreviation thereof. The name shall not contain any word or phrase indicating or implying it is organized to conduct the business of insurance, assurance, indemnity, acceptance of savings deposit, banking or corporate fiduciary.
The name shall be distinguishable from the name of any domestic or foreign corporation authorized to transact business or a name exclusive right to which is, at the time, reserved or registered. Name fee is $25, and the reservation remains effective for 90 days.

Director Information

- Minimum number: one or more
- Residence requirements: no provision
- Age requirements: none
- Directors are not required to be listed in the articles of incorporation

Report Filing Requirements

Domestic Illinois corporations must file a domestic profit corporation annual report.

Detailed Tax Information

Illinois Department of Revenue
www.revenue.state.il.us

State and Federal Tax Forms

www.irs.ustreas.gov/formspubs/index.html

Securities Registration Information

www.cyberdriveillinois.com/departments/securities/home.html

Indiana

Indiana Secretary of State/Business Services Division
302 W. Washington Street
Room E018
Indianapolis, IN 46204
1.317.232.6576
www.state.in.us/sos/business/corps/general.htm

Where to Get Forms and Background

www.state.in.us/sos/business/corps/sched.html

State Filing Fees

(Does not include processing fees specific to counties or types of industries)

• Domestic profit corporation	$90
• Foreign corporation	$90
• Domestic LLCs	$90

Naming Procedures for Corporations

The name must include the word Corporation, Incorporated, Company, Limited or an abbreviation thereof. The name cannot imply purpose or power not possessed by corporations organized under Indiana Business Corporation Law or in the articles of incorporation. The name must be distinguishable from a reserved name or the name of any other corporation then existing under the laws of the state, unless consent of the other user is obtained. Name registration fee is $20 to reserve a name for 120 days.

Director Information

- Minimum number: one or more
- Residence requirements: no provision
- Age requirements: none
- Directors are not required to be listed in the articles of incorporation

Report Filing Requirements

Indiana corporations and qualified foreign corporations must file a biennial corporate report with the secretary of state and a $30 fee.

Detailed Tax Information

Indiana Department of Revenue
www.in.gov/dor

State and Federal Tax Forms

www.irs.ustreas.gov/formspubs.index.html

Securities Registration Information

www.in.gov/sos/securities/index.html

Iowa

Business Services Division
Office of the Secretary of State
First Floor, Lucas Building
Des Moines, IA 50319
1.515.281.5204
www.sos.state.ia.us

Where to Get Forms and Background

www.sos.state.ia.us/business/handbookintro.html#3

Where to Get Forms

www.sos.state.ia.us/business/form/html

State Filing Fees

(Does not include processing fees specific to counties or types of industries)

• Domestic corporation	$50
• Foreign corporation	$100
• Domestic LLCs	$50

Naming Procedures for Corporations

The name must contain the words Corporation, Incorporated, Company, Limited or the abbreviation Corp., Inc., Co., Ltd. or words or abbreviations of like import in another language. Name reservation costs $10 for 120 days.

Director Information

- Minimum number: one or more
- Residence requirements: no provision
- Age requirements: none
- Directors are not required to be listed in the articles of incorporation

Report Filing Requirements

Each domestic profit corporation and each foreign corporation is required to file a biennial report according to IC § 490.1622. The first biennial report shall be delivered to the secretary of state for filing between January 1 and April 1 of the first even.numbered year following the calendar year in which a domestic profit corporation was incorporated or a foreign corporation was authorized to transact business. Subsequent biennial reports must be delivered to the secretary of state between January 1 and April 1 of the following even.numbered calendar years.

Detailed Tax Information

Iowa Department of Revenue
www.state.ia.us/tax

State and Federal Tax Forms

www.irs.ustreas.gov/formspubs/index.html

Securities Registration Information

www.iowa/gov/state/main/business_portal/index/html

Kansas

Kansas Secretary of State/Business Services
Memorial Hall, First Floor
120 SW 10th Avenue
Topeka, KS 66612
1.785.296.4564
www.kssos.org/business/business.html

Where to Get Forms and Background

www.kssos.org/forms/forms.html

State Filing Fees

(Does not include processing fees specific to counties or types of industries)

• Domestic profit corporation	$90/$84 online
• Foreign corporation	$115
• Domestic LLCs	$165/$160 online

Naming Procedures for Corporations

The name shall contain the word Association, Church, College, Company, Corporation, Club, Foundation, Fund, Incorporated, Institute, Society, Union, Syndicate, Limited or the abbreviation Co., Corp., Inc. or Ltd. The name shall be distinguishable upon the records of the secretary of state from names of other corporations, limited liability companies and limited partnerships.

Director Information

- Minimum number: one or more
- Residence requirements: no provision
- Age requirements: none
- Directors are not required to be listed in the articles of incorporation

Report Filing Requirements

Kansas corporations must file a corporate annual report and must pay a minimum franchise tax of $20.

Detailed Tax Information

Kansas Department of Revenue
www.ksrevenue.org

State and Federal Tax Forms

www.irs.ustreas.gov/formspubs/index.html

Securities Registration Information

www.securities.state.ks.us

Kentucky

Kentucky Secretary of State
700 Capital Avenue
Suite 152, State Capitol
Frankfort, KY 40601
1.502.564.3490
www.sos.ky.gov

Where to Get Forms and Background

www.sos.ky.gov/business/filings/forms

State Filing Fees

(Does not include processing fees specific to counties or types of industries)

• Domestic profit corporation	$40
• Foreign corporation	$90
• Domestic LLCs	$40

Naming Procedures for Corporations

The corporate name must be distinguishable upon records of secretary of state from the name of existing business entities filed with the secretary of state. The corporation may use one of these names if another corporation consents in writing or in certain other enumerated cases. The name must include the word Corporation, Incorporated, Company, Limited or an abbreviation thereof. The name shall not contain language stating or implying the corporation is organized for a purpose other than that permitted by the act or the articles.

Director Information

- Minimum number: one or more
- Residence requirements: no provision
- Age requirements: none
- Directors are not required to be listed in the articles of incorporation

Report Filing Requirements

Kentucky corporations and qualified foreign corporations must file an annual report due by June 30 of each year. The filing fee is $15.

Detailed Tax Information

Kentucky Department of Revenue
http://revenue.ky.gov

State and Federal Tax Forms

www.irs.ustreas.gov/formspubs/index.html

Securities Registration Information

www.dfi.state.ky.us

Louisiana

Secretary of State
Commercial Division
P.O. Box 94125
Baton Rouge, LA 70804
1.225.925.4704
www.sec.state.la.us/comm/comm.index.htm

Where to Get Forms and Background

www.sec.state.la.us/comm/corp/corp.filings.htm

State Filing Fees

(Does not include processing fees specific to counties or types of industries)

• Domestic profit corporation	$60
• Foreign corporation	$100
• Domestic LLCs	$75

Naming Procedures for Corporations

The name of the corporation shall contain the word Corporation, Incorporated, Limited or an abbreviation thereof. The name may contain the word Company or the abbreviation Co., if Company or Co. is not immediately preceded by the word and or the symbol &. The name must not be the same or deceptively similar to any other reserved or registered names of another corporation. The name cannot use certain enumerated words relating to banking, savings and loans or insurance. Name reservation is $25.

Director Information

• Minimum number: not less than one natural person

• Residency requirements: no provision

• Age requirements: none

• Directors are not required to be listed in the articles of incorporation

Report Filing Requirements

Louisiana corporations must file annual reports before the anniversary date of incorporation. The filing fee is $25.

Detailed Tax Information

Louisiana Department of Revenue
www.rev.state.la.us

State and Federal Tax Forms

www.irs.ustreas.gov/formspubs/index.html

Securities Registration Information

www.ofi.state.la.us/securit.htm

Maine

Department of the Secretary of State
Burton M. Cross State Office Building
Fourth Floor
101 State House Station
Augusta, ME 04333
1.207.624.7736
www.maine.gov/sos/cec/corp

Where to Get Forms and Background

www.maine.gov/sos/cec/corp

State Filing Fees

(Does not include processing fees specific to counties or types of industries)

• Domestic profit corporation	$145
• Foreign corporation	$250
• Domestic LLCs	$175

Naming Procedures for Corporations

A corporate name may not contain language stating or implying that the corporation is organized for a purpose other than that permitted by or entity's articles of incorporation or organization. A name must be distinguishable on the records of the secretary of state from:

(a) The name of a corporation, nonprofit corporation, limited liability company, limited liability partnership or limited partnership that is incorporated, organized or authorized to transact business or carry on activities in this state;

(b) Assumed, fictitious, reserved and registered name filings for all entities; and

(c) Marks registered under Title 10, chapter 301.A unless the registered owner or holder of the mark is the same person or entity as the corporation seeking to use a name that is not distinguishable on the records of the secretary of state and files proof of ownership with the secretary of state. Name reservation fee is $20.

Director Information

- • Minimum number: one or more
- • Residence requirements: no provision
- • Age requirements: none
- • Directors are elected at the first annual shareholders' meeting and at each annual meeting thereafter unless their terms are staggered

Report Filing Requirements

All domestic and foreign corporations and LLCs must file an annual report with a fee of $85 for domestic entities and $150 for foreign entities.

Detailed Tax Information

Maine Revenue Services
www.state.me.us/revenue/homepage.html

State and Federal Tax Forms

www.irs.ustreas.gov/formspubs/index.html

Securities Registration Information

www.state.me.us/pfr/sec/sec_about.htm

Maryland

Maryland State Department of Assessments and Taxation (SDAT)
Corporate Charter Division
301 W. Preston Street
Baltimore, MD 21201
1.410.767.1340
www.dat.state.md.us

Where to Get Forms and Background

www.dat.state.md.us/sdatweb/charter.html

State Filing Fees

(Does not include processing fees specific to counties or types of industries)

• Domestic profit corporation	$120
• Foreign corporation	$120
• Domestic LLCs	$100

Naming Procedures for Corporations

The name must indicate the corporate status and contain the word Corporation, Incorporated, Limited or an abbreviation thereof. The name may also contain or end with the word Company, which can never be preceded by the word and or the symbol &. Names shall not imply any purpose that is not authorized by the charter. They shall not be the same as and must be distinguishable upon the record of the department from other domestic or qualified foreign corporations. This rule and standard applies to domestic and registered foreign LPs, LLCs and LLPs as well. The cost of reserving a name is $7.

Director Information

- Minimum number: at least one initial director must be listed in the articles of incorporation
- Residence requirements: no provision
- Age requirements: none
- Directors are not required to be listed in the articles of incorporation

Report Filing Requirements

Maryland corporations must file an annual Personal Property Report no later than April 15. The annual report fee is $300 a year.

Detailed Tax Information

Maryland Department of Assessments and Taxation
www.dat.state.md.us

State and Federal Tax Forms

www.irs.ustreas.gov/formspubs/index.html

Securities Registration Information

www.oag.state.md.us/Securities

Massachusetts

Massachusetts Secretary of the Commonwealth
Corporations Division
1 Ashburton Place, 17th Floor
Boston, MA 02108
1.617.727.9640
www.state.ma.us/sec/cor

Where to Get Forms and Background

www.sec.state.ma.us/cor/corfees.htm

State Filing Fees

(Does not include processing fees specific to counties or types of industries)

• Domestic profit corporation	$275
• Foreign corporation	$400 ($375 by fax)
• Domestic LLCs	$500

Naming Procedures for Corporations

The corporation may assume any name indicating it is incorporated. The name may not be the same as the name or trade name of a Massachusetts corporation, foreign corporation, firm, association, person carrying on business in Massachusetts or name under reservation, nor so similar as to be mistaken for that other name unless given the written consent of existing corporation, firm, association or person.

Director Information

- Minimum number: not less than three, unless there are only one or two shareholders of record; then the number of directors may be less than three but not less than the number of shareholders
- Residence requirements: no provision
- Age requirements: none
- Directors are required to be listed in the articles of incorporation

Report Filing Requirements

Massachusetts corporations must file an annual report before the fifteenth day of the third month after the close of the corporation's fiscal year. Filing fee is $125.

Detailed Tax Information

Commonwealth of Massachusetts Department of Revenue
www.dor.state.ma.us

State and Federal Tax Forms

www.irs.ustreas.gov/formspubs/index.html

Securities Registration Information

www.sec.state.ma.us/sct/sctidx.htm

Michigan

Michigan Department of Consumer & Industry Services
Bureau of Commercial Services—Corporation Division
7150 Harris Drive
P.O. Box 30054
Lansing, MI 48909
1.517.241.6470
www.michigan.gov/businessstartup

Where to Get Forms and Background

http://michigan.gov/cis/0,1607,7.154.10557_12901...,00.html

State Filing Fees

(Does not include processing fees specific to counties or types of industries)

• Domestic LLCs	$500
• Domestic profit corporation	$60
• Domestic LLCs	$50

Naming Procedures for Corporations

The name shall contain the word Corporation, Company, Incorporated, Limited or an abbreviation thereof. The name shall not indicate that the corporation was formed for a purpose other than one or more purposes permitted in the articles. The name shall be distinguishable from the corporate name of domestic or foreign corporations, domestic or foreign limited partnerships or names currently reserved. The name cannot use the words Bank, Industrial Bank, Deposit, Surety, Security, Trust or Trust Company.

Director Information

- Minimum number: one or more
- Residence requirements: no provision
- Age requirements: none
- Directors are not required to be listed in the articles of incorporation

Report Filing Requirements

Michigan corporations must file an annual report at $15 a year.

Detailed Tax Information

Michigan Department of Treasury
www.michigan.gov/treasury

State and Federal Tax Forms

www.irs.ustreas.gov/formspubs/index.html

Securities Registration Information

www.michigan.gov/cis/0,1607,7.154.10555_13044_13209---00.html

Minnesota

Secretary of State
Business Services Division
180 State Office Building
100 Rev. Dr. Martin Luther King Jr. Boulevard
St. Paul, MN 55155
1.651.296.2803
www.sos.state.mn.us/business/index.html

Where to Get Forms and Background

www.sos.state.mn.us/business/bc.html

State Filing Fees

(Does not include processing fees specific to counties or types of industries)

• Domestic profit corporation	$135
• Foreign corporation	$200
• Domestic LLCs	$135

Naming Procedures for Corporations

The name shall not be deceptively similar to the names of any other domestic corporation, limited partnership, limited liability partnership, limited liability company, foreign corporation, foreign limited partnership, foreign limited liability partnership or foreign limited liability company authorized to do business in the state unless: (1) such other corporation is about to change its name, cease business, dissolve or withdraw and (2) written consent therefrom is obtained. The name shall contain the word Corporation, Incorporated, Limited or the abbreviation thereof, or shall contain the word Company or the abbreviation Co., only if it is not immediately preceded by the word and or the character &. Name reservation fee is $15.

Director Information

• Minimum number: one or more

• Residence requirements: no provision

• Age requirements: none

• Directors are not required to be listed in the articles of incorporation

Report Filing Requirements

Minnesota corporations must file an annual statement each year by February 15.

Detailed Tax Information

Minnesota Department of Revenue
www.taxes.state.mn.us

State and Federal Tax Forms

www.irs.ustreas.gov/formspubs/index.html

Securities Registration Information

www.state.mn.us/cgi.bin/portal/mn/jsp/content.do?subchannel=.536881759&id=.536881351&agency=Commerce

Mississippi

Office of the Mississippi Secretary of State
700 N. Street
Jackson, MS 39202
1.800.256.3494
1.601.359.1633
www.sos.state.ms.us/busserv/corp/corporations.asp

Where to Get Forms and Background

www.sos.state.ms.us/busserv/corp/corporations.asp

State Filing Fees

(Does not include processing fees specific to counties or types of industries)

• Domestic profit corporation	$50
• Foreign corporation	$50
• Domestic LLCs	$50

Naming Procedures for Corporations

The name must contain the word Corporation, Company, Incorporated, Limited or the abbreviation Corp., Co., Inc., Ltd. or words or abbreviations of like import in another language. The name may not contain language implying that the corporation is organized for any unauthorized purpose. The name must be distinguishable from that of domestic or foreign corporations entitled to do business in the state, or to reserved or registered names.

Director Information

- Minimum number: one or more
- Residence requirements: no provision
- Age requirements: none
- Directors are not required to be listed in the articles of incorporation

Report Filing Requirements

Mississippi corporations must file a corporate annual report with a filing fee of $25.

Detailed Tax Information

Mississippi State Tax Commission
www.mstc.state.ms.us

State and Federal Tax Forms

www.irs.ustreas.gov/formspubs/index.html

Securities Registration Information

www.sos.state.ms.us/regenf/securities/SecAct/SecuritiesAct.asp

Missouri

State of Missouri
Corporations Division
P.O. Box 778
600 W. Main Street, Rm. 322
Jefferson City, MO 65101
1.573.751.4153
www.sos.mo.gov/business/corporations

Where to Get Forms and Background

www.sos.mo.gov/business/corporations/forms.asp

State Filing Fees

(Does not include processing fees specific to counties or types of industries)

• Domestic profit corporation	Missouri domestic profit corporation fees are based on dollar amount of authorized capital. The fee is $50 for the first $30,000 or less of authorized shares, and a further sum of $5 for every additional $10,000 of authorized shares
• Foreign corporations	$155
• Domestic LLCs	$105

Naming Procedures for Corporations

The name shall contain the word Corporation, Company, Incorporated, Limited or an abbreviation thereof. The name may not contain any word or phrase indicating or implying the corporation is a governmental agency or that it is organized for any purpose other than the purpose for which corporations may be organized under the laws of Missouri. The name shall be distinguishable from the name of any domestic or foreign corporation authorized to do business in Missouri, or any limited partnership, limited liability company or reserved name filed with the state.

Director Information

- Minimum number: not less than three, unless there are only one or two shareholders of record; then the number of directors may be less than three but not less than the number of shareholders
- Residence requirements: no provision
- Age requirements: directors must be natural people who are at least 18 years of age
- Directors are not required to be listed in the articles of incorporation

Report Filing Requirements

Missouri corporations must file an annual report due by the fifteenth day of the fourth month of the corporation's fiscal year.

Detailed Tax Information

Missouri Department of Revenue
www.dor.state.mo.us

State and Federal Tax Forms

www.irs.ustreas.gov/formspubs/index.html

Securities Registration Information

www.sos.mo.gov/securities

Montana

Bob Brown
Secretary of State
P.O. Box 202801
Helena, MT 59620
1.406.444.3665
www.sos.mt.gov

Where to Get Forms and Background

www.sos.state.mt.us/css/BSB/Filing_Forms.asp#CORPORATIONS

State Filing Fees

(Does not include processing fees specific to counties or types of industries)

• Domestic profit corporation	$70
• Foreign corporation	$70
• Domestic LLCs	$70

Naming Procedures for Corporations

The name must be distinguishable from that of any corporation authorized to transact business in the state, a reserved or registered name, the fictitious name of a foreign corporation or any assumed business name, limited partnership, limited liability company, trademark or service mark. The name must contain the word Corporation, Company, Incorporated, Limited or an abbreviation thereof. The state also requires a registered agent's name, Montana address and signature on file.

Director Information

- Minimum number: one or more
- Residence requirements: no provision
- Age requirements: none
- Directors are not required to be listed in the articles of incorporation

Report Filing Requirements

Montana corporations must file an annual corporation report with a $15 fee if filed on or before April 15. Online filing fee is $10.

Detailed Tax Information

Montana Department of Revenue
www.state.mt.us/revenue

State and Federal Tax Forms

www.irs.ustreas.gov/formspubs/index.html

Securities Registration Information

www.discoveringmontana.com/sao/securities

Nebraska

Corporations Division
Room 1301
State Capitol
P.O. Box 94608
Lincoln, NE 68509
1.402.471.4079
www.sos.state.ne.us

Where to Get Forms and Background

www.sos.state.ne.us/business/corp_serv/corp_form.html

State Filing Fees

(Does not include processing fees specific to counties or types of industries)

• Domestic profit corporation	$60 (for capitalization up to $10,000)
• Foreign corporation	$60 (for capitalization up to $10,000)
• Domestic LLCs	$100

Naming Procedures for Corporations

The name must contain the word Corporation, Company, Incorporated, Limited or the abbreviation Corp., Inc., Co. or Ltd. The name shall be distinguishable from the name of a corporation incorporated in or authorized to transact business in the state, a corporate name reserved or registered, the fictitious name of a foreign corporation, the corporate name of a not-for-profit corporation incorporated in or authorized to transact business in this state, a trade name registered in the state, the trade name of domestic or foreign corporations entitled to do business in the state, or a name that is reserved or registered. However, the similar name may be registered if corporation affected consents in writing or by court decree.

Director Information

- Minimum number: one or more
- Residence requirements: no provision
- Age requirements: none
- Directors are not required to be listed in the articles of incorporation

Report Filing Requirements

Nebraska corporations must file an Annual Corporation Occupation Tax Report. The fee is based upon the paid.up capital stock for domestic profit corporations and the real estate and personal property in use in Nebraska for foreign corporations.

Detailed Tax Information

Nebraska Department of Revenue
www.revenue.state.ne.us/index.html

State and Federal Tax Forms

www.irs.ustreas.gov/formspubs/index.html

Securities Registration Information

www.ndbf.org/press/press.shtml

Nevada

Secretary of State
New Filings Division
202 N. Carson Street
Carson City, NV 89701
1.775.684.5708

or

555 East Washington Blvd.
Las Vegas, NV 89101
Corporations Division Suite #4000
1.702.486.2880
http://secretaryofstate.biz/comm_rec/crforms/crforms.htm

Where to Get Forms and Background

http://secretaryofstate.biz/comm_rec/crforms/domestic_index.htm

State Filing Fees

(Does not include processing fees specific to counties or types of industries)

• Domestic profit corporation	$75 (for corporations $75,000 or less in capitalization)
• Foreign corporation	$75 (for corporations $75,000 or less in capitalization)
• Domestic LLCs	$75

Naming Procedures for Corporations

The name must contain the word Corporation, Company, Incorporated, Limited or the abbreviation Corp., Inc., Co. or Ltd. The name shall be distinguishable from the name of a corporation incorporated in or authorized to transact business in the state, a corporate name reserved or registered, the fictitious name of a foreign corporation, the corporate name of a not.for.profit corporation incorporated in or authorized to transact business in this state, a trade name registered in the state, the trade name of domestic or foreign corporations entitled to do business in the state or a name that is reserved or registered. However, the similar name may be registered if corporation affected consents in writing, or by court decree. Name reservation costs $25.

Director Information

- Minimum number: one or more
- Residence requirements: no provision
- Age requirements: none
- Directors are not required to be listed in the articles of incorporation

Report Filing Requirements

Nevada corporations must file an initial list of officers and directors form by the first day of the second month following the incorporation date. Filing fee is $125.

Detailed Tax Information

Nevada Department of Taxation
http://tax.state.nv.us

State and Federal Tax Forms

www.irs.ustreas.gov/formspubs/index.html

Securities Registration Information

http://sos.state.nv.us/securities

New Hampshire

Secretary of State
Corporation Division
107 N. Main Street
Concord, NH 03301
1.603.271.3244
www.state.nh.us/sos/coporate/index.htm

Where to Get Forms and Background

www.sos.nh.gov/corporate/Corpforms.html

State Filing Fees

(Does not include processing fees specific to counties or types of industries)

• Domestic profit corporation	$100
• Foreign corporation	$100
• Domestic LLCs	$35

Naming Procedures for Corporations

The name must contain the word Corporation, Company, Incorporated, Limited or the abbreviation Corp., Inc., Co. or Ltd. The name shall be distinguishable from the name of a corporation incorporated in or authorized to transact business in the state, a corporate name reserved or registered, the fictitious name of a foreign corporation, the corporate name of a not.for.profit corporation incorporated in or authorized to transact business in this state, a trade name registered in the state, the trade name of domestic or foreign corporations entitled to do business in the state or a name that is reserved or registered. However, the similar name may be registered if corporation affected consents in writing, or by court decree. Name reservation costs $25.

Director Information

- Minimum number: one or more
- Residence requirements: no provision
- Age requirements: none
- Directors are not required to be listed in the articles of incorporation

Report Filing Requirements

New Hampshire corporations must file an annual report at a cost of $100.

Detailed Tax Information

New Hampshire Department of Revenue Administration
www.state.nh.us/revenue

State and Federal Tax Forms

www.irs.ustreas.gov/formspubs/index.html

Securities Registration Information

www.sos.nh.gov/securities

New Jersey

New Jersey Department of Treasury
Division of Revenue/Corporate Filing
P.O. Box 308
Trenton, NJ 08625
1.609.292.9292
www.state.nj.us/treasury/revenue/dcr/programs/corpfile.html

Where to Get Forms and Background

www.state.nj.us/treasury/revenue/gettingregistered.htm

State Filing Fees

(Does not include processing fees specific to counties or types of industries)

• Domestic profit corporation	$125
• Foreign corporation	$125
• Domestic LLCs	$125

Naming Procedures for Corporations

The name shall not contain any word, phrase, abbreviation or derivative thereof indicating or implying it is organized for any purpose other than one or more purposes permitted by its certificate of incorporation. The name shall be distinguishable from the names of other for.profit and nonprofit domestic corporations, foreign corporations, domestic and foreign limited partnerships, and current name reservations or registrations. The name shall not contain any word, phrase, abbreviation or derivative thereof which use is prohibited or restricted by any other statute of New Jersey. The name shall contain the word Corporation,

Company, Incorporated, an abbreviation thereof or the abbreviation Ltd. Name reservation fee is $50.

Director Information

- Minimum number: one or more
- Residence requirements: no provision
- Age requirements: directors must be a natural person at least 18 years of age
- Directors are not required to be listed in the articles of incorporation
- Registered agents must have a New Jersey street address

Report Filing Requirements

New Jersey corporations must file an annual report with a fee of $50.

Detailed Tax Information

New Jersey Division of Taxation
www.state.nj.us/treasury/taxation

State and Federal Tax Forms

www.irs.ustreas.gov/formspubs/index.html

Securities Registration Information

www.state.nj.us/lps/ca/bos.htm

New Mexico

Public Regulations Commission
Corporations Division
P.O. Box 1269
Santa Fe, NM 87504
1.505.827.4502
www.nmprc.state.nm.us/corporations/corpshome.htm

Where to Get Forms and Background

www.nmprc.state.nm.us/corporations/corpsforms.htm

State Filing Fees

(Does not include processing fees specific to counties or types of industries)

- Domestic profit corporation $100 (minimum)
- Foreign corporation $200 (minimum)
- Domestic LLCs $50

Naming Procedures for Corporations

The name must contain the word Corporation, Incorporation, Company, Limited or an abbreviation thereof. The name must not be the same as, or confusingly similar to, a name of any domestic or foreign corporation, or a name reserved by or registered by another corporation, unless written permission of other corporation is obtained. The name must not imply a purpose other than that contained in the charter. Name reservation fee is $25.

Director Information

- Minimum number: one or more
- Residency requirements: registered agent/registered office must be maintained in New Mexico
- Age requirements: none
- Directors are required to be listed in the articles of incorporation

Report Filing Requirements

New Mexico corporations must file a first report within 30 days of letter confirming filing. Filing fee is $25.

Detailed Tax Information

State of New Mexico Taxation and Revenue
www.state.nm.us/tax

State and Federal Tax Forms

www.irs.ustreas.gov/formspubs/index.html

Securities Registration Information

www.rld.state.nm.us/Securities

New York

Department of State
Division of Corporations
41 State Street
Albany, NY 12231
1.518.473.2281
www.dos.state.ny.us/corp/corpwww.html

Where to Get Forms and Background

www.dos.state.ny.us/corp/corpfees.html

State Filing Fees

(Does not include processing fees specific to counties or types of industries)

• Domestic profit corporation	$125
• Foreign corporation	$225
• Domestic LLCs	$200

Naming Procedures for Corporations

The name must contain the word Corporation, Incorporated, Limited or an abbreviation thereof. The name may not be the same as, or so similar or confusing to, that of any domestic or authorized foreign corporation or reserved name. The name may not contain any word or phrase indicating the corporation is formed for any purpose other than the purpose for which the corporation may be and is formed. The use of certain enumerated words and abbreviations including banking, insurance and various professions is prohibited or restricted. Name reservation fee is $20.

Director Information

- Minimum number: not less than three, unless there are only one or two shareholders of record; then the number of directors may be less than three but not less than the number of shareholders.
- Residence requirements: no provision
- Age requirements: directors must be a natural person at least 18 years of age
- Directors are not required to be listed in the articles of incorporation.

Report Filing Requirements

New York corporations must file a biennial statement with a $9 filing fee.

Detailed Tax Information

New York State Department of Taxation and Finance
www.tax.state.ny.us

State and Federal Tax Forms

www.irs.ustreas.gov/formspubs/index.html

Securities Registration Information

www.oag.state.ny.us/investors/investors.html

North Carolina

Corporations Division
P.O. Box 29622
Raleigh, NC 27626
1.919.807.2225
www.secstate.state.nc.us/corporations

Where to Get Forms and Background

www.secretary.state.nc.us/corporations/ThePage.aspx

State Filing Fees

(Does not include processing fees specific to counties or types of industries)

• Domestic profit corporation	$125
• Foreign corporation	$125
• Domestic LLCs	$125

Naming Procedures for Corporations

The name must contain the word Corporation, Incorporated, Company, Limited or the abbreviation Corp., Inc., Co. or Ltd. Names may not contain language stating or implying the corporation is organized for purposes not permitted by the act and its articles. The name must be distinguishable from the name of any domestic, foreign or nonprofit corporation, or the reserved or registered name of a limited liability company or partnership. Name reservation fee is $30.

Director Information

- Minimum number: one or more
- Residence requirements: no provision
- Age requirements: none
- Directors are not required to be listed in the articles of incorporation

Report Filing Requirements

North Carolina corporations must file an annual report with a $20 fee.

Detailed Tax Information

North Carolina Department of Revenue
www.dor.state.nc.us

State and Federal Tax Forms

www.irs.ustreas.gov/formspubs/index.html

Securities Registration Information

www.secretary.state.nc.us/SEC/ThePage.aspx

North Dakota

Business Division
Secretary of State
State of North Dakota
600 E. Boulevard Avenue, Dept. 108
Bismark, ND 58505
1.701.328.4284
www.state.nd.us/sec/businessreg/register.htm

Where to Get Forms and Background

www.state.nd.us/sec/businessserv/registrations/types/corporations/general/index.html

State Filing Fees

(Does not include processing fees specific to counties or types of industries)

• Domestic profit corporation	$80 (minimum)
• Foreign corporation	$125
• Domestic LLCs	$125

Naming Procedures for Corporations

The name must contain the word Corporation, Incorporated, Limited, Company or an abbreviation thereof. It must be in the English language or any other language expressed in English letters or characters. It may not contain words implying it is incorporated for a purpose other than business for which a company may be incorporated. The name may not be the same as, or deceptively similar to, the name of a domestic or foreign corporation, limited liability company, limited partnership, reserved name, registered fictitious name or trade name, unless consent is given. Name reservation fee is $10.

Director Information

- Minimum number: one or more
- Residence requirements: no provision
- Age requirements: directors must be a natural person at least 18 years of age
- Directors are required to be listed in the articles of incorporation

Report Filing Requirements

North Dakota corporations must file an annual report by August 1 with a fee of $25.

Detailed Tax Information

North Dakota Office of State Tax Commissioner
www.state.nd.us/taxdpt

State and Federal Tax Forms

www.irs.ustreas.gov/formspubs/index.html

Securities Registration Information

www.ndsecurities.com

Ohio

Secretary of State
P.O. Box 670
Columbus, OH 43216
1.614.466.3910
www.sos.state.oh.us/sos/busiserv/index.html

Where to Get Forms and Background

www.sos.state.oh.us/sos

State Filing Fees

(Does not include processing fees specific to counties or types of industries)

• Domestic profit corporation	$125
• Foreign corporation	$125
• Domestic LLCs	$125

Naming Procedures for Corporations

The name shall contain the word Company, Corporation, Incorporated or the abbreviation Co., Corp. or Inc. The name must be distinguishable from the name of another domestic or foreign corporation authorized to do business in the state or from any trade name. The name shall not contain language implying it is connected with a government agency of the United States. Name reservation is $50.

Director Information

- Minimum number: not less than three, unless there are only one or two shareholders of record; then the number of directors may be less than three but not less than the number of shareholders
- Residence requirements: no provision
- Age requirements: must be 18 years old
- Directors are not required to be listed in the articles of incorporation

Report Filing Requirements

Ohio corporations must file an annual report.

Detailed Tax Information

Ohio Department of Taxation
http://tax.ohio.gov

State and Federal Tax Forms

www.irs.ustreas.gov/formspubs/index.html

Securities Registration Information

www.securities.state.oh.us

Oklahoma

Secretary of State
2300 N. Lincoln Boulevard, Room 101
Oklahoma City, OK 73105
1.405.521.3912
www.sos.state.ok.us

Where to Get Forms and Background

www.sos.state.ok.us/forms/FORMS.HTM#Oklahoma%20Corp

State Filing Fees

(Does not include processing fees specific to counties or types of industries)

• Domestic profit corporation	$50 (minimum)
• Foreign corporation	$300 (minimum)
• Domestic LLCs	$100

Naming Procedures for Corporations

The name must contain the word Corporation, Company, Incorporated, Limited, Association, Club, Foundation, Fund, Institute, Society, Union, Syndicate or an abbreviation thereof. The name must be distinguishable from the name of any other corporation, limited partnership, trade name, fictitious name, reserved name, limited liability company, limited partnership or any limited liability company name filed with the secretary of state. Name reservation fee is $10.

Director Information

- Minimum number: one or more
- Residence requirements: no provision
- Age requirements: none
- Directors are not required to be listed in the articles of incorporation

Report Filing Requirements

Oklahoma corporations must file an annual report each year by July 1. Filing fee is $25.

Detailed Tax Information

Oklahoma Tax Commission
www.oktax.state.ok.us/oktax

State and Federal Tax Forms

www.irs.ustreas.gov/formspubs/index.html

Securities Registration Information

www.securities.state.ok.us

Oregon

Corporation Division
Business Registry Section
Public Service Building, Suite 151
55 Capitol Street NE
Salem, OR 97310
1.503.986.2200
www.filinginoregon.com

Where to Get Forms and Background

www.filinginoregon.com/forms/index.htm

State Filing Fees

(Does not include processing fees specific to counties or types of industries)

• Domestic profit corporation	$50
• Foreign corporation	$50
• Domestic LLCs	$50

Naming Procedures for Corporations

The name must contain the word Corporation, Company, Incorporated, Limited or an abbreviation thereof. The name shall not contain the word Cooperative. It must be distinguishable from the name of any corporation, reserved name, registered name, professional corporate name, nonprofit corporate name, cooperative name, limited partnership name, business trust name or assumed business name. The name shall be in the English alphabet. Name reservation fee $10.

Director Information

- Minimum number: one or more
- Residence requirements: no provision
- Age requirements: directors must be natural people at least 18 years of age
- Directors are not required to be listed in the articles of incorporation

Report Filing Requirements

Oregon corporations must file an annual report with a fee of $30.

Detailed Tax Information

Oregon Department of Revenue
http://egov.oregon.gov/DOR

State and Federal Tax Forms

www.irs.ustreas.gov/formspubs/index.html

Securities Registration Information

www.cbs.state.or.us/external/dfcs

Pennsylvania

Department of State Corporation Bureau
P.O. Box 8722
Harrisburg, PA 17105
1.717.787.1057
www.dos.state.pa.us/corps/site/default.asp

Where to Get Forms and Background

www.dos.state.pa.us/corps/cwp/view.asp?a=1093&Q=431210&corpsNav=

State Filing Fees

(Does not include processing fees specific to counties or types of industries)

• Domestic profit corporation	$125
• Foreign corporation	$250
• Domestic LLCs	$125

Naming Procedures for Corporations

The name shall contain the word Corporation, Company, Incorporated, Limited or an abbreviation thereof. The name may be in any language but must be expressed in English letters or characters or Arabic or Roman numerals. Name reservation fee is $70.

Director Information

- Minimum number: one or more
- Residence requirements: no provision
- Age requirements: directors must be natural people at least 18 years of age
- Directors are not required to be listed in the articles of incorporation

Report Filing Requirements

Pennsylvania corporations are not required to file annual reports.

Detailed Tax Information

Pennsylvania Department of Revenue
www.revenue.state.pa.us

State and Federal Tax Forms

www.irs.ustreas.gov/formspubs/index.html

Securities Registration Information

www.psc.state.pa.us

Rhode Island

Office of the Secretary of State
Matthew A. Brown Corporations Division, First Floor
100 N. Main Street
Providence, RI 02903
1.401.222.3040
www.state.ri.us

Where to Get Forms and Background

www2.corps.state.ri.us/corporations/forms

State Filing Fees

(Does not include processing fees specific to counties or types of industries)

• Domestic profit corporation	$230
• Foreign corporation	$310
• Domestic LLCs	$150

Naming Procedures for Corporations

The corporate name must contain the word Corporation, Company, Incorporated, Limited or an abbreviation thereof. The name must not be deceptively similar to any domestic or foreign corporation, limited partnership, foreign limited partnership authorized to do business in the state, or reserved or registered name, unless written consent is obtained from the holder of such name. The name may not contain any word implying the corporation was formed for a purpose for which it is not organized. Name reservation fee is $50.

Director Information

All director information is dependent on the type of corporate structure chosen. Contact the state at www.state.ri.us for more detail.

Report Filing Requirements

Rhode Island domestic and foreign corporations must file annual reports at a filing fee of $50.

Detailed Tax Information

Rhode Island Division of Taxation
www.tax.state.ri.us

State and Federal Tax Forms

www.irs.ustreas.gov/formspubs/index.html

Securities Registration Information

www.dbr.state.ri.us/securities.html

South Carolina

Secretary of State
P.O. Box 11350
Columbia, SC 29211
1.803.734.2158
www.scsos.com/corporations.htm

Where to Get Forms and Background

www.scsos.com/forms.htm

State Filing Fees

(Does not include processing fees specific to counties or types of industries)

• Domestic profit corporation	$135
• Foreign corporation	$135
• Domestic LLCs	$110

Naming Procedures for Corporations

The name must contain the word Corporation, Incorporated, Company, Limited, the abbreviation Corp., Inc., Co., or Ltd. or abbreviations of words with similar meanings in another language. The name cannot contain language indicating a purpose other than that permitted by state law and the articles of organization. It must be distinguishable upon records of the secretary of state from the name of a domestic or qualified foreign corporation, reserved or registered corporate name, nonprofit corporation or limited partnership. Name reservation fee is $10.

Director Information

- Minimum number: one or more
- Residence requirements: no provision
- Age requirements: none
- Directors are required to be listed in the articles of incorporation

Report Filing Requirements

South Carolina corporations must file an annual report and a fee of $10 a year.

Detailed Tax Information

South Carolina Department of Revenue:
www.sctax.org/default.htm

State and Federal Tax Forms

www.irs.ustreas.gov/formspubs/index.html

Securities Registration Information

www.scsecurities.com

South Dakota

Secretary of State
State Capitol
500 E. Capitol Avenue
Pierre, SD 57501
1.605.773.4845
www.sdsos.gov/corporations

Where to Get Forms and Background

www.sdsos.gov/corporations/forms2005.htm

State Filing Fees

(Does not include processing fees specific to counties or types of industries)

• Domestic profit corporation	$125
• Foreign corporation	$550
• Domestic LLCs	$125

Naming Procedures for Corporations

The name must contain the word Corporation, Company, Incorporated, Limited or an abbreviation thereof. It must be distinguishable upon the records of the secretary of state from the name of any other corporation, whether for profit or not for profit organized under the laws of this state; the name of any foreign corporation, whether for profit or not for profit, authorized to engage in any business in this state; or any corporate name reserved or registered as permitted by the laws of this state; or the name of any limited partnership certified or registered in this state; or the name of any limited liability company. The name must not imply it is organized for any purpose other than that stated in the articles of incorporation. The name may not be the same as any corporation, limited partnership or limited liability company on file in South Dakota. Name reservation fee is $20.

Director Information

- Minimum number: one or more
- Residence requirements: no provision
- Age requirements: directors must be a natural person at least 18 years of age
- Directors are required to be listed in the articles of incorporation

Report Filing Requirements

South Dakota corporations must file an annual report and pay a fee of $30.

Detailed Tax Information

South Dakota Department of Revenue and Regulation
www.state.sd.us/drr2/revenue.html

State and Federal Tax Forms

www.irs.ustreas.gov/formspubs/index.html

Securities Registration Information

www.state.sd.us/drr2/reg/securites

Tennessee

Department of State
Corporate Filings
312 Eighth Avenue North
William R. Snodgrass Tower, Sixth Floor
Nashville, TN 37243
1.615.741.2286
www.state.tn.us/sos/bus_svs/index.htm

Where to Get Forms and Background

www.state.tn.us/sos/bus_svc/forms.htm

State Filing Fees

(Does not include processing fees specific to counties or types of industries)

• Domestic profit corporation	$100
• Foreign corporation	$100
• Domestic LLCs	$300

Naming Procedures for Corporations

The name must include the word Corporation, Incorporated, Company or an abbreviation thereof, including words or abbreviations in a foreign language. The name must be distinguishable in the secretary of state's records from any corporate or assumed name of a domestic or qualified foreign corporation, a reserved or registered name under Tennessee law or the name of a not.for.profit corporation, limited partnership or limited liability company. Name reservation fee is $20.

Director Information

- Minimum number: one or more
- Residence requirements: no provision
- Age requirements: none
- Directors are required to be listed in the articles of incorporation

Report Filing Requirements

Tennessee corporations must file an annual report on or before the first day of the fourth month following the close of the corporation's fiscal year. The annual report filing fee is $20.

Detailed Tax Information

Tennessee Department of Revenue:
www.state.tn.us/revenue

State and Federal Tax Forms

www.irs.ustreas.gov/formspubs/index.html

Securities Registration Information

www.state.tn.us/commerce/securities

Texas

Corporations Section
Secretary of State
P.O. Box 13697
Austin, TX 78711
1.512.463.5555
www.sos.state.tx.us/corp/index.shtml

Where to Get Forms and Background

www.state.tx.us/sos/corp/forms.shtml

State Filing Fees

(Does not include processing fees specific to counties or types of industries)

• Domestic profit corporation	$300
• Foreign corporation	$750
• Domestic LLCs	$200

Naming Procedures for Corporations

The name must contain the word Corporation, Company, Incorporated or an abbreviation thereof. The name must not imply a purpose other than that stated in the articles of incorporation. It may not be the same as, or deceptively similar to, the name of any domestic or foreign corporation, or reserved or registered name. However, a name already in use may be used if the corporation or LLC gets written consent from the user filed with the secretary of state. The name may not contain the word Lottery. Name reservation fee is $40.

Director Information

- Minimum number: one or more
- Residence requirements: no provision
- Age requirements: directors must be a natural person at least 18 years of age
- Directors are required to be listed in the articles of incorporation

Report Filing Requirements

Texas corporations must file an initial franchise tax report and public information report within one year and 89 days after the corporation's original filing date. Afterward, the corporation must file an annual report every May 15.

Detailed Tax Information

Texas Comptroller's Office
www.window.state.tx.us/fm

State and Federal Tax Forms

www.irs.ustreas.gov/formspubs/index.html

Securities Registration Information

www.ssb.state.tx.us

Utah

State of Utah
Division of Corporations & Commercial Code
160 E. 300 South, Second Floor
Box 146705
Salt Lake City, UT 84114
1.801.530.4849
www.utah.gov/business

Where to Get Forms and Background

www.commerce.utah.gov/cor/corpforms.htm

State Filing Fees

(Does not include processing fees specific to counties or types of industries)

• Domestic profit corporation	$52
• Foreign corporation	$52
• Domestic LLCs	$52

Naming Procedures for Corporations

The name must contain the word Corporation, Incorporated, Company or an abbreviation thereof, or words or abbreviations with the same meaning in another language. It must be distinguishable from the name of any domestic profit corporation, authorized foreign corporation, domestic or foreign limited liability company or partnership or reserved or registered name in the state of Utah. Name reservation fee is $22.

Director Information

- Minimum number: not less than three, unless there are only one or two shareholders of record; then the number of directors may be less than three but not less than the number of shareholders

- Residence requirements: no provision

- Age requirements: directors must be natural people who are at least 18 years of age

- Directors are not required to be listed in the articles of incorporation

Report Filing Requirements

Utah corporations must file an annual application for renewal form with a $10 fee.

Detailed Tax Information

Utah State Tax Commission
http://tax.utah.gov

State and Federal Tax Forms

www.irs.ustreas.gov/formspubs/index.html

Securities Registration Information

www.securities.state.ut.us

Vermont

Vermont Secretary of State
81 River Street, Drawer 09
Montpelier, VT 05609
1.802.828.2386
www.sec.state.vt.us/corps/corpindex.htm

Where to Get Forms and Background

www.sec.state.vt.us/tutor/dobizdoc.htm

State Filing Fees

(Does not include processing fees specific to counties or types of industries)

• Domestic profit corporation	$75
• Foreign corporation	$100
• Domestic LLCs	$75

Naming Procedures for Corporations

The name must contain the word Corporation, Incorporated, Company, Limited or an abbreviation thereof. The name may not contain language stating or implying the corporation is organized for purposes other than those permitted by state law. The name shall not have the word Cooperative or any abbreviation thereof. The name shall be distinguishable from, and not the same as, deceptively similar to, or likely to be confused with or mistaken for any name granted, registered or reserved under chapter or with the secretary of state. Name reservation fee is $20.

Director Information

- Minimum number: not less than three, unless there are only one or two shareholders of record; then the number of directors may be less than three but not less than the number of shareholders
- Residence requirements: no provision
- Age requirements: none
- Directors are not required to be listed in the articles of incorporation

Report Filing Requirements

Vermont corporations must file an annual report with a fee of $15.

Detailed Tax Information

Vermont Department of Taxes
www.state.vt.us/tax/index.shtml

State and Federal Tax Forms

www.irs.ustreas.gov/formspubs/index.html

Securities Registration Information

www.bishca.state.vt.us/SecuritiesDiv/securindex.htm

Virginia

Clerk of the State Corporation Commission
P.O. Box 1197
Richmond, VA 23218
1.804.371.9733
www.scc.virginia.gov/division/clk/index.htm

Where to Get Forms and Background

www.scc.virginia.gov/division/clk/corp.htm

State Filing Fees

(Does not include processing fees specific to counties or types of industries)

• Domestic profit corporation	$75 (minimum)
• Foreign corporation	$75 (minimum)
• Domestic LLCs	$100

Naming Procedures for Corporations

The name shall contain the word Corporation, Incorporated, Company, Limited or an abbreviation thereof. The name shall not contain any prohibited word or phrase implying it is organized for any purpose other than that stated in the articles of incorporation. The name may not be confusingly similar to that of any domestic or qualified foreign corporation. Name reservation fee is $10.

Director Information

- Minimum number: one or more
- Residence requirements: no provision
- Age requirements: none
- Directors are not required to be listed in the articles of incorporation

Report Filing Requirements

Virginia corporations must file an annual report with an annual registration fee ranging from $50 to $850.

Detailed Tax Information

Virginia Department of Taxation
www.tax.virginia.gov

State and Federal Tax Forms

www.irs.ustreas.gov/formspubs/index.html

Securities Registration Information

www.scc.virginia.gov/division/srf

Washington

Corporations Division
801 Capitol Way South
P.O. Box 40234
Olympia, WA 98504
1.360.753.7115
www.secstate.wa.gov/corps

Where to Get Forms and Background

www.secstate.wa.gov/corps/registration_forms.aspx

State Filing Fees

(Does not include processing fees specific to counties or types of industries)

• Domestic profit corporation	$175
• Foreign corporation	$175
• Domestic LLCs	$175

Naming Procedures for Corporations

The corporate name must include the word Corporation, Incorporated, Company, Limited or the abbreviation Corp., Inc., Co. or Ltd. The name must not imply a purpose other than the purpose stated in the charter. The name must be distinguishable from the name of any other domestic profit corporation or of any foreign corporation authorized to do business in state. The name must not include certain enumerated words indicating it is a bank or savings and loan, or any other words or phrases prohibited by any state statute. Name reservation fee is $30.

Director Information

- Minimum number: one or more
- Residence requirements: no provision
- Age requirements: none
- Directors are not required to be listed in the articles of incorporation

Report Filing Requirements

Washington corporations must file an annual report.

Detailed Tax Information

Washington tax site
http://access.wa.gov/business/taxes.aspx

State and Federal Tax Forms

www.irs.ustreas.gov/formspubs/index.html

Securities Registration Information

www.dfi.wa.gov/sd/default.htm

West Virginia

Business Organizations Division
Secretary of State
Building 1, Suite 157-K
1900 Kanawha Boulevard East
Charleston, WV 25305
1.304.558.8000
www.wvsos.com/common/startbusiness.htm

Where to Get Forms and Background

www.wvsos.com/business/services/formindex.htm

State Filing Fees

(Does not include processing fees specific to counties or types of industries)

• Domestic profit corporation	$50
• Foreign corporation	$100
• Domestic LLCs	$100

Naming Procedures for Corporations

The name must contain the words Company, Corporation, Incorporated, Limited or an abbreviation thereof. An optional name reservation fee is $15.

Director Information

- Minimum number: for for.profit corporations, there is no required number of directors
- Residency requirements: no provision
- Age requirements: no age requirement
- Directors are not required to be listed in the articles of incorporation

Report Filing Requirements

West Virginia corporations must file an annual report with a fee of $25.

Detailed Tax Information

West Virginia Department of Revenue
www.wvrevenue.gov

State and Federal Tax Forms

www.irs.ustreas.gov/formspubs/index.html

Securities Registration Information

www.wvauditor.com/securities/securities.shtml

Wisconsin

Department of Financial Institutions
P.O. Box 7846
Madison, WI 53707
1.608.261.7577
www.wdfi.org/corporations

Where to Get Forms and Background

www.wdfi.org/corporations

State Filing Fees

(Does not include processing fees specific to counties or types of industries)

• Domestic profit corporation	$100
• Foreign corporation	$100 (minimum)
• Domestic LLCs	$170

Naming Procedures for Corporations

The name of the corporation shall contain the word Corporation, Incorporated, Company, Limited or an abbreviation thereof, or words or abbreviations of words with similar meanings in another language. The name may not contain language stating or implying the corporation is organized for a purpose other than as permitted. The corporate name must be distinguishable upon the records of the Department of Financial Institutions from other corporations, LLCs, and other business entities authorized in the state.

Director Information

- Minimum number: one or more
- Residence requirements: no provision
- Age requirements: none
- Directors are not required to be listed in the articles of incorporation
- Statutory close corporations can elect to operate without a board

Report Filing Requirements

Wisconsin corporations must file an annual report with a $25 fee.

Detailed Tax Information

Wisconsin Department of Revenue
www.dor.state.wi.us

State and Federal Tax Forms

www.irs.ustreas.gov/formspubs/index.html

Securities Registration Information

www.wdfi.org/fi/securities

Wyoming

Wyoming Secretary of State Corporations Division
The State Capitol Building
Cheyenne, WY 82002
1.307.777.7311
http://soswy.state.wy.us/corporat/corporat.htm

Where to Get Forms and Background

http://soswy.state.wy.us/corporat/corporat.htm

State Filing Fees

(Does not include processing fees specific to counties or types of industries)

• Domestic profit corporation	$100
• Foreign corporation	$100
• Domestic LLCs	$100

Naming Procedures for Corporations

The name of the corporation may not contain language implying a different purpose from the purpose or purposes in the articles of incorporation. The name shall not be the same as or similar to the name of any domestic or foreign profit or nonprofit corporation, trade name, trademark or service mark registered in this state, limited liability company, statutory trust company or limited partnership or other business entity. Naming reservation fee is $50.

Director Information

- Minimum number: one or more
- Residence requirements: no provision
- Age requirements: none
- Directors are required to be listed in the articles of incorporation

Report Filing Requirements

Wyoming corporations must file an annual report on or before the anniversary month of the corporation's initial filing.

Detailed Tax Information

Wyoming Department of Revenue
http://revenue.state.wy.us

State and Federal Tax Forms

www.irs.ustreas.gov/formspubs/index.html

Securities Registration Information

http://soswy.state.wy.us/securiti/securiti.htm

SOURCES: Secretary of state offices, staff members and state Web sites.

Glossary of
Incorporation Terms

Please note: The terms described below are just part of the comprehensive Business Law and Accounting & Finance Dictionaries available to readers of this book at www.socrates.com/books/ready-incorporate.aspx.

abandonment To give up, voluntarily, an ownership or leased interest in a property. When a lease is involved, the property reverts to the owner; when an owner is involved, the property usually reverts to the state.

abatement The cancellation of a levy imposed by the government. Levies are commonly for taxes or for special assessments that an individual (or organization) has not paid.

absorption costing A type of costing in which all manufacturing expenses are treated as cost of goods (or product cost) and non manufacturing expenses (e.g., marketing costs) are treated as cost of sales (or period cost). In other words, the cost of sales is not included in the inventory value of the product and cannot be reported as part of that value.

abusive tax shelter A limited partnership that the Internal Revenue Service determines is claiming illegal tax deductions. A common scenario is a partnership overvaluing property, thus allowing itself greater tax write-offs for depreciation. When the IRS disallows such write-offs, it usually claims back-taxes and imposes interest and penalties on the partnership.

accelerated cost recovery system (ACRS) A method of depreciation against taxes created by the Economic Recovery Act of 1981. The type of property determines its class, and each class is assigned a depreciation rate. For example, for 3-, 5-, 7- and 10-year classes, the depreciation is 200 percent against the declining balance. The purpose of the ACRS is to encourage capital investment by businesses.

account The relationship between a creditor and debtor (one is said to have an account with the other) and the record of each financial category within an individual business, separately reported in that company's financial records (e.g., an account for a particular asset, customer or a vendor, cash on hand).

account form A kind of balance sheet, one in which assets are positioned to the left, liabilities and equity to the right. The more common form, the report form, puts assets above liabilities and equity.

accountability The responsibility of ensuring that the financial records of a business or organization are in order and accurate. The chief financial officer of a company is accountable to that company's board of directors. A company's auditors are responsible to those using that company's financial statements (including the Internal Revenue Service and to government entities in general) that the statements are true and in no way fraudulent.

accountancy Generally a British term; what Americans refer to as accounting (i.e., the theories and practice of the profession).

accountant Someone who performs accounting services (i.e., a person who creates financial plans, monitors those plans, and prepares financial statements and tax returns). In firms of accountants or in the largest corporations, accountants customarily specialize in a particular branch of the discipline (e.g., taxes or cost accounting). Accountants may also act as advisers to management. See certified public accountant.

accountant-in-charge During an audit, that person who is ultimately responsible for the final report and to whom the assistants report. The accountant-in-charge will also report to the management of the company being audited, is ultimately responsible to his own firm for the audit and is the point person to whom the IRS (and any other government agencies) refers if they have any queries.

accounting change Any variation in the way that accounts are prepared. There could be various reasons for the change (e.g., new IRS regulations or the adoption of new methods in, say, allowing for doubtful, probably non collectable, accounts receivable). Whenever such a change occurs, accountants are expected to footnote any financial statement, offering a full explanation of the reason for the change.

accounting principles The rules of the profession (i.e., the ways in which certain accounting problems are handled). Generally, these rules are those of generally accepted accounting principles (GAAP), which are based mainly on the pronouncements of the American Institute for Certified Public Accountants.

accounting system That which is followed by a particular company or organization to record, store, and communicate its finances. Any such system must of course conform to industry standards, to professional rules of conduct and to government regulations.

accounts payable Undertakings to pay for goods and services rendered to a company by outside suppliers/vendors. Accounts payable are a crucial part of a company's short-term debt and are recorded as a liability on the balance sheet.

accounts receivable Amounts a company is owed from customers who have purchased its goods or services. Accounts receivable are recorded as an asset in the company's balance sheet.

accretion Growth in the value of assets.

accrual accounting The opposite of cash basis accounting. Accrual accounting recognizes revenue when earned (when the company renders a bill) and expenses when incurred (when the company is invoiced). In other words, transactions are treated as if cash has been received or paid out.

acid test ratio Slang for a test of liquidity. Dividing liabilities by liquid assets (cash and accounts receivable, not inventory). The goal is to determine whether assets are equal to or greater than liabilities.

acquisition cost The real price of goods or services. That is, the base costs as well as incidental costs (e.g., transportation of a manufactured item from manufacturer to user).

activity analysis An evaluation designed to determine the most cost-effective way of creating a particular product or providing a particular service.

activity-based costing (ABC) An attempt to identify the various tasks performed in a company as a way of assigning overhead costs to goods or services.

adequate disclosure A comprehensive explanation included within financial statements to the extent that readers of those statements will feel that they fully understand what has been presented.

adjustable rate loan A loan with an interest rate based on an outside factor. For example, the interest on business loans is often based on U.S. prime rate. A bank may give its best customers a prime-rate loan; other customers may pay more than prime. As the prime rate changes, the interest on these loans will change.

adjusted basis The value used as a base against which depreciation is calculated. Normally, the adjusted basis is the original cost.

adverse opinion An auditor's claim that a company's accounts do not fairly present its financial position or that they are not produced in accordance with generally accepted accounting principles. An adverse opinion is not common: it must be included (with reasons) in any audit opinion and is usually the result of an auditor's being unable to convince a client to revise the company's financial statements.

affiliated company One with which there is a close relationship, though neither company holds a majority interest in the other. The term is also used to describe two companies that are subsidiaries of a third, controlling company.

age discrimination Unfair treatment, especially in the hiring or laying off of current or potential employees aged 40 to 70 years, which is illegal under the Age Discrimination Unemployment Act. The main challenge by the claimant is to prove age discrimination.

age discrimination in employment act (ADEA) A federal law prohibiting discrimination against workers older than 40 years of age in employment decisions, especially those regarding which workers should be laid off. Under the law, no worker can be forced to retire.

agent A person who, by mutual consent, is authorized to act for the benefit of and under the direction of another person when dealing with third parties. The person who appoints the agent is the principal. The agent is in a fiduciary relationship with the principal, can enter into binding agreements on behalf of the principal and could potentially create liability for her or him.

aging of accounts The classification of accounts according to the length of time that has elapsed since the invoice date or the due date. An aging schedule customarily breaks down invoices into 1-30 days, 31-60 days, 61-90 days, and over 90 days. In general, the longer an account is outstanding, the more difficult it is to collect.

aggregate par value Aggregate par value is the par value multiplied by the number of authorized shares. This amount is important in determining initial fees and annual franchise taxes in many states.

alimony payments Support payments from one former spouse to another—generally husband to wife. The person making the payments may deduct them as part of the calculation of adjusted gross income (AGI). The person receiving the payments must, for tax purposes, treat them as income.

allocate Charging the expenses of achieving revenue to a number of different departments or spreading a cost over two or more accounting periods (e.g., a lawyer is engaged and paid a 3 -year retainer of $30,000: $10,000 of that amount would be charged in each annual accounting for the next three years).

allowance This term has three meanings: (1) reducing the value of an asset; (2) reduction in the amount owed to a vendor because of delays or because of damaged goods; and (3) the acceptable amount of spoilage in the manufacture of some product.

allowance for bad debts/allowance method A provision in accounts for the possibility of failure to collect some of a company's accounts receivable. In a well-done company balance sheet, gross receivables are reduced to reflect what the accountant believes is the likely net amount to be collected.

all-purpose financial statement A financial statement that will be regarded as thorough and as meeting the needs of all potential users—from employees to creditors to stockholders.

amortize/amortization The reduction of the value of an asset over a period of time (e.g., the reduction in the value of a piece of equipment).

analytical procedures Evaluations of financial information performed by a qualified auditor. These evaluations range from the simple (comparison of last year's earnings with this year's) to the complex (predicting future growth or contraction).

analyze To evaluate any accounting-related item.

angel investor An individual who provides capital to one or more startup companies. The individual is usually affluent or has a personal stake in the success of the venture. Such investments are characterized by high levels of risk and a potentially large return on investment.

annual budget A budget prepared for either a calendar or fiscal year.

annualize To predict expenditure on a particular business cost for a year based on the experience of a few months. For example, an accountant might assume that if the cost of telephone services has been running at $200 a month, then the annualized cost (for a fiscal or calendar year) is going to be an estimated $2,400. This technique is commonly used in creating an annual budget or forecast.

annual meeting In corporations, a general meeting of shareholders or directors. Shareholders' meetings are held to elect directors or to vote on major changes to the corporation, such as amendments to the articles of incorporation or merging of the business with another. A meeting of directors might consider raising funds by borrowing and other financial decisions, buying property, and hiring or replacing key staff.

annual report The financial document prepared by companies to summarize the previous year. It usually consists of the company's financial statements for the year, annotated with explanations; the report of the company's auditors; and a letter from the president or CEO of the company. The annual report is intended for the use of the company's shareholders, banks, employees, creditors, or any entity that has dealings with the company.

annuity Any kind of periodic payment of more or less the same amount (e.g., a company's receipt of dividends on its holdings of preferred stock).

antitrust laws Three sets of U.S. government laws designed to encourage competition by ensuring that one company (or group of companies) do not unfairly control the market for particular goods or services.

appreciation An increase in the value of an asset (e.g., the increase in value of property or shares).

arbitrage Buying an asset in one market and selling it in another in order to realize a profit.

arm's-length transaction A transaction between unrelated parties (e.g., an online transaction in which one party bids for the goods another has for sale).

arrears Past due payments on an account.

articles of incorporation Those documents prepared for individuals who wish to found a corporation in a U.S. state. They must file these documents with the relevant government official, usually the secretary of state. A copy of these documents is returned to the individuals. Along with the state-issued certificate of incorporation, these papers become the new corporation's license to begin operations.

articles of partnership Similar to articles of incorporation in that they are filed with the state authority, the acceptance of which allows the partnership to begin operations—appropriate to partners but not shareholders. Typically, these articles include commentary on the capital contributions, the purpose of the partnership, and the duties of partners, which in a corporation is generally covered by its bylaws, a separate document setting out the internal workings of the corporation.

assessment An official (government) valuation of property for the purpose of levying a tax on it.

asset Any resource that is expected to provide a future economic benefit to a business. Assets are usually described according to their monetary value. In accounting, an asset is referred to as having tangible or intangible value. A tangible asset is one the value of which can be easily determined (e.g., a company car). The value of an intangible asset is much more difficult to quantify (e.g., goodwill or a trademark).

assignment of accounts receivable Using accounts receivable as collateral on a promissory note. If the assignor defaults, the assignee may collect the accounts receivable; they then belong to the assignee.

assumed name A name under which a corporation conducts business that is not the legal name of the corporation as shown in its articles of incorporation. Assumed names (also called a fictitious name and doing business as or DBA) could be filed at the city, county or state level depending on state requirements. A corporation can use multiple assumed names.

at par At face value. A share that has a face value of $50 and is being traded at $50 is said to be trading at par. If the share is trading above $50, it is trading at a premium; if less than $50, it is trading at a discount.

audit An audit refers to four kinds of company procedure: (1) compliance audit—a determination of whether a company is operating according to national rules and regulations, as well as the regulations of the jurisdiction in which it operates; (2) management audit—an evaluation of the effectiveness of a company's executives; (3) internal audit—an investigation by a senior member of staff (not necessarily the company's chief financial officer or accountant) to determine that a company's procedures (including both financial controls and the day-to-day activities of the company) are operating consistently with company goals; and (4) financial audit, that which most people understand by the term audit—the formal examination of a client's financial records by a licensed certified public accountant to decide whether they are accurate and whether they conform to generally accepted auditing procedures (GAAP), leading to an audit opinion.

audit committee A committee set up by a company, and composed of outside directors, to oversee audit operations and to appraise the performance of the company's certified public accountants.

audit evidence That information that an auditor uses to arrive at the conclusions on which the audit opinion or audit report is based. The auditor is also determining the quality of the information (i.e., how sound the financial procedures of a client may or may not be).

audit liability The legal responsibility of auditors to make sure that the accounts they audit and the resulting financial statements are correct, that their audit opinion is sound. There is precedent for suing auditors for their mistakes.

audit opinion The report made by the certified public accountant after that accountant has conducted an investigation of a company's records at the end of its financial year. The purpose of the opinion is to verify that the company's records are true; that it has been operating in accordance with generally accepted auditing procedures (GAAP). The CPA may conclude that the company is not in compliance and is then obliged to say so in the audit opinion.

audit planning The setting out—by an auditor—of the steps an audit will involve.

audit program The procedures to be followed in an audit, generally prepared by the head CPA, to guide the assistants who will be helping the CPA. Usually, completion of each step is noted on a written program, and the person responsible for having completed the step signs his or her name.

audit report/auditor's report One of two kinds of report: a short form, which includes the CPA's statement about whether a company has fairly expressed its financial condition in its financial statements; or a long form, usually rendered for a large or complicated business in which the CPA also discusses scope of the audit, offers extensive commentary on the financial position of the company, makes suggestions about the future, and comments on the effectiveness of the company's accounting procedures.

bad debt One that cannot be collected despite the best efforts of a company to do so.

balance sheet A statement that shows a company's financial position at the end of a particular period. The year's financial statements always include a balance sheet, but many companies also produce one at the end of each month to accompany their profit and loss statement. A balance sheet offers three component's of a company's financial position: its assets, its liabilities, and what it owes to shareholders (i.e., the equity shareholders have contributed to the company by buying its shares plus any unpaid earnings on those shares). The balance is achieved in this way: assets equal liabilities plus shareholder's equity. Balance sheets are used extensively in business for the reason that they provide an overall view of the condition of a company and help executives, directors, and their professional advisors easily see the resources of a company as well as what it owes. Balance sheets are regarded as the single most pertinent document illustrating a company's financial condition.

balloon A term commonly used in real estate to describe a kind of mortgage or equity loan. In effect, a balloon is the payment on any loan substantially greater than previous payments—one that pays off the loan.

bankruptcy A situation in which debts of a business are substantially greater than the value of its assets and the business files for court protection. The court supervises the liquidation of assets and the payment to creditors, prorated, of what this liquidation yields. See Chapter 7; Chapter 11.

bankruptcy trustee A court-appointed individual who oversees the case of a person or business that has filed for bankruptcy. In a consumer Chapter 7 case, the trustee gathers the debtor's nonexempt property, liquidates it, and distributes it proportionally to the creditors. In a Chapter 13 case, the trustee receives the debtor's monthly payments and distributes them proportionally to the creditors.

benchmarking Comparing the procedures of a company to those of companies that are highly efficient and profitable in an effort to improve productivity or competitiveness.

blanket insurance A policy that covers several items of property for the amount of their fair market value.

blue chip stock One that has a long record of growth or dividend payments. Such stocks are usually regarded as the best long-term investments, appropriate for those who wish to invest but do not wish to speculate in the stock market.

board of advisors A board of advisors provides essential guidance, information and services to a company. Often the board will play devil's advocate, pointing out potential markets and flaws in what you're doing. It is a tremendous think-tank resource to keep you on track and find the resources you need to succeed. Advisors usually serve as unpaid advisors and do not have voting power when it comes to major company decisions and the hiring and firing of executives and officers.

board of directors A group of people chosen by the shareholders of either a public or private corporation to run the business according to the company's charter and bylaws. It is common for a board to consist of a company's high-ranking executives (e.g., its president or CEO) as well as outside directors who it is hoped will bring a more generalist perspective to the group. Among other things, a board of directors has ultimate responsibility for a company's financial practices.

boilerplate That part of any contract that is more or less common to all contracts.

bond Any written undertaking by a company, government agency, or other organization to pay the holder of the instrument a fixed amount on maturity. Interest payments are involved, and are usually paid semiannually. Bonds are either secured or unsecured. Secured bonds (e.g., a mortgage bond) have a claim on real estate or other securities; unsecured bonds have no specific claim on any assets (they are often referred to as junk bonds).

book inventory The value of inventory as shown in company records. It is not necessarily true inventory, which because of spoilage/damage can be determined only by a physical inventory.

book value the net value (net = original cost less depreciation) shown for an asset on a company's balance sheet.

bookkeeper/bookkeeping The person(s) within a company who is in charge of various accountancy support functions. Duties could include making entries in various company ledgers, doing the payroll, and reconciling bank statements. A bookkeeper is usually not a trained accountant but often someone who has gained expertise through on-the-job training.

bottom line A company's net income after taxes or the end result (i.e., the final consequence of an activity).

branch accounting The practice of maintaining different accounts for each branch of one business entity. The purpose is to provide management the means of determining how well each branch is doing. Customarily, these different accounts are combined at the end of the financial year.

breakeven analysis A determination of when a company's revenues equal its costs in producing the goods or services that create those revenues. Any revenues beyond the breakeven point are profits. If costs are greater than revenues, however, the company is operating at a loss.

bridge loan A short-term loan, often carrying a higher rate of interest, that is made in anticipation of a long-term loan. The most common example is money advanced by a lender so that an individual may purchase a home before that person has sold his or her current home; the bridge loan is paid back when the current home is sold, and the lender (the same lender or another one) provides a long-term mortgage on the new home.

brokerage fee An amount, usually a commission—though it can be a straight set fee—paid to a broker for buying or selling securities.

budget committee A company group, usually comprised of that company's senior executives and chief financial officer, that reviews, vets, and potentially revises a company's budget for the year.

business cycle A theoretical construct that economies periodically expand or contract; such cycles affect an individual company's growth and income.

business entity An organization that possesses a separate existence for tax purposes. Some types of business entities include corporations and limited liability companies.

business opportunity These are prepackaged business concepts that are sold by branded companies, and though they look like franchises, they are not. They differ in important ways. Once purchased, owners are pretty much on their own to make the business a go. There are no stringent rules for operations, nor is the seller involved directly in the business after purchase. Training and marketing assistance is rarely part of the deal. Also franchises are generally subject to more state and federal regulation. Business opportunity purchases should be checked through the Better Business Bureau and state attorneys general offices to check for complaints.

business plan A written document that details a proposed or existing venture. It will typically explain the vision, current status, expected needs, defined markets and projected results of the business.

bylaws Bylaws are the rules and regulations adopted by a corporation for its internal governance. It usually contains provisions relating to shareholders, directors, officers and general corporate business. The bylaws are adopted at the corporation's initial meeting.

C corporation A C corporation is simply a standard business corporation. It is called a C corporation because it is taxed under subsection C of the IRS code.

cafeteria plan Slang for a benefit plan that permits employees to make their own choices among various company benefits on offer.

canadian institute of chartered accountants Founded in 1902, the primary professional organization for Canadian chartered accountants (the same as CPAs in the United States).

capital In accounting, capital has four meanings: (1) long-term assets that are not themselves sold in the normal course of business, such as a factory building or equipment; (2) a company's resources (i.e., the difference between its current assets and current liabilities); (3) any goods purchased for use in the production of goods or services (e.g., computers); and (4) the interest of an owner in a business, the difference between assets and liabilities that constitutes the value of the business—also called equity or net worth. (In a corporation, stockholders' equity is the capital.)

capital gain Any profit involved in selling a capital asset. Both individuals and corporations are taxed on capital gains, though some gains (e.g., an individual selling a personal residence) are exempt to certain limits.

cash Money that a company has deposited in a bank as well as any instrument that a bank will accept as cash (e.g., checks or money orders). Notes receivable or accounts receivable are not regarded as cash and may not be entered as such on financial statements.

cash basis accounting Recognizing income and expenses when cash is received or disbursed as opposed to when goods are sold or debt incurred (i.e., the opposite of accrual basis accounting). The method is generally only possible for a small service business that does not maintain any kind of inventory.

cash flow Cash receipts less cash disbursements for a particular period of time. If, in a given month, a company pays out $30,000 and collects $40,000, its cash flow for the month is said to be $10,000.

certificate of authority or application for authority Is a document issued by the proper state authority to a foreign corporation granting the corporation the right to do business in that state upon filing an application of authority.

certificate of good standing A certificate issued by a state official as conclusive evidence that a corporation or LLC is in existence or authorized to transact business in the state. The certificate generally sets forth the corporation's or LLCs name; that it is duly incorporated or organized and authorized to transact business; that all fees, taxes and penalties owed the state have been paid; that its most recent annual report has been filed; and, that articles of dissolution have not been filed. Also known as a certificate of existence or certificate of authorization.

certificate of incorporation A document issued in some states confirming that a corporation has filed articles of incorporation; in other states, the articles themselves are sufficient proof.

certified public accountant (CPA) An accountant who has passed the Uniform SPA Examination administered by the American Institute of Certified Public Accountants (AICPA) and is therefore licensed by the state in which the accountant practices to use that title. A CPA is authorized to write an audit opinion or audit report on a company's financial statements and can act as a final auditing authority.

change in reporting entity Notification to government taxing agencies that two of more formerly independent companies are now combined into one and will jointly prepare financial statements and tax returns in the future. It is common for companies in this situation to restate their financial results for the previous 5 years as if they were combined during that period.

chapter 7 A type of bankruptcy in which, after a company has liquidated many of its assets to pay off most creditors, the court appoints a trustee to make management changes in the company, arrange for further financing, and run the business with a view to avoiding further loss. The underling assumption of a Chapter 7 bankruptcy is that, with a fresh start, the company can prove itself to be a viable business.

chapter 11 A kind of bankruptcy that is effectively a reorganization of the business. Managers remain in control of their business while the court provides them protection from their creditors. The company and its creditors work together to restructure its debt (i.e., reschedule payments to its creditors). The assumption of a Chapter 11 bankruptcy is that, allowed to restructure its debt, the company will survive.

Class action A lawsuit in which all members of a group of persons who have suffered the same or similar injury join together in an action against the alleged wrongdoer. The group must be sufficiently numerous that it is impractical for them all to be before the court individually, so they are represented collectively by only a few members, or by one. All members are bound by the court's decision. Typical class actions involve a manufactured product that has injured many people or a group that has suffered discrimination by an organization.

closely held corporation A company that has only a few shareholders. It is different from a privately held corporation in that it does trade shares (i.e., although it is a public company, very few shares are actually traded).

collateralize To pledge company assets to secure a debt. Common forms of collateral include company fixed assets, inventory and accounts receivable.

collection period The number of days it customarily takes a company to collect its accounts receivable. A long collection period (more than 30-60 days) can prove a burden to a company because it disallows the company from discharging its own accounts payable in a timely manner.

combined financial statement A financial statement in which income statements and balance sheets of related business entities (e.g., subsidiaries of the same holding company) are combined so that they may considered as one reporting entity. Inter-company transactions are eliminated in a combined financial statement.

commercial law That part of the law (including statutes, cases and precedents) that encompasses the rights, relations, and conduct of persons and businesses engaged in commerce, merchandising, trade and sales. This body of law is now codified in the Uniform Commercial Code, which has been adopted, at least in part, by all states.

common stock A share in a public or privately held company. Common stockholders have dividend and voting rights. In a bankruptcy, common stockholders are paid after bondholders and preferred stockholders. The advantage of common stock is that it involves the possibility of substantial appreciation.

company A formal business enterprise that is set up to make a profit. Examples include corporations, partnerships and sole proprietorships.

condensed financial statement An income statement, balance sheet, or changes in financial position statement in which less essential detail has been combined into general categories. A document that provides a quick perspective on a particular business.

consolidated omnibus budget reconciliation act (COBRA) A federal law that requires employers to offer employees—and their spouses and dependents—continuing insurance coverage if their work hours are cut or they lose their jobs for any reason other than gross misconduct. The act also states that an ex-spouse and children are eligible to receive group-rate health insurance provided by the other ex-spouse's employer for three years after a divorce. However, the employer is not responsible for paying the insurance premiums.

contract A legally enforceable agreement, not contrary to any law, to do or not to do something. A contract involves two or more people or businesses; it sets forth what they will or will not do and can be either oral or written (though real estate and larger commercial contracts must be in writing to be enforceable). A contract involves competent parties—usually adults of sound mind or business entities—one of whom makes an offer to which the other agrees by acceptance, by which each provides the other some benefit (called consideration), such as a promise to pay money in return for a promise to deliver, or the actual delivery of, particular goods or services, within a stated time frame. Contracts are at the heart of most business dealings, and contract law is one of the most significant areas of legal concern.

controller The head accounting executive in a business, though such a post may not exist in a company that also has appointed a chief financial officer. The alternate British spelling, comptroller, is sometimes used in the United States, particularly in the federal government.

corporate kit A binder usually containing essential items for the routine maintenance and administration of a corporation. Corporate kits include sample minutes, resolutions and bylaws, stock certificates, a corporate seal, and stock ledger.

corporate joint venture Any cooperation between two or more otherwise unrelated companies to achieve a particular goal (e.g., a cooperative pact between two manufacturers to build an airline: one of them provides the frame, the other provides the motor).

corporate record book Maintaining the proper records is very important to assure limited liability to corporate shareholders. The corporation should have a record book which contains a copy of the articles of incorporation, bylaws, initial and subsequent minutes of directors and shareholders meetings and a stock register.

corporate seal A device made to either emboss or imprint certain company information onto documents. This information usually includes the company's name and date and state of formation. Corporate seals are often required when opening corporate bank accounts, distributing stock or conducting other corporate business.

corporation A business entity, with legal status, in which ownership is vested in those who purchase its stock and in so doing contribute capital to fund the business; a corporation is, however, regarded (in terms of taxation or responsibility for liabilities) as a legal entity separate from its shareholder-owners. A corporation is formed when its founders file articles of incorporation with the relevant state authority, usually the secretary of state. Shareholders may sell their shares to other investors.

credit analysis The process by a lender (usually a bank) of determining whether an applicant (an individual or a business) is a good risk and how much credit can be extended to that applicant without the loan's being risky.

current asset An asset that, with rare exceptions, has a life of 1 year or less.

current cost The price it would cost to replace a company asset.

current liability A debt that a company must pay within 1 year.

debenture A long-term debt that is not secured by a lien on specific property. Because it is unsecured debt, it is generally issued by large and financially sound companies about which there is unlikely to be any doubt, in the minds of investors, about the possibility of repayment.

debit An entry on the left side of an account: expenses as opposed to revenues.

debt-equity ratio An analysis of a company's financial statements to ascertain the kind of protection available to its creditors (e.g., whether or not the company is overextended in its borrowings against the value of its equity).

debt financing Raising money either by borrowing it from a bank or other financial institution or by selling bonds or notes payable.

debtor Any individual or company that has a legal obligation to pay money to another individual or company.

debtor in possession In bankruptcy proceedings, a debtor who has filed for the right to submit a plan for reorganization or refinancing under Chapter 11, and is allowed to continue to manage her or his business without an appointed trustee.

debt restructuring A change in a company's debt structure, which reflects concessions granted by its creditors, usually involving giving the company more time to pay its debts. Debt restructuring is usually an indication that a company is in financial difficulties. It may be agreed by the creditors privately or it may be imposed on them by the court (e.g., in a Chapter 11 bankruptcy).

deficit A debit balance in a company's retained earnings account because of accumulated losses.

defined benefit plan A type of occupational pension in which the pension provision is defined (e.g., a fixed monthly amount for each year of service) and guaranteed. The employer has to make up the difference if the scheme fails to perform as well as expected. Also known as a final salary pension scheme, in which the benefit is calculated as a percentage of the final salary.

defined contribution plan A type of occupational pension that has a fixed contribution rate but does not guarantee any particular pension amount on retirement. The employer pays into the pension fund a certain amount every month or every year for each employee; this is usually a fixed percentage of the employee's wages or salary but may be a percentage of the company's profits. The plan is based on these contributions rather than on the employee's final salary immediately before retirement. At retirement, the pension fund is used to purchase an annuity, the value of which depends on the level of contributions made to the fund on behalf of the employee, the investment returns received by the fund as a whole, and annuity rates at the time.

derivative action A lawsuit brought by a corporation shareholder against the directors, management and/or other shareholders for a failure by management. The suing shareholder claims to be acting on behalf of the corporation because the directors and management are failing to exercise their authority in the best interests of the business and its shareholders. A derivative action suit often arises when there are claims of fraud, insider trading, self-dealing, misuse of a corporate opportunity, mismanagement, and other acts that are being ignored by the officers or board of directors.

derivatives Financial instruments that are based on some underlying asset, such as stocks, bonds, commodities or currencies.

descriptive mark A trademark or service mark (e.g., Jet Fast hamburger service) that describes the characteristics of a product or service (in this example, speed). Such marks initially receive little protection from the courts, and at the federal level are placed on the Supplemental Register rather than the Principal Register of trademarks. After a descriptive mark has been in active use for five years, however, it can be moved to the Principal Register because by then it may have become fairly widely known.

detailed audit One in which virtually all of a company's transactions and record keeping are thoroughly examined. This kind of audit is much more comprehensive than what is normally done at most companies. It can be provoked by suspicions of illegal activities or as one of the ways of preparing for a major change (e.g., the sale or merger of the company).

dilution The weakening of an item in a financial statement. The term commonly refers to the phenomenon of a company's issuing more common stock, thus reducing the equity interest of each common stock that then exists.

director A member of the board of directors of a corporation. The board, selected by shareholders, is the chief governing body of the corporation, though generally it is not involved with the day-to-day running of the company, which is the responsibility of its senior executives (though, generally, the head executive—the CEO—is a member of the board). The board's responsibilities include selecting a company's corporate officers; declaring dividends; deciding on major expansion or contraction of the company's activities; and advising officers on long-term strategy.

disbursement Payment by cash or by check.

discharge in bankruptcy An order given by a judge in a bankruptcy court, at the conclusion of all legal steps in processing a bankrupt person's assets and debts, which forgives (i.e., discharges) those remaining debts that cannot be paid—with exceptions. Debts for fraudulent or illegal actions, alimony and child support, and taxes are not dischargeable and remain owed (which does not mean they can be collected).

dividend Periodic distribution of earnings to shareholders. Dividends are declared per individual share.

divestiture The giving up of a possession (e.g., part of a business) or right. If voluntary, divestiture may be an attempt to improve efficiency by cutting a loss-making business or concentrating on one product or business area. If court-ordered, it may be the result of an antitrust action to prevent monopoly or other restraint of trade.

doing business as (DBA) A DBA, also known as an assumed name, is typically completed by making a filing at the county level where the business is located. This filing does not change the official name of the corporation; however, it allows the company to use additional names.

domain name A combination of letters and numbers that identifies a specific computer or Web site on the Internet. The owner of a domain name can stop another business from using the same name only if the domain name is being used in the sale of goods or services to consumers and is thus a trademark.

domestic corporation A company that is incorporated in the United States rather than a foreign country.

double-entry bookkeeping The kind of financial record-keeping that involves two entries for each transaction—a debit and a credit.

double taxation (dual taxation) Corporations are treated as a separate legal taxable entity for income tax purposes. Therefore, corporations pay tax on their earnings. If corporate earnings are distributed to shareholders in the form of dividends, the corporation does not receive the reasonable business expense deduction, and dividend income is taxed as regular income to the shareholders. Thus, to the extent that earnings are distributed to shareholders as dividends, there is a double tax on earnings at the corporate and shareholder level. S corporations and LLCs are pass-through entities which are not subject to the double tax.

earnings The income of a business in a specific accounting period—revenues less all costs and expenses.

electronic fund transfer system (EFTS) System for electronically transferring funds between buyers and sellers. EFTS is also used by many companies to transmit the payroll of their employees directly to employees' individual accounts.

elements of balance sheet Those components that traditionally appear on a balance sheet: assets, liabilities, and the equity account. The detail for these components appears in the company's chart of accounts.

employee retirement income security act (ERISA) A federal law that regulates private pension plans that supplement Social Security. The Act sets minimum standards for such plans, provides workers with some protection if a plan cannot pay the benefits to which they are entitled, and requires employers to provide full information about their employees' pension rights and to ensure that the administration of their pension funds is transparent.

employee stock ownership plan (ESOP) A plan that encourages employees to invest in their company's stock. Depending on the extent of their stock ownership, employees may also participate in the management of the company.

entrepreneur An individual with the initiative and drive to start a business and assume its risks. Customarily, the entrepreneur founds/creates the business and then hires people to work for him or her.

equal employment opportunity commission (EEOC) The federal agency that deals with discrimination in the workplace. The EEOC was set up by the Civil Rights Act of 1964.

equity Also called net worth. In accounting, equity equals assets minus liabilities. In a sole proprietorship, equity belongs to the owner; in a corporation, it belongs to the stockholders.

equity financing Obtaining financing by issuing preferred or common stock—or both.

ESOP See employee stock ownership plan.

escape clause A provision in a contract that allows a party to be relieved from any obligation if a certain event occurs or does not occur.

escrow An account held by a third party (i.e., an escrow agent) in which documents and funds are held in trust before a transfer of real estate, the completion of a sale, or some other transaction. When the funding is complete or other specified conditions are met, the escrow agent will release the documents and funds to the buyer and seller. As a verb, to escrow means to place documents and funds in an escrow account.

estimated tax Corporations must remit to the Internal Revenue Service in quarterly payments 90 percent of what they judge their tax to be for the year.

excise tax A tax levied on specific products, usually for a particular purpose or goal. For example, such a tax on cigarettes might be used to fund public health care; a tax on gasoline might be used to fund the repair of roads.

expenses The outgoings of any business, subtracted from revenues to arrive at the company's net income.

extraordinary item Something in a company's accounts that is highly unusual or that occurs infrequently (e.g., a loss as a result of a fire).

 fair labor standards act (FLSA) of 1938 A federal law that applies to all employees of companies that engage in interstate commerce, including minimum wage laws. Except for very small retail establishments, most companies are involved in trading in more than one state and therefore are subject to minimum wage and other regulations of the act.

family and medical leave act (FMLA) A federal law that requires employers to provide an employee with 12 weeks of unpaid leave over the course of a year for the birth or adoption of a child, family health needs, or personal illness. Employees must be allowed to return to the same or a similar position to the one held before taking leave. The Act applies only to employers with 50 or more employees, so about half the workforce is not covered by it.

FASB See financial accounting standards board.

federal tax identification number This is a number assigned to a corporation or other business entity by the federal government for tax purposes. Banks generally require a tax identification number to open bank accounts. The federal tax identification number is also known as the Employer Identification Number (EIN).

federal trade commission (FTC) The federal agency (established in 1914) responsible for prosecuting unfair competition and preventing monopolies in U.S. business.

federal unemployment tax act (FUTA) The law that requires employers to pay an unemployment tax based on the size of the company's workforce, which in turn funds unemployment insurance. State and federal governments are involved in the administration of this tax, and some states also tax employees.

Fees Charges for services rendered. The term is generally used to describe the remuneration of such professionals as lawyers or auditors, who generally work on a per-job basis rather than for a salary or hourly wages.

fictitious name See doing business as.

fiduciary (Latin, fiduciary: trust) An individual or business (e.g., a bank or brokerage) that has the power to act for another in circumstances of trust. Often, a fiduciary is a trustee of a trust, but others filling this role can be attorneys, guardians, administrators of estates, real estate agents, stockbrokers or title companies. A fiduciary relationship is one in which one person places complete confidence in another regarding a particular transaction or more general affairs.

financial accounting standards board (FASB) The organization with the authority to enforce generally accepted accounting principles (GAAP). That is, although FASB is not a government body, certified public accountants are required to follow its dictates in their auditing and reporting practices.

financial statements A report setting out the financial information about a company. It is itself comprised of three required documents: a profit/loss statement (income statement), a balance sheet, and a statement detailing changes in the company's financial position.

fiscal year The 12 consecutive months for which companies traditionally (and by law) account for their business operations. Typically, the fiscal year is the calendar year, but some organizations (notably government units) use a different year. The term is also used in taxation to mean any 12-month period other than the calendar year.

fixed asset An asset that produces income, has physical reality and has a life of longer than 1 year.

fixed cost A cost that remains constant over a given period (e.g., the rate of taxes).

fixed overhead Anything in overheads that remains a constant, no matter what the level of activity in a business (e.g., rent).

footnote The explanatory notes to a financial statement, regarded as a crucial and integral part of that statement. Subjects that footnotes generally cover include accounting policies, pending litigation, and tax matters.

foreign corporation A corporation that is incorporated under the laws of a state different from the one in which it is doing business, or of another country. Such a corporation must file a notice of doing business in any state in which it does substantial regular business, and name an agent for acceptance of service in that state (a state's secretary of state is sometimes the agent) so that customers or suppliers can bring legal actions locally.

form 10-K The form that publicly traded companies must submit each year to the Securities and Exchange Commission (SEC). Financial statements, supporting documents, important disclosures, and general information about the business are included in this submission.

401(k) plan An investment plan that allows employees to defer part of their gross salary and invest that money in stocks, bonds, or money market funds. The employer commonly provides a choice of investments, and many employers match (partially or wholly) their employees' contributions. The contributions and any of the earnings on plan's investments are tax free until the employee withdraws them, commonly when that employee retires (when the rate of taxation will be lower than it would have been when the employee was working) or when the employee leaves the company—in which case the 401(k) plan can be transferred to a new employer.

franchise A license that awards rights from a franchisor to a franchisee to use specific trademarks, business systems and support for a business concept.

franchise agreement The franchise agreement is the legal, written document that governs the relationship and specifies the terms of the franchise purchase. Area Development Franchise Agreements, Master Franchise Agreements, and Single or Direct-Unit Franchise Agreements are varieties of franchise agreements.

It is more specific than the UFOC about the terms of the business relationship. A typical franchise agreement may include specifics about:
• the franchise system, such as use of trademarks and products;
• territory;
• rights and obligations of the parties: standards, procedures, training, assistance, advertising, etc.;
• term (duration) of the franchise;
• payments made by the franchisee to the franchiser; and
• termination and/or the right to transfer the franchise.

franchise consultant A business advisor with direct experience in the franchising industry who works primarily for prospective franchisors in setting up a franchise system.

franchise fee A one-time fee paid by the franchisee to the franchisor to buy into the franchise. It can range anywhere from $10,000 into the millions, depending on the particular company and its industry. Home-based franchises are generally the least expensive; hotels are generally the most expensive. Generally, the fee reimburses the franchisor for the costs of initial training and support for new franchisees.

franchise rule The FTC-administered rule requires franchisors to provide all potential franchisees with a disclosure document that contains 23 categories of information about the franchise, the officials and other franchisees, among other important information. If the franchisor makes any claim about financial performance, the rule requires it to have a reasonable basis for those claims and provide documents substantiating them. The rule, also known as FTC RULE 436, was established in 1978.

franchise system A group of franchised businesses with common trademarks, operating standards and products.

franchising A method of business expansion launched by a company that grants trademarks, operating systems and support to independent business people known as franchisees who pay Fees and Royalties to use these assets to build businesses for themselves.

franchiser The person or company that grants the franchisee the right to do business under their trademark or trade name.

garnishment A legal proceeding in which a creditor (or other plaintiff) obtains a court order compelling a third party (e.g., a bank, the employer of a debtor or other defendant) to pay money earned by the defendant to the plaintiff. Up to a quarter of a debtor's wages can be deducted in this way. The garnishee is the person or entity (i.e., the bank or employer) that receives the court order not to release funds. If the garnishee mistakenly gives the money to the debtor, the garnishee will be liable to pay the creditor the amount that should have been set aside.

general accounting office (GAO) A federal agency that acts as an auditor of the different units of the federal government.

general agreement on tariffs and trade (GATT) A treaty in effect among various western countries. Its purpose is to foster international trade relations by encouraging bilateral agreements that reduce tariffs and other trade restrictions. In other words, it is a treaty/agency devoted to free trade among nations.

general partner One of the owners of a partnership, which is a joint business for profit. Unlike the owners of a corporation, a general partner is personally liable for all the business' debts and obligations. A general partner can take actions (e.g., signing contracts) that legally bind the entire business, including the other general partners. A general partner differs from a limited partner, who is liable only to the extent of the money he or she has invested in the business. In some states, the term may also refer to the managing partner of a limited partnership who is responsible for partnership debts over and above his or her individual investment.

generally accepted accounting principles (GAAP) The standards and practices that accountants follow in creating financial statements. These standards are to an extent based on convention, but they are codified by publications of the American Institute of Certified Public Accountants. In any audit report, the certified public accountant must assure readers that GAAP have been followed by the client and by the auditor's own staff.

generally accepted auditing standards (GAAS) Guidelines that are published by the American Institute of Certified Public Accountants (AICPA) that auditors follow in preparing (and certifying) financial statements for clients. Any certified public accountant who does not follow these guidelines is in violation of AICPA rules and can be held legally liable by clients.

general partner A participant in a partnership who is jointly liable for the debts incurred by the partnership.

golden parachute A lucrative contract offered to a senior executive as an inducement: the executive gains compensation (a large bonus, stock options) if his or her job is lost as a result of a merger or acquisition. Sometimes these contracts involve so much money as to be a disincentive to would-be purchasers, which can be one of their purposes in the first place.

gross profit Sales minus the direct cost of those sales before any other expenses are subtracted. When expenses are subsequently subtracted, the result is called net profit or net income.

gross sales Total sales before discounts or any reductions for returns.

holding company A corporation that holds more than 50 percent of the stock of other companies, thus effectively controlling them.

home office deduction A deduction allowed a taxpayer for maintaining an office in what is otherwise the taxpayer's home. The requirement is that stated portion of the home is regularly used for office purposes.

incorporate To obtain articles of incorporation or an official charter from a state for an organization (a profit-making business, a professional business such as a law office or medical office, or a nonprofit entity). The steps include having one or more incorporators (most states require a minimum of three for profit-making companies); choosing a name that is not currently used by (or confusingly similar to) any corporation; preparing articles and filing them with the relevant state's secretary of state; appointing an agent for acceptance of service; deciding on the share structure; adopting a set of bylaws; holding a first meeting of incorporators to launch the enterprise; electing a board of directors; selecting officers; and issuing shares according to state laws.

incorporation Legal existence of a corporate entity (i.e., recognized by the state and allowed to operate according to the corporation's articles of incorporation). All incorporated entities share certain characteristics: limited liability of shareholders; paid-in-capital; independence of operation from stockholders; and a name protected from use by other business entities.

incorporator The person or entity that prepares, files and signs the articles of incorporation. For example, the company, Business Filings Incorporated acts as an incorporator for many new companies.

independent contractor A person who is hired (i.e., contracted) to work for another to do a specific job, and who retains control over how the job is done. Such a contractor does not qualify as a statutory employee under the day-to-day control of the employer (i.e., the person who did the hiring) and is not protected by most employment laws.

initial public offering (IPO) Also called going public. The means by which shares of common stock are first offered for sale in public markets (via the exchanges or via over-the-counter methods).

inside director A member of a company's board of directors who also works for the company, as opposed to an outside director, who is not an employee of the company.

insider information Facts achieved by a corporate director, officer of the company, or shareholder, who, given the opportunities of his or her position, obtains knowledge that may be used primarily for personal gain or that of someone else with whom this person is closely associated. For example, this person knows that the company earnings for the year will be bad, and, in advance of the publication of those results, sells stocks at a price higher than they will command after the results are published.

insider trading Illegal transactions made on the basis of privileged information. This may involve using confidential information (e.g., proposed management changes, forthcoming profit and loss reports, unreleased sales figures, merger talks) about a business, gained through an individual's employment in a company or a stock brokerage, to profit from buying and selling shares and bonds based on that confidential information. Normal investors are the victims. Insider trading is a crime under the Securities and Exchange Act.

institutional investor Any entity that trades large volumes of securities (e.g., a pension fund or a mutual fund). A very high percentage of the trading of U.S. exchanges each day involves buying and selling by institutional investors.

intangible assets Assets that have no physical substance yet are of value to a company (e.g., goodwill) or one that represents a right (e.g., a patent or a franchise).

internal revenue service (IRS) That branch of the federal government in charge of collecting most kinds of national personal and corporate income taxes. Through the U.S. Tax Court, the IRS can also prosecute a taxpayer. If the IRS suspects wrongdoing on the part of a taxpayer, it may also audit that taxpayer. IRS audits of business tend to be time-consuming and extensive, often involving more than 1 year's returns.

inventory A company's goods on hand (or in transit or on consignment) at any particular time. A physical count of inventory usually occurs at year's end to resolve any discrepancy between what a company shows on its books and what is available for sale (i.e., is not damaged or miscounted).

invoice A bill prepared by a seller of goods or services and given to the buyer, as the buyer's notification that payment should be made.

involuntary bankruptcy Bankruptcy provoked by a petition of a company's creditors, not by the company itself.

joint venture Two or more companies that join together for the purpose of completing a particular project.

keogh retirement plan A retirement plan for self-employed individuals who may defer taxes (up to a certain limit) until they withdraw funds (their contributions and the earnings on those contributions) during their retirement. The current annual maximum contribution is $40,000.

key man insurance Life insurance on a business partner or an especially important manager that is intended to help a business through the loss of a contributor of money and expertise, and to help pay for hiring and training a replacement.

letter of credit A document issued by a buyer's bank that guarantees payment to the seller (up to a stated limit) for merchandise when that merchandise is delivered. In other words, the buyer's credit is replaced by that of a bank, which is a comfort to the seller who may or may not be familiar with the buyer but will be familiar with the reputation and stability of the bank. Letters of credit are often used when the buyer is in one country and the seller is in another.

leveraged buyout The acquisition of one company by another in which the assets of the target company are used as collateral for loans to the acquiring company, enabling it to accomplish the takeover. These loans are paid back by the earnings of the acquired company. The term is also used of a company using its own assets as security for loans to accomplish a takeover.

levy Collection, usually by the government, of a specified amount (e.g., a tax levy).

liability The obligation to pay funds for goods or services received. The person or company having a liability is called a debtor. Liabilities can be of three kinds: an actual liability is one that exists—goods/services have been received, and an invoice has been rendered; an estimated liability is one that is certain to exist but the precise amount is unknown (e.g., taxes on a business for the year); and a contingent liability is one that may or may not occur (e.g., a shipment is for the moment lost; it might not be found and would have to be replaced).

lien The right of some person or organization to hold someone else's property as security that a debt will be paid. Liens are imposed by the government (e.g., a tax lien imposed by the Internal Revenue Service). Liens can also be private: the most common example is a mortgage, in which the lender has a lien on the property (can collect by selling the property if there is a default) until such time as the borrower has paid off all the principal and interest on the property.

life cycle The progress of a company (or its products) through the phases of development, growth, maturity, and decline.

limited liability Liability that does not extend beyond the owners' investment in a business; that is, the owners can lose that investment, but they are not held responsible for the debts of the business. Corporations and limited partnerships are limited liability business structures; sole proprietorships and usual partnerships are not.

limited liability company (LLC) A business structure in which personal liability is limited, as it is in a corporation. It otherwise operates as a partnership: the partners—called members in an LLC—are allocated the profits (or losses) of the company, depending on their ownership stake, and they, not the LLC, are responsible for taxes on profits or may use losses to offset any other income.

limited liability partnership (LLP) A type of partnership that offers protection to each partner from personal liability for negligent acts committed by any other partner or by an employee not under his or her direct control. LLPs are recognized in most states, but are often restricted to partnerships of professionals (e.g., lawyers, doctors, accountants, architects).

limited partnership A business structure recognized in most states that allows one or more partners (called limited partners) to have limited personal liability for partnership debts, while another partner or partners (called general partners) have unlimited personal liability. The defining difference between a general partner and a limited partner concerns the management of the business: general partners run it, whereas limited partners (often straightforward investors) are not involved in business decisions. A limited partner who becomes too involved may come to be regarded as a general partner in terms of liability.

LLC kit A binder usually containing essential items for the routine maintenance and administration of a limited liability company. LLC kits include membership certificates, an LLC seal and sample operating agreements.

LLC seal A device made to either emboss or imprint certain company information onto documents. This information usually includes the company's name and date and state of formation. LLC seals may be required when opening bank accounts, distributing membership certificates or conducting other company business.

line of credit A bank's agreed obligation to make loans to a company up to a specified maximum for a specified period of time, usually one year. A line of credit is typically operated in conjunction with a company's bank account (i.e., if a company needs additional funds, these funds are deposited in the company's current bank account).

LLC See limited liability company.

loan An agreement between a lender and a borrower by which the lender will loan the borrower cash in return for interest and an agreement to pay back the cash by a certain date.

margin A technique used by some investors: the investor purchases stocks or commodities from a broker with a down payment but not the full amount due. The broker retains the instruments as collateral and charges the investor interest on the money owed. Buying on margin is a speculative investment strategy: if the price of the instrument rises, the investor can sell, pay off the broker, and pocket the profit. If the value of the instrument declines, the investor has lost money, as the investor is committed to paying the broker the original sale price.

merger Combining two or more companies, with one company (typically) retaining its previous identity. A larger company will often buy a smaller company (or companies) by making a direct offer to the smaller company's management or by purchasing a controlling interest in the shares of the smaller company.

minutes A written record which details the events of the corporation. These records should be kept in the corporation's or LLCs record book.

mortgage A lien securing a loan that has as its collateral real property: the lien stays in place until the loan, and the interest on that loan, has been completely repaid.

name reservation The name of a corporation or LLC must be distinguishable on the records of the state government. If the name is not unique, the state will reject the articles of incorporation or articles of organization (for LLCs). A name can be reserved, usually for 120 days, by applying with the proper state authorities and paying a fee.

NASD/NASDAQ See National Association of Securities Dealers.

national association of accountants (NAA) Professional association comprised mainly of accountants who are not certified public accountants.

national association of securities dealers (NASD) The organization of brokers who handle over-the-counter securities (i.e., those not handled by the traditional stock exchanges). The association is self-regulating, and it operates a computerized system that provides running quotes on the price of OTC securities. The system is known as NASDAQ (National Association of Securities Dealers Automated Quotations).

national labor relations board (NLRB) A five-member independent commission created in 1935 by the National Labor Relations Act (Wagner Act) that is charged with regulating the process of collective bargaining, protecting employees' rights to unionize, preventing abuses by employers or unions, and overseeing union elections. Members are appointed for five-year terms by the President, with the approval of the Senate.

natural person A real human being, as distinguished from a corporation, which is often treated in law as a fictitious person.

net income Also called net profit. Revenue less all costs and expenses.

net loss Amount by which revenues for any given accounting period are less than costs and expenses.

next-in, first out (NIFO) A method of valuing inventory that uses the cost of replacement rather than the original (historic) cost. This method is not a common one.

no-par-value stock Stock with no minimum value. Most states allow no-par stock. If the stock is no-par stock then the amount of stated capital is typically an arbitrary amount assigned by the board of directors. Some states, though, assign a value of $1 to stock when filed as being no-par-value stock. Further, the value of capital for franchise tax purposes is determined by the state and this may result in higher franchise taxes in comparison with low par-value stock.

nonprofit organization Such organizations as charities, religious institutions, and educational entities that operate on the basis that profit, if any, will not be shared with investors. Most such organizations are exempt from federal income taxes.

occupational safety and health act (OSHA) Administered by the U.S. Department of Labor, OSHA is a federal law that mandates the standards that employers must maintain with regard to their health and safety of their employees.

officers The directors appoint officers. They manage the daily affairs of the corporation. A corporation's officers usually consist of a president, vice-president, treasurer, and secretary. In most states, one person can hold all of these posts.

offshore corporation A corporation that is chartered under the laws of a country other than the United States. Some countries (particularly in the Caribbean) are often used as places of incorporation because they have little corporate regulation and low tax rates. Professional trustees and nominal officials in the country of incorporation deal with the necessary contacts with the local government but are not active in the management of the business. Offshore corporations may be useful in a number of areas, such as tax avoidance, easier international operations, and reduced state and banking regulations.

operating expenses Those that are associated not with the production but with the selling and administrative activities of a company. They are a period cost (i.e., they refer to a time period rather than to the creation of the product).

operating income Revenue less cost of goods, less any expenses related to the normal operations of the company. Operating income does not include investment income or interest income or expense.

organizational meeting The initial meeting where the formation of the corporation is completed. At the organizational meeting a number of initial tasks are completed such as: the articles of incorporation are ratified, the initial shares are issued, officers are elected, bylaws approved, and a resolution authorizing the opening of bank accounts is passed.

outside director A member of the board of directors who is not an employee of the company.

outsourcing Acquisition of products or services from outside sources as opposed to producing them within the company making the acquisition. One common kind of outsourcing is having a company's payroll prepared by an outside organization expert at the task.

paid-in capital Stockholders' equity, plus any premium (price above par) they may have paid for the stocks they hold.

paid-in surplus Paid-in capital that is in excess of the par value of the stocks themselves.

parent corporation The owner of a subsidiary company or companies. The parent company may be a holding company—that is, one that does not trade itself but administers the activities of its subsidiaries.

partner One of the co-owners or investors in a partnership, an ongoing business enterprise entered into for profit.

partnership A kind of business organization in which two or more persons contribute capital and their services to the organization. It is easy to form, but the disadvantage to some people is that partners are personally liable for the debts of their operation, unlike corporations, in which owners' risk is only that they may lose their equity (i.e., the money they have paid for their shares).

pass-through taxation The income to the entity is not taxed at the entity level; however, the entity does complete a tax return. The income or loss as shown on this return is passed through the business entity to the individual shareholders or interest holders, and is reported on their individual tax returns. S corporations and LLCs are both pass-through tax entities.

patent An exclusive right, mandated by the federal government, to allow a particular company the right to use, manufacture, or sell a product/process for a period of 20 years. Usually, the individual or company holding the patent has invented the product/process.

payroll taxes Those taxes applied to employees' salaries (or the net income of self-employed individuals). Social security taxes are also imposed on employees, with employers responsible for a matching amount. Employers also pay unemployment taxes based on the number of their employees.

pension fund A retirement fund set up and administered by a trustee for the benefit of a company's employees. Employees contribute to the fund, and very often employers contribute or, in some instances, are the sole contributors. The pension fund and its earnings are retained by the trustee until individual employees retire.

pension plan A retirement plan administered by the employer in which the employer provides employees a guaranteed retirement income. The employer may deduct these expenses from taxes.

piercing the veil A judicial doctrine that allows a plaintiff to hold otherwise immune corporate officers and directors personally liable for damages caused by a corporation under their control. The veil (of immunity) is pierced when officers have acted intentionally and illegally, when their actions exceeded the powers authorized by the company's articles of incorporation, or when the corporation is merely a completely controlled alter ego (i.e., front) for an individual or management group.

preferred stock A class that has preference over common stock in the distribution of earnings and in the event of company liquidation. There is usually a fixed dividend on preferred stock, which makes them preferred over common stock, which, though likely to pay a greater dividend if a company is doing well, pay nothing if the company is doing poorly.

price-earnings ratio (P/E ratio) A mathematical calculation: the market price of a share divided by the current earnings per share. Generally used as an indicator of how well a particular business is doing, though fast-growing companies (which are usually young companies) often have very good P/E ratios that they do not sustain in the long term.

private corporation/privately held company A company that is owned by only a few individuals; its shares are not publicly traded on any of the country's stock exchanges.

professional corporation A corporation which is organized for the purpose of engaging in a learned profession such as law, medicine or architecture. Professional Corporations must file articles of incorporation with the state which meet the state's requirements for professional corporations.

profit margin The ratio, stated as a percentage, of a company's net income to sales. In other words, if a company's share, after costs/expenses, on a sale of a $100 is $20, then the company is said to have a 20 percent profit margin.

profit-sharing A plan that allows employees to share in some part of a company's annual net income, usually involving criterion such as an employee's years of service to the company.

profitability The ability of any company to generate revenues in excess of its costs and expenses (i.e., its net income is positive, not negative).

prospectus This term has two meanings: (1) an informational document issued by a company when it is planning a new issue of its stock: it offers potential investors the story of the company, a list of its officers, its financial statements, and its plans for the future; and (2) an informational document issued by a company's director when they plan to sell the company—used for the benefit of potential buyers; it lists much the same information.

proxy Any situation in which a person transfers voting rights, via power of attorney, to another individual. The most common of these situations is that in which an individual gives rights to another person to vote the first person's stockholding when that first person cannot attend a stockholders' meeting.

public offering the act of offering stocks in a company to the general public via a stock exchange and after registering with the U.S. Securities and Exchange Commission. An intermediary, an investment banker, is usually involved, handling the transaction on behalf of the company.

publicly held company A company that is owned by a great number of investors, the shares of which are traded on one of the country's stock exchanges.

quorum The minimum attendance required to conduct business at a shareholder or board of directors meeting. Usually, a quorum is achieved if a majority of directors are present (for directors meetings) or outstanding shares are represented (for shareholder meetings).

registered agent The agent named in the articles of incorporation. The agent will receive service of process on the corporation and other important documents. The agent must be named in the articles of incorporation, and must be located in the state of incorporation or organization.

registration statement Extensive statement that a company issuing new securities to the public statement must submit to the U.S. Securities and Exchange Commission. It contains complete facts, historical and financial, about the issuing company.

reorganization That which is allowed certain companies that would otherwise be bankrupt—called a Chapter 11 bankruptcy. The company is allowed to negotiate with its creditors to create long-term payments plans; simultaneously, it reorganizes with a view to operating more efficiently in future.

S corporation A business term for a profit-making corporation whose shareholders have received subchapter S corporation status from the Internal Revenue Service. Shareholders of an S corporation have limited liability status (as they would in any corporation) but are taxed as a partnership or sole proprietor. Thus, instead of being taxed as a separate entity (as is a C corporation), the profits and losses of an S corporation are passed through to the shareholders and are reported and paid by them on their personal tax returns.

securities and exchange commission (SEC) The U.S. government agency that regulates that regulates the trading of stocks by, and financial reporting of, U.S. corporations.

sole proprietor An unincorporated business with just one owner, usually a small business. The disadvantage of such a business entity is that the sole proprietor is directly responsible for all the debts of the business.

spreadsheet Numbers arranged in fixed rows and columns, universally used for financial calculations. Computers now greatly reduce the work of compiling spreadsheets via software packages.

stock certificate A documents that is evidence of an investor's partial ownership of a corporation. The certificate commonly shows the number of shares the investor owns, par value, class of stock, and voting rights. Stock certificates can be traded.

stock split A corporation's act of issuing a substantial number of new shares, thus reducing the par value of its exiting stock. The usual reason for such an action is that the company wishes to reduce the price of its shares in the marketplace, to make them more attractive to a greater number of buyers.

stockholder Any individual or entity that owns shares in a corporation. Return on the investment is in the form of dividends or in an increase in the value of the stock—because it is trading at a higher price than that for which it was purchased.

subchapter S corporation A corporation in which the income of the corporation is regarded as the income not of the entity itself but, proportionately, of its stockholders. Same as an S Corporation.

subordinated debt Securities that have a right to a firm's assets only after the claims of holders of senior securities have been paid.

tax-exempt organization Any organization that is determined by the IRS to be exempt from federal taxation of income. This determination is based off of IRS acceptance of Form 1023. A tax-exempt organization may be required to operate exclusively for charitable, religious, literary, educational or similar types of purposes.

10-K The form that publicly traded companies must submit each year to the Securities and Exchange Commission. Financial statements, supporting documents, important disclosures, and general information about the business are included.

tender offer An attempt to buy a large block of shares at a specified price, usually one in excess of the current market price. The objective is to gain a sufficient number of shares to takeover a target company. Usually a tender offer is made directly to the company's stockholders. If the company making the offer accumulates more than five percent of the shares, that company must disclose its ownership position to the Securities and Exchange Commission.

treasurer That person in a company who deals with its financial problems, different from a controller who supervises all of its accounting functions. In all but large companies, the two jobs are usually combined.

underwriting Acceptance of risk as a means of making money if the risk pays off. An underwriter, in this instance an investment banker, buys a new issue of shares at a fixed, discounted price from the company issuing them. The underwriter's goal is to sell them at a higher offering price, thereby making a profit. The company has its money, but the underwriter is taking a risk—the shares may not be popular, may not sell.

venture capital Funding from wealthy individuals or from investment companies (that have generally pooled funding from numerous such individuals) who money in new businesses or those businesses in an early stage of development. The risk is great, but so is the potential for substantial returns if the companies funded are successful.

W-2 form A form sent by an employer to an employee at the end of the calendar year; it shows gross earnings, taxes paid, and FICA deductions. The employer sends copies of the W-2 to the relevant tax authorities; the employee attaches copies to the various income tax returns the employee is obliged to file.

work made for hire For copyright purposes, a work that is created by an employee within the scope of employment, or a work that is created by an independent author on commission under a written contract. The owner of a work made for hire is considered the author of the work, and is therefore the copyright owner. If a company commissions a technical writer to produce a manual as a work made for hire, the company is considered to be the author and owns the copyright in the manual.

workers' compensation Rights that are found in various Workers' Compensation Acts, state statutes that establish the liability of employers for injuries to workers that are sustained on the job or illnesses that result from their employment, and that require employer insurance to protect the workers. Workers' compensation is not based on employer negligence, but is absolute liability for medical coverage, a percentage of lost wages or salary, costs of rehabilitation and retraining, and payment for any permanent injury (usually based on a medical evaluation). If compensation is granted, it becomes the only remedy against an employer and prevents workers or their dependents from suing the employer for injury or death. Some injured workers waive workers' compensation and sue the employer for damages caused by the employer's negligence. If a third party contributed to the damages, the injured worker may sue that party for damages even though he or she receives workers' compensation. Formerly known as workmen's compensation.

Index

SOCRATES™
KNOW HOW TO DO MORE
AND SAVE

Are You Ready to Incorporate? Saving Time & Money through Sound Business Tactics

Partnerships Software (SS4310)
INCLUDES E-BOOK AND 11 FORMS.

Save time and money by learning how to set up and maintain an effective business partnership—from choosing the type that's right for you to obtaining financing and creating an agreement that satisfies all concerned.

Small Business Home Business Kit (K321)
INCLUDES INSTRUCTION MANUAL AND 21 FORMS.

Be your own boss. With this convenient, comprehensive kit, you'll be able to set up your own business and achieve your personal goal of financial independence.

Last Will & Testament Kit (K307)
INCLUDES INSTRUCTION MANUAL AND 17 FORMS.

Protect your loved ones, make your wishes known and award your assets as you desire. Contains the forms and instructions you need to plan your estate responsibly and affordably.